Cost-Benefit
Analysis
and Manpower
Programs

Cost-Benefit Analysis and Manpower Programs

Steve L. Barsby
University of Arizona

Lexington Books
D.C. Heath and Company
Lexington, Massachusetts
Toronto   London

to my wife, Sue,
and my daughters
Denise and Pamela

Table of Contents

List of Figures and Tables

Acknowledgements

Mrs. Marjorie Parker, in the Division of Economic and Business Research at the University of Arizona, deserves words of gratitude for her many editing hours. Professor Phillip Bryson read an earlier version of the manuscript and made numerous helpful suggestions. Unfortunately, I am unable to blame either of them for any errors that remain.

The Arizona Research Coordinating Unit made the research for this book possible by providing financial support. I am especially grateful to Dr. Arthur Lee, Director of the Arizona Research Coordinating Unit, who suggested that this research project be undertaken. The conclusions reached in the book are mine, and may not reflect those of the Arizona Research Coordinating Unit.

Cost-Benefit Analysis and Manpower Programs

1 The Application of Cost-Benefit Analysis in the Manpower Area

Introduction

Between fiscal years 1964 and 1969, annual federal expenditures on manpower programs rose from around $403 million to about $2.2 billion. Table 1-1 containing federal obligation figures for most programs conducted during the 1960s, shows that this increase was the result both of expanding already existing programs—vocational rehabilitation, training under the Manpower Development and Training Act (MDTA), and vocational education — and of inaugurating new programs.

Most important of the newer programs (in terms of expenditures in 1969) are:

1. Neighborhood Youth Corps (NYC; $321 million), established by the Economic Opportunity Act of 1964, which conducts three separate programs—

   . . . an in-school program designed to provide paid jobs for youth inclined to drop out of school and thus encourage their continued school enrollment; a summer program with similar objectives; and an out-of-school program for those who have already left school and need work experience and remedial education to compete in the job market.[1]

2. Concentrated Employment Program (CEP; $114 million), established in 1967 and funded by the Economic Opportunity Act and MDTA, which serves hard-core unemployed youths and adults in specific poverty areas by providing a broad range of services including training;
3. Job Opportunities in the Business Sector (JOBS; $153 million), started in 1968 and funded through the Economic Opportunity and MDT Acts to subsidize employers who hire, train, and up-grade hard-core unemployment;
4. Job Corps ($278 million), established in 1965 and funded by the Economic Opportunity Act, which provides residential training and education for youths with severe problems requiring a change in environment to benefit from such aid; and
5. Work Incentive and Training Program (WIN; $101 million), designed to re-

Table 1-1
Federal Funds Obligated Under Manpower Programs, Fiscal Years 1963–1969[a] (in millions of dollars)

Program	1963	1964	1965	1966	1967	1968	1969
Manpower Development and Training							
Institutional	$ 55.2	$135.5	$249.3	$ 281.7	$ 215.5	$ 218.3	$ 196.6
On-The-Job	.8	6.6	37.2	57.9	106.9	94.9	56.4
Vocational Rehabilitation	65.1	78.9	90.9	143.0	220.5	312.5	374.8
Vocational Education	54.6	55.0	156.9	151.6	225.9	191.8	192.0[b]
Bureau of Indian Affairs Training	7.7	8.2	8.8	10.0	10.8	11.8	12.0[b]
Neighborhood Youth Corps	—	—	127.7	263.3	219.1	155.0	320.6
Job Corps	—	—	183.0	310.0	211.0	285.0	278.1
Work Experience and Training Program	—	—	20.7	76.2	98.8	15.0	—
Concentrated Employment Program	—	—	—	25.0	78.8	93.1	114.2
Operation Mainstream	—	—	—	—	23.6	22.3	41.0
New Careers	—	—	—	—	15.6	7.6	18.5
Job Opportunities in the Business Sector	—	—	—	—	—	60.1	153.3
Work Incentive and Training Program	—	—	—	—	—	9.0	100.8
Total	$183.4	$284.2	$874.5	$1,318.7	$1,426.5	$1,476.4	$1,858.3

Sources: U. S. Treasury Department, Annual Report of the Secretary of the Treasury (Washington, D.C.: Government Printing Office, 1963–69); U.S. Department of Health, Education and Welfare, HEW Annuals (Washington, D.C.: Government Printing Office, 1963–69); Sar A. Levitan and Garth L. Mangum, Federal Training and Work Programs in the Sixties (Ann Arbor, Mich.: Institute of Labor and Industrial Relations, University of Michigan, 1969); U. S. Department of Labor, Manpower Report of the President (Washington, D. C.: Government Printing Office, 1969); U. S. Department of Labor, Manpower Report of the President (Washington, D. C.: Government Printing Office, 1970); and U. S. Department of Health, Education and Welfare, Office of Education, Vocational and Technical Annual Report-Fiscal Year 1968 (Washington, D. C.: Government Printing Office, various issues).

[a]A major exclusion from this list is the operation of the United States Employment Service.
[b]1969 figures not available. Figures are 1968 obligations.

place the Work Experience and Training Program (WEP) in 1968, is funded through the Social Security Act of 1935, and provides broad services including child care and subsidized employment to family heads with dependent children.[2]

These five programs listed above are just a few of the many established after 1963. (The *1970 Manpower Report of the President* itemized 28 separate manpower programs operating in fiscal 1969.) Without exception, new programs were aimed at various disadvantaged or poor groups. Even those programs operating prior to 1963 have been reoriented toward serving disadvantaged persons. MDTA programs originally stressed skill training, and were primarily aimed at unemployed and underemployed persons with previous labor force experience who could be trained quickly for occupations characterized by labor shortages. MDTA now has a dual role—training for labor-short occupations *and* training the disadvantaged. Vocational education was conceived of originally to train persons for skills needed in agriculture and industry. This emphasis remained during the 1960s, but special provisions have been made to aid specific disadvantaged groups.

Changes in the orientation of manpower programs are well illustrated by changes in characteristics of persons aided by them. As the charts in Figure 1-1 show, selected characteristics of trainees of MDTA institutional programs in 1963 differ substantially from those in the same programs in 1969, and from those in other programs in 1969. Participants in MDTA in 1963, relative to their 1969 counterparts (see Figure 1-1a), were more likely to be male, aged 22 and above, white, heads of households, have completed high school, and be experienced members of the labor force.

NYC and Job Corps, aimed primarily at disadvantaged youth, clearly served this group (Figure 1-1b). Only about 3 percent of out-of-school NYC participants and 0 percent of Job Corps participants were aged 22 or above, compared with the nearly 75 percent of those in institutional MDTA in 1963. At the same time, only 4 percent and 12 percent of those in NYC and Job Corps, respectively, had completed high school, while 59 percent in MDTA had done so six years earlier.

CEP and JOBS were designed to serve both youths and adults, and the percentages of those aged 22 and above in these programs (63 percent and 52 percent, respectively) reflect this, so that the broad age compositions are similar to that of MDTA in 1963 (Figure 1-1c). But CEP and JOBS were aiding persons who were more disadvantaged. Only 28 percent and 13 percent of their participants, respectively, were white, compared with 76 percent in MDTA in 1963; and only around 30 percent of those in CEP and JOBS had completed high school, compared to 59 percent who had done so in the 1963 MDTA programs.

4

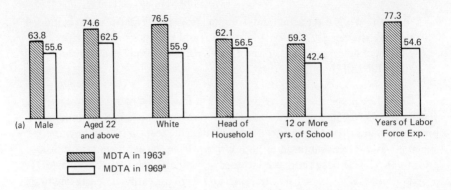

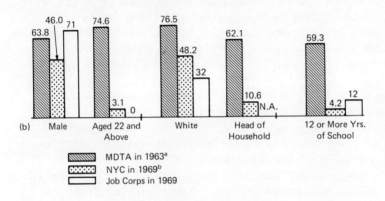

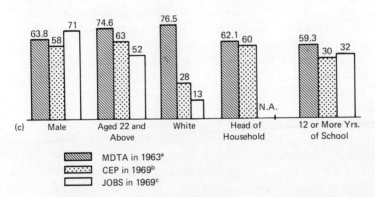

Figure 1-1. Percentages of Trainees with Selected Characteristics in Various Manpower Programs. Source: U. S. Department of Labor, *Manpower Report of the President* (Washington, D.C.: GPO, 1970); and U. S. Department of Labor, *Manpower Report of the President* (Washington, D.C.: GPO, March, 1969).

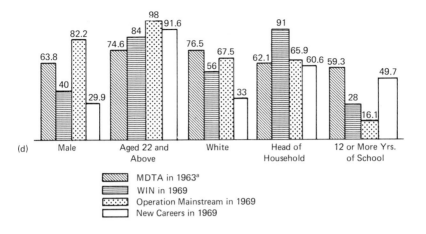

(d)

MDTA in 1963[a]
WIN in 1969
Operation Mainstream in 1969
New Careers in 1969

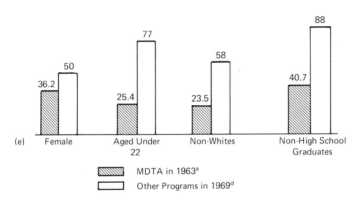

(e)

MDTA in 1963[a]
Other Programs in 1969[d]

[a] Institutional programs only.
[b] Out-of-school only.
[c] 1968 and 1969.
[d] Weighted averages of NYC, Job Corps, CEP, JOBS, WIN, Operation Mainstream, and New Careers.

WIN, Operation Mainstream, and New Careers were aimed primarily at older persons, who respectively comprised 84 percent, 98 percent, and 92 percent of participants in these programs (Figure 1-1d). Again, substantially fewer of the participants had completed high school than was the case in MDTA programs in 1963.

Figure 1- 1e summarizes the changes in participant characteristics between MDTA in 1963 and the newer programs contained in Figures 1-1b through 1-1d. Compared to MDTA institutional training in 1963, programs established after 1963 had higher participation rates of

1.   females (50 percent versus 36.2 percent),
2.   youths (77 percent versus 25.4 percent),
3.   nonwhites (58 percent versus 23.5 percent), and
4.   non-high school graduates (88 percent versus 40.7 percent).[a]

The magnitude of expenditures on manpower programs is sufficient justification for requiring careful evaluation of their operation. The wide range of programs initiated following 1963, and the duplication of programs serving similar groups, indicates that the past seven years have been a period of experimentation as well as one of intensified efforts toward reducing poverty. The fiscal effort, the number of programs available and their changing emphasis — illustrated in Table 1-1 and Figure 1-1 — add urgency to evaluation activities. Which program or combination of programs is most effective in reducing poverty, and in giving persons skills needed to participate in the competitive labor market, can only be determined through research.

It becomes apparent, then, that evaluation of manpower programs is a necessary adjunct to their operation.[b] Proper evaluation gives us a mirror that lets us see past results, allows us to compare relative success in achieving stated goals; it enables us to adjust the composition of existing programs and devise new ones to increase the efficiency with which the goals are reached. Careful evaluation can help in another way. "It requires a clear articulation of objectives and a precise methodology for determining exactly how these objectives are being met."[3] [c]

---

[a]The extremely large enrollments in NYC, in which very few participants have completed high school, distorts the relative size of the change in educational achievement change in manpower program participants. Ignoring NYC results in an estimate of 73 percent in place of 88 percent.

[b]The importance of research is recognized. The 1962 MDTA charged the Secretary of Labor with the responsibility of evaluating the operation of the nation's manpower programs (*Manpower Report of the President, 1970*). This evaluation has been an integral part of all manpower programs since then.

[c]Glen G. Cain and Robinson G. Hollister, ("Evaluating Manpower Programs for the Disadvantaged," *Cost-Benefit Analysis of Manpower Policies. Proceedings of a North American Conference,* ed. G. G. Somers and W. D. Wood [Ontario: Industrial Relations

Evaluation can take many forms and be concerned with many different aspects of activity. For example, a manpower training program can be evaluated from the standpoint of the efficiency of its management structure, the skill or learning achievements of its participants, how it uses its facilities, the way it is viewed by present and past participants and by the community, whether it is achieveing its goals, the economic efficiency with which it is achieving those goals, etc. Evaluation of various manpower programs from the standpoint of economic efficiency, generally referred to as cost-benefit analysis, attempts to indicate whether the value of the outputs of a program exceeds the value of the inputs; and if so, by how much. It can compare the costs and results of alternative programs or of alternative methods of conducting any one program, and direct investment into the better path.

As noted above, cost-benefit analysis is only one of many ways by which a program's success can be judged. It does not give any final answers as to whether a program is "justified," or "good," or should be expanded or contracted. It merely suggests how well a program is operating when viewed in a specific manner. Cain and Hollister suggest that cost-benefit analysis is a way of increasing rationality in the decision-making process, encouraging the use of "rules of evidence." [4]

Since our demands for resources exceed supplies, the efficiency with which we use those resources is (or should be) an important consideration in the way they are allocated. Cost-benefit analysis has the potential for increasing the efficiency of resources used in manpower programs. Its contribution, however, has been limited by the lack of an agreed-upon methodology for conducting cost-benefit studies, a shortage of skilled persons qualified to perform the research, the lack of funds for conducting cost-benefit research, and the seeming fear of administrators that the outcome of the studies will be unfavorable. Cost-benefit studies are not included routinely as a part of program evaluation; when such studies are performed, the results are accepted as valid only when they cast a favorable light on the program. Peter Rossi has stated that the only programs he knows of that were ended because of poor evaluation results were those in which the evaluation was used as an excuse for a decision already made. He feels that the main reason for the lack of impact of negative evaluations is that those conducting the program had not considered the possibility of those results.[5] He points out that administrators first attack the

---

Centre, Queens University at Kingston, 1969], pp. 122–125.), suggest that this is not necessarily an easy task, because few programs have one well-defined objective or even one dominant objective. The difficulty is increased because some objectives that appear to be important are not amenable to measurement (such as students' attitudes toward a program). They also suggest that we cannot tell what a program's goals are until it has been operating for a while and we can observe what it has been doing. To the extent that this is true, it reflects poorly on designers of manpower programs. What rules does one follow in setting up a program if precise goals are not known?

methodology of the research, attempting to cast doubts on the results.
(Researchers themselves may add to this problem by setting standards of proof
that cannot be met because of the nature of the programs being examined.
Thus it is easy to criticize almost any study.[6]) Or administrators indicate that
more study is needed before any conclusions can be reached; or suggest
that the goals the researchers examined were not the real goals of the program
after all.

Components of Cost-Benefit Analysis

Bruce Davie has outlined compactly the various components that go into
cost-benefit analysis and how they are combined to reach the various "decision
rules" that may be applied.[7] Benefits and costs can be viewed appropriately
from the standpoint of society, the individual, and the different levels of
government. The lists of costs and benefits are not the same for each, nor are the
lists of goals and the relative importance attached to each identical. Thus,
society benefits from a program to the extent that total income is increased,
without regard to the distribution of income gains or what happens to taxes.
However, the benefitting individuals who pay the resulting taxes do not
benefit directly from them, so they must be subtracted from increased earnings
when private benefits are calculated. The government also does not gain
the full benefit from increased earnings, but only the increases in tax revenues
stimulated by increased earnings.

Society benefits to the extent that fewer resources have to be utilized in
administration of government transfer payment programs, and to the extent that
costs of crime are reduced. These benefits are not captured by the individual
who undergoes the training. On the other hand, various governmental units will
have their budget situations improved by the total reduction in transfer
payment programs (both the payments themselves and the administration costs
of the programs), saving more from this source of benefits than society.
Savings to government will not be the total savings from crime reduction, but
only that portion reflected in lower crime enforcement costs. Looking at
the three lists of benefits, society has the greatest number of sources of benefits,
and probably experiences total gains in excess of either individuals or
government.

This does not imply that society always will receive the greatest *net* benefits,
because costs must be included in the calculations also. Depending on who
pays for the program, any of the three groups may experience the most net
benefits. In government programs, the normal situation would be for the
government and society to bear more program costs than the individual; and for
society to capture more gains than either the individual or the government.

Table 1-2
Components of Benefit-Cost Calculation of a Given Activity

Benefits		
Society	*Individual*	*Government*

1. Increase in earnings of program participants (gross of taxes)	1. Increase in earnings (net of taxes)	1. Increase in taxes
		   a. From participants
		   b. From others

2. Increases in other income (gross of taxes)
   a. To pay for fringe benefits
   b. Due to other resources becoming more productive
   c. Due to increasing the productivity of future generations as children become better educated (inter-generation effect)
   d. Due to previously unemployed workers taking jobs vacated by program participants (vacuum effect)
	2. Additional fringe benefits due to increased income	2. Decrease in expenses of
		   a. Unemployment insurance
		   b. Employment service
		   c. Welfare programs
		   d. Crime control

3. Reduction in administrative expenses of transfer payment programs
   a. Unemployment administration
   b. Employment service operation
   c. Welfare program administration		

4. Reduced costs to society due to bad citizenship
   a. Economic loss to others
   b. Crime control system		

Table 1-2, (continued)

Society	Costs	
	Individual	*Government*
1. Opportunity costs (gross of taxes)	1. Opportunity costs (net of taxes)	1. Costs of instruction and supplies (net of taxes)
2. Operating costs of training or education agency	2. Loss of transfer payments a. Welfare support b. Unemployment insurance c. Other subsidies	2. Capital costs
3. Capital expenses of training or education agency	3. Extra costs related to program participation a. Tuition b. Books, supplies, etc.	3. Additional administrative costs (net of taxes)
4. Induced reductions in income (gross of taxes) of workers displaced by program participants (displacement effect)		4. Additional subsidies paid during training

Source: Bruce F. Davie, "Benefit/Cost Analysis of Vocational Education: A Survey," *Occupational Education: Planning and Programming,* ed. Arnold Kotz (Menlo Park, Calif.: Stanford Research Institute, September 1967), vol. 2, fig. V-1, pp. 310–11.

Note: This outline of various costs and benefits that should be considered comes largely from Davie, although, as he notes, no one person can be credited with development of these concepts.

Table 1-3
The Three Methods of Comparing Benefits and Costs

Type of Comparison	Method of Calculation[a]	Decision Rule
1. Present Value of Net Benefits	1. $\sum_{t=0}^{n} \dfrac{B_t - C_t}{(1 + i)^t}$	1. Select the project with the highest net benefits first, then pursue successive projects in descending order of net benefits.
2. Rate of Return	2. $\sum_{t=0}^{n} \dfrac{B_t - C_t}{(1 + r)^t} = 0$	2. Select the project with the highest rate of return (r), then pursue successive projects in descending order of r until r equals some predetermined interest rate (i).
3. Benefit-Cost Ratio	3. $\dfrac{\sum_{t=0}^{n} \dfrac{B_t}{(1 + i)^t}}{\sum_{t=0}^{n} \dfrac{C_t}{(1 + i)^t}}$	3. Select the project with the highest B/C, then pursue projects in descending order until $B/C=1$ or budget exhausted.

where B_t = benefits in year t

C_t = costs in year t
n = number of years spanned by the analysis
i = social discount rate
r = rate of return

Source: Bruce F. Davie, "Benefit/Cost Analysis of Vocational Education: A Survey," Occupational Education: Planning and Programming, ed. Arnold Kotz (Menlo Park, Calif.: Stanford Research Institute, September 1967), vol. 2, fig. V-2, p. 313.
[a]Davie's notation is used here because of its simplicity.

When cost and benefit components of a cost-benefit analysis are compared, the comparison must be made at a given point in time. Since in most cases both costs and benefits accrue over a period of years, they must be discounted in order to take into account the time factor. There are three common methods of comparing costs with benefits: (1) present value of net benefits, (2) rate of return, and (3) benefit-cost ratio. (See Table 1-3)

The present value of net benefits is calculated by discounting the stream of future benefits back to the present (usually defined as the time a person or group finishes a program), and subtracting accumulated costs from this total (including interest) calculated at that same point in time. This will tell us the absolute size of gain due to the program. Rate of return is calculated by finding the interest rate that will equalize the present value of costs and benefits. This tells us the rate of interest the "investment" in the program is earning.

The benefit-cost ratio is calculated by dividing present value of benefits by present value of costs. This tells us how large the gain is *relative* to the size of the investment. The benefit-cost ratio differs from the present value of net benefits because the latter tells us the *absolute size* of the gain. The benefit-cost ratio is usually best to use when there are budget constraints, because it allows attention to focus on gain per dollar spent.[d] Since manpower programs are conducted under conditions of sometimes severe budget constraints, the rest of this book will be concerned primarily with benefit-cost ratios, framing discussions in those terms but recognizing that the same data can be used to calculate present value of net benefits and rate of return as well.

So far the only benefits mentioned have been those which could be measured in economic terms. Other measures can be introduced to assess a program's effectiveness. When these types of benefits are discussed and measured, but not entered formally into the calculations, the analysis is still referred to as cost-benefit analysis. However, when they explicitly enter into the benefit calculations, either with economic benefits or as separate calculations, the analysis may be referred to as cost-effectiveness analysis.[e]

Cost-benefit analysis is much more common than cost-effectiveness analysis for two reasons. First, economists have had a substantial influence on the development of cost-benefit analysis and are concerned primarily with efficiency in the use of resources. The most direct way to compute efficiency is to measure the dollar value of inputs against dollar value of outputs of an activity. Second, effectiveness measures are ambiguous. Values determined for various measures of effectiveness must be arbitrarily determined and weighted. Subjectiveness is more evident in cost-effectiveness than in cost-benefit analysis (although it permeates both kinds of analysis). The emphasis on the economic consequences of manpower programs as opposed to, say, social consequences and the resulting "prominence" of cost-benefit analysis relative to cost-

---

[d]Each of the methods described above for comparing costs and benefits of a program has deficiencies that, under certain conditions, can result in an "incorrect" decision. These deficiencies are discussed in many places. See, for example, Jacob J. Kaufman et al., "A Cost-Effectiveness Study of Vocational Education," *A Comparison of Vocational and Non-vocational Education in Secondary Schools* (University Park, Penn.: Institute for Research on Human Resources, Pennsylvania State University, March, 1969), pp. 49–59.

[e]Garth Mangum has differentiated cost-benefit and cost-effectiveness analysis in a different manner. He considers cost-benefit analysis to encompass cost-effectiveness analysis, as I have defined it above, whenever the evaluation considers only one program. Thus he defines cost-benefit analysis as the process of determining whether a given program is "worth" more than it costs, however "worth" may be defined. Cost-effectiveness analysis, as Mangum defines it, is the search for the "least-cost method" of achieving any specified result. Using Mangum's definition, cost-effectiveness analysis includes comparing costs of several different programs serving the same group and of analyzing alternative activity patterns within any one program in order to find which is least expensive (Mangum, "Determining the Results of Manpower and Antipoverty Programs," *The Analysis and Evaluation of Public Expenditures: The PPB System,* Vol. III [Joint Economic Committee, Washington, D.C., 1969], pp. 1174–1175.). I prefer the definitions used in this book, but do not know which usage is more common.

effectiveness analysis has been criticized frequently.[8] However justified these criticisms may be, they do not invalidate the cost-benefit studies for four reasons. First, many studies *do* concern themselves extensively with noneconomic aspects of manpower programs (e.g. Kaufman et al., [9] and Sullivan [10]), although these aspects have not been integrated into the cost-benefit calculation. Second, manpower programs are not the only source of noneconomic benefits (good citizenship, appreciation of environment, etc.). General education in particular is regarded as a better means for achieving them.[11] Third, when administrators list a large number of program goals, they usually can be reduced to two — increasing income and achieving more equity in society.[12] Fourth, the main goal of the war on poverty, of which the many manpower programs are a part, is to raise incomes. Other (noneconomic) goals that can be cited are secondary.[13]

When cost-effectiveness analysis is performed, the lists of costs remain unchanged from cost-benefit analysis. Measures of effectiveness that can be selected to evaluate a program, however, are limited only by the imagination and ingenuity of the investigators. Some of the more obvious are listed below.

Measures of Program Effectiveness

1. Academic improvement between pre- and post-program tests
2. Skill improvement between pre- and post-program tests
3. Absolute levels of achievement in both academic and skill tests at end of program
4. Percentage of persons completing program who are placed in occupations using skills in which they trained
5. Percentage of persons completing program
6. Percentage of persons completing program who are placed
7. Employment-unemployment experience following training (both absolute and relative to nonparticipants)
8. Opinions of program graduates as to how well the program prepared them for future employment
9. Opinions of program graduates' immediate supervisors as to how well the program prepared them for employment (both absolute and relative to nonparticipants)
10. Extent to which program is serving those persons for whom it was designed.

Problems Encountered in Estimating Costs

Accounting Costs

The most obvious problem in determining the cost of some activity is lack of good accounting data. For some reason, all levels of government have been slow to adopt accounting practices that permit cost calculation for specific activities within any one agency. The federal government has been moving more rapidly than state governments in this regard, but even at the federal level no firm commitment has yet been made to provide detailed cost data by activity. The result is a dependence by investigators on educated guesses for determining program costs.

This introduces a more subtle problem — the use of average, rather than marginal, costs — a problem made more serious by its very subtlety. Average costs can be calculated with less detailed data than can marginal costs. Given the generally "lumped" nature of accounting information available, it is natural that average costs are most often used. However, average costs can be used only to "look in the mirror to see where we have been" and to decide whether we should have been there in the first place. Average cost data cannot tell us whether we should expand, hold constant, or decrease the level of a program. To get this information we need marginal costs. Marginal costs tell us how much the total costs of some activity will change when we change the level of activity by some small amount.

Benefit-cost studies that rely on average cost calculations to make suggestions concerning the appropriate level of some program (i.e., should a program be expanded or contracted) have this serious, often unrecognized, deficiency. Since researchers generally caution the reader that (average) cost data have been estimated, results can be interpreted with this in mind. But since the researcher rarely warns the reader that the use of even complete average cost data has certain limitations, unjustified conclusions may be drawn (by the researcher as well as by the reader). Of all the studies examined in this book, only that by Cain and Stromsdorfer [14] makes a conscious effort actually to develop marginal cost data. Others, Corazzini [15] and Taussig [16] for example, warn the reader that their use of average costs may have resulted in overstatement of costs of expanding a program.

Joint-Costs

The so-called "joint-cost" problem arises when a given expenditure (e.g., for a capital facility or administrative services) serves more than one activity either simultaneously or in sequence. The problem is to decide what portions of those costs to allocate to various activities. Some researchers have allocated joint costs on the basis of relative sizes of activities which they serve; others have ignored them. There is no "right" way to do this, although the question "How much have those costs been increased by the presence of this particular activity?" is the one that should be asked. In many cases the answer will be "None." In each case, the decision on how to handle joint-cost items should depend on the particular questions the study is trying to answer.

Opportunity Costs

The determination of opportunity costs (what one must give up in order to do what he is doing) is one of the more formidable problems encountered. In the case of manpower programs, opportunity costs generally consist of earnings the participants of some program gave up in order to participate. There is no direct way to measure this loss. It may be estimated as the participants' earnings prior to their entering the program. A better way of measuring lost earnings is to use a control group with the same characteristics as the participants except for participation in the program.

A yet unsolved problem in calculating opportunity costs is to find a means of estimating the "vacuum" effect — the number of jobs vacated by program participants that were filled by workers who otherwise would have been unemployed. To the extent that the vacuum effect operates, opportunity costs for society are reduced, (they are not reduced for the individual in this case because he does not receive any of the benefits accruing to the previously unemployed workers), and the use of control groups overstates program costs. The vacuum effect generally is assumed to be zero,[f] at least partly because of the difficulties encountered in trying to measure it.[17]

Price Distortions

Two kinds of price distortions can enter the cost-benefit calculation. The first emerges because of the price advantage held by governmental units in purchasing materials. Nonpayment of sales and property taxes enables the government to purchase more resources for a given sum of money than could be purchased by the private sector. Economists disagree over whether a price adjustment should be made so that resources are valued at what they are worth in the private sector. Normal practice is not to make an adjustment.[g]

The second type of price distortion is more difficult to detect. It is possible for a government project to be large enough to distort the prices of resources it purchases and "products" it sells. For example, the demand for technicians to teach courses in skilled areas pulls them out of the labor market and tends

[f]Michael E. Borus, ("A Benefit-Cost Analysis of the Economic Effectiveness of Retraining the Unemployed," *Yale Economic Essays,* vol. 4, no. 2[Fall, 1964], pp. 371–429) makes a notable exception to this practice. He assumes that every job vacated by program participants is filled by a previously unemployed or underemployed person.

[g]Again, Borus ("A Benefit-Cost Analysis") is an exception. Ernst W. Stromsdorfer ("Economic Benefits and Criteria for Investment in Vocational and Technical Education," *Occupational Education: Planning and Programming,* ed. Arnold Kotz, Vol. II [Menlo Park, Calif.: Stanford Research Institute, September, 1967], p. 342) also argues for their inclusion.

to increase the wages of all technicians. Additionally, program graduates may be plentiful enough to force wages down (or keep them from increasing as rapidly as they otherwise would have increased) in those occupations for which they were trained. These types of price distortion are generally ignored, [18] because there is no sure way to detect their existence or magnitude and because most manpower programs are of a modest size relative to the labor markets which they utilize and serve. These distortions are probably small or temporary when they do exist. None of the studies examined in this book has attempted to estimate the extent of these distortions.

Problems Encountered in Estimating Benefits

Control Groups

Most economists agree that "before and after" analysis (in which the participants serve as their own control group) is seriously deficient.[19] It is almost impossible to show that improvements experienced by program participants in earnings and employment result from participation in the program and not from other causes, e.g., the passage of time and changes in economic conditions. Cain and Hollister point out that the "before" situation may not even be representative of the participant's general experience.[h] Consequently, researchers have used one or more separate control groups in order to isolate a program's effect on its participants.

Finding an appropriate control group is difficult. Economists disagree about requirements for determining and selecting one that is both relevant and adequate. Regardless of the control group that one researcher uses, another one can point out why that control group is inadequate. Ideally, a control group would be identical in all respects to the participants (or "experimental" group) except for program participation. To achieve this kind of control group, one would have to pick at random from persons who had applied and qualified for the program in question.[i] Administrators have not shown a willingness

---

[h]Loren C. Scott ("The Economic Effectiveness of On-the-Job Training: The Experience of the Bureau of Indian Affairs in Oklahoma," *Industrial and Labor Relations Review,* vol. 23, 2 [January, 1970],220–236) and Dale Bruce Rasmussen ("Determinants of Rates of Return to Investment in On-the-Job Training," Ph.D. dissertation, Southern Methodist University, 1969) have used this approach by attempting to compensate for changes in general economic conditions before the program commenced and after it is completed. In each case it is up to the reader to decide if the researcher adequately handled the problem.

[i]Even this method is not guaranteed to give identical groups, since being rejected may affect the behavior of the control group. Chernick et al. (*The Selection of Trainees Under MDTA,* report prepared for the Office of Manpower Policy, Evaluation and Research, U.S. Department of Labor [New Brunswick, N.J.: Institute of Management and Labor Relations, Rutgers State University, 1966] have found that persons rejected for participation in an MDTA program are disappointed and discouraged; some are bitter toward the Employment Service.

to do this, although Rossi [20] has suggested that this problem can at least partially be avoided if we adopt some techniques utilized by the medical profession and give the control group some kind of "placebo" treatment – e.g., placement, counseling, or testing. He does not feel it is necessary to hold back all "treatment" of the control group.[j]

Given that the "ideal" control group is unavailable (or nonexistent), researchers have relied mainly on one or more of the following groups;

1. Those who completed the program but did not utilize the training
2. Those who entered the program but dropped out prior to completion
3. Those who applied for and qualified for the program, but did not show up
4. Workers who were registered with the Employment Service as needing jobs, but did not apply for the program
5. Friends and neighbors of program participants.

Use of each of these groups involves problems that reduce the reliability of results to some degree. Use of groups 1 and 2 is based on the assumption that no benefits can be attributed to the program unless two criteria are met: first, that the job was obtained because the course was completed; and second, that the skills learned in the course were needed for the job. As Hardin [21] points out, how to determine if these criteria have been met is a problem in itself. Additionally, very real benefits may result from program participation even if the skills learned are not necessary in the job received, or if the participant dropped out prior to completion. One such benefit might be the acquisition of better personal habits. Hardin argues that groups 1 and 2 should be included in the experimental group.[22]

Use of qualified applicants who did not participate in the program (group 3), avoids the above problems, but runs into difficulty because these people may have found jobs attractive enough to keep them out of the program.[k] That some qualified applicants may have failed to show up for training because they found good jobs does not invalidate the use of this control group if it can be assumed that the reasons for not showing up are random. Hardin states that he finds some "comfort" in the fact that "randomness" does

---

[j]This idea is good if we can be sure of finding some kind of "treatment" that does not affect labor market behavior. There is some suspicion, for example, that placement and counseling are two of the most important parts of manpower retraining programs, and that many of the benefits may flow from these activities even in the complete absence of training and education.

[k]Borus ("A Benefit-Cost Analysis") has attempted to avoid this problem as well as those mentioned in the preceding paragraph by utilizing multiple control groups. In each case when someone withdrew from training or failed to report at the beginning of the program, he excludes those who did so because they found attractive employment. He is then caught on the other horn of the dilemma, because he ends up with a range of annual benefit estimates ($424 to $1,033) depending on which control group he uses. This forces him to decide what estimate of the benefits is "best."

play a role throughout the selection process and in determining who actually reports for training — erratic judgment of the Employment Service in initial screening of applicants, failure of applicants to receive their notice of acceptance, temporary illness, and failure to qualify for training allowances for a number of reasons.[23]

Control group 4 is good because it helps to match the labor market conditions of the control and experimental groups, but suffers because matching the personal characteristics is more difficult. Using personal interviews to gather additional information concerning personal characteristics of the control groups and controlling for differences in these characteristics through statistical techniques reduces this problem.[1]

Use of control group 5 (selected by the method sometimes referred to as "snowballing") runs into the problem that characteristics of the control group may not be sufficiently like those of the experimental group to give good results. Use of this group is based on the assumption that relatives' and neighbors' characteristics will be similar to the trainees'. The most common method used to compensate for deficiencies in the use of any specific control group is to explore the type of bias introduced through its use and warn the reader accordingly.

A different kind of difficulty in the use of control groups is the necessity of assuming that experiences of the experimental and control groups are independent. An increase in the supply of better-trained workers due to a training program will make it more difficult than before for the untrained to get jobs. Thus some workers tend to be "displaced" (hence the term "displacement" effect) from their jobs by the increased supply of better trained and educated workers.[m] Operation of the displacement effect can result in an overstatement of benefits. No good way has yet been devised to measure the displacement effect, so the normal assumption is that it is zero.[n] Solie, for example, does not

---

[1]Use of multiple regression analysis is advantageous if the differences in characteristics between the experimental and control groups are subject to measurement. Herbert A. Chesler ("The Retraining Decision in Massachusetts: Theory and Practice," *Retraining the Unemployed*, ed. G. G. Somers [Madison, Wis.: University of Wisconsin Press, 1968], p. 165) indicates that many of these differences may in fact be the sort that are difficult to measure. In comparing personal characteristics of the two groups, he has found that relative to those who volunteered for the program, those who did not usually gave at least one of the following reasons—little interest in the skill training offered, a feeling that program participation would not enhance their employability, a " . . . relatively high aversion to uncertainty; . . . " a feeling that the training program would be too difficult to complete, and a " . . . failure to perceive a real need for effecting any change in one's general labor market situation." On the other hand past occupation, employment, earnings and mobility experiences *are* measurable.

[m]This might be thought of as the "other side of the coin" of the vacuum effect discussed earlier.

[n]Two notable exceptions are Borus ("A Benefit-Cost Analysis"), who assumes that anyone who did not complete the program and utilize his new skills in his first job displaced someone else; and Michael K. Taussig ("An Economic Analysis of Vocational Education in the New York City High Schools," *Journal of Human Resources,* Vol. 3, Supp. (1968), pp. 59-87), who assumes that unless the wage *rates* were increased by training, the training was merely being used as a screening device by employers.

attempt to measure it, but tries to compensate for it by repeatedly warning the reader that displacement may be occurring.[24]

Size of the control group also is important. Large control groups cannot be selected at random, and if questionnaires are used, the data gathering is expensive and time consuming. Small control groups can be picked at random, but they may not be large enough to permit treatment of a large number of variables (either because of statistical constraints or because all the desired characteristics may not be represented). Small control groups also may have a "hot house" environment in which conditions are special and cannot be re-created anyplace else.[25]

Lack of agreement over what determines an adequate control group has resulted in use of different control groups in different studies. Page uses unemployment insurance applicants with characteristics similar to program enrollees as the control group; and all enrollees, both graduates and dropouts, as the experimental group.[26] Cain and Stromsdorfer's control group consists of unemployed nonapplicants, and their experimental group is composed of all the program graduates. Main and Blume use the "before and after" technique.[27, 28] Borus uses a number of different control groups.[29] This variability in control groups makes the different cost-benefit studies hard to compare with each other because altering the control group will affect results.[o]

Lack of Data

Researchers have followed the practice of estimating the economic benefits of government programs by calculating the increases in income that may be attributed to them. As a practical matter only the earnings of program participants are included.[p] It is recognized, however, that this measure of benefits probably excludes significant unmeasured economic benefits. Some of these benefits may accrue to society (and to the individual) through reductions in crime, increased productivity because of improved health, increased earnings of the children (the intergeneration effect), increased nonwage job benefits, and increased productivity of other resources. Lack of good data for measuring these benefits has discouraged their inclusion in most studies, although often these types of benefits are recognized as existing and possibly quite large.[30]

In addition to the often nonmeasured economic benefits noted above, significant benefits may exist that do not lend themselves to quantification. Several more obvious "noneconomic" benefits are: (1) consumption value

---

[o]This is only one of several difficulties encountered in comparing the results of various cost-benefit studies. Other problems are discussed throughout the book.

[p]Some studies include estimates of reductions in the costs of operating transfer payment programs. Researchers rarely attempt to include increases in income induced in other groups, whether they result from increased productivity of complementary resources or the multiplier effect.

of the training and education (Many people enjoy the training and education process itself, and thus derive benefits simply from participating.); (2) benefits society may receive from its citizens participating more in public affairs (assuming that those with more education and income do more of those things included under "good citizenship"); (3) the individual's satisfaction in being successful in his chosen vocation; (4) value of options to the trainee of further education and training made possible by participating in any one program;[q] and (5) value of redistributing income in a more "equitable" manner. This last source of benefits is particularly important in the context of this book because one of the important goals of manpower programs is to reduce poverty.[r]

Other Problems

Benefits and costs of an activity must be related to each other at a given point in time in order to have meaning. This necessitates selecting a discount rate and time horizon (the period of time over which benefits and costs are to be considered) so that present values of the streams of costs and benefits can be calculated.[s] Unfortunately, little agreement exists over how the discount rate should be selected, let alone what the resulting "correct" rate is. The Army Corps of Engineers has used a rate as low as 3 1/4 percent. Borus has utilized several rates, one of them 15 percent. Most studies in the manpower area utilize discount rates ranging between 5 and 10 percent.

Selection of the time horizon also is subjective. Since most studies observe the benefit stream over a relatively short period of time (one to two years), benefits must be estimated by some kind of extrapolation if a longer time horizon is desired. This introduces the problem of determining the basis on which the extrapolation is made. Kaufman et al. refuse to extrapolate, calculating the benefit-cost ratios on the basis of the four-year earnings actually observed. Kaufman and Lewis extrapolate earnings until age sixty-five on the assumption the observed earnings advantage of vocational graduates will

---

[q]To the extent that participation in a vocational curriculum in high school makes a college education more difficult, these benefits are reduced. On the other hand, nontechnical post-high school education is not a real option for many students in the first place.

[r]A discussion in Chapter 6 of the extent to which excluding these factors from cost-benefit analysis reduces its value suggests that they are not as important as often is thought.

[s]Discounting is justified for two reasons. First, use of funds in one endeavor precludes their use in another. Thus some other opportunity is foregone, and the discount rate represents the value of these opportunities foregone. Also, people have a positive time preference for goods. That is, they value having things now more than they value having the same things sometime in the future. The discount rate reflects this also (Kenneth J. Arrow, "The Social Discount Rate," *Cost-Benefit Analysis of Manpower Policies;* Kaufman et al., "A Cost-Effectiveness Study of Vocational Education," pp. 59–66; and Stromsdorfer, "Economic Benefits and Criteria for Investment in Vocational and Technical Education," pp. 344–346.)

remain constant. Weisbrod utilizes census data to make the extrapolation.[31]
Carroll and Ihnen make two extrapolations to age sixty-five: one under the
assumption that the earnings advantage of junior college vocational graduates at
the end of the period of observation (four years) remains constant; the other
based on census data (in which the differential increases at 2 percent annually).
Borus uses a 5 percent discount rate and a ten-year time horizon, while
adjusting the earnings advantage of trainees downward to reflect the movement
of trainees out of the occupations for which they were trained.

The various ways in which the extrapolations have been made reflect
differences in approach to handling uncertainty. Uncertainty arises because we
do not know the actual path of benefits, and have no good way of predicting
what events might occur to affect those paths. Industrial composition might
change and bring a change in demands for skills. Dramatic technological
breakthroughs might eliminate the need for some skill almost overnight.
Institutional arrangements might change and affect earnings. These possibilities
cannot be predicted. One factor, mortality, can be taken into account.[32]
If we could wait long enough, and defer judgments concerning the value of some
activity, we could observe the actual results of a program over several genera-
tions. However this is not practical. Stromsdorfer suggests that uncertainty might
be adjusted for by using higher rates of discount, calculating what are expected
to be the "best" and "worst" estimates of what might happen, or using
"sensitivity" analysis, and systematically varying assumptions concerning
employment, wages, interest, etc., to see how sensitive the results are to changes
in them and presenting a range of solutions.[33] The reader then can decide
how to interpret the results. This is the most common method. Another
approach would be for the researcher to provide sufficient information to enable
the reader to make calculations on the basis of varying assumptions.

Conclusions

Cost-benefit analysis often is thought of as a potentially valuable tool in the
design and operation of manpower programs. Utilized correctly, it may help
decision makers increase the efficiency of the activities with which they are
involved. However, cost-benefit analysis presently is neither used routinely nor
considered a key factor in decision-making when used. Data problems and
the lack of an agreed-upon methodology probably explain much of this. Often
desired cost and benefit data are not available. Researchers sometimes must
be arbitrary in the allocation of joint costs and the calculation of opportunity
costs. No agreement obtains over what constitutes an adequate control group,
what the "proper" discount rate is, how uncertainty should be handled or what
benefits should be included in the explicit calculations.

The formidable problems of the researcher attempting to conduct a cost-benefit study may convince some that another approach would be more fruitful. Goldfarb has surveyed the problems involved and concluded that we would be better off not to attempt to calculate benefit-cost ratios.[34] Davie feels that benefits that cannot be quantified are important enough to ". . . make it impractical to undertake strict cost-benefit analyses of vocational education on a widespread scale."[35] But most researchers would not advocate altering the activities of a program or changing its priorities on the basis of a benefit-cost ratio alone. They recognize that the ratio may be one of the lesser considerations in guiding decision-making in these (manpower) areas. But the uncertainties involved in the answers provided through the analysis need not prevent cost-benefit analysis from contributing to decision-making.

An assessment of the contributions that cost-benefit analysis has made in the past and can make in the future in conducting manpower programs is best left until after a series of actual cost-benefit studies have been examined.

Chapter 2 examines four studies of the benefits and costs of vocational education in high schools. While the resulting benefit-cost ratios exceed one, the value of these findings is somewhat limited by methodological problems experienced in several of the studies, and by the narrow range of questions investigated.

Chapter 3 summarizes the results of two cost-benefit studies of vocational education in post-secondary schools. High opportunity costs attendant with such education result in ratios substantially lower than those associated with vocational education in high schools, and greater than one only under low discount rate and long time horizon assumptions.

Chapters 4 and 5 contain cost-benefit studies of out-of-school manpower programs; Chapter 4 concentrating on institutional training programs and Chapter 5 on programs with an OJT component and on several miscellaneous programs. Benefit-cost ratios exceeding one are found in every major manpower program examined, although calculations based on Job Corps operations require liberal discount rate and time horizon assumptions to achieve these results.

Chapter 6 summarizes the results of Chapters 2 through 5, and concludes that while we may get satisfaction out of finding benefit-cost ratios greater than one for manpower activities during the 1960s, such studies must be compared with each other with care and have not been performed in sufficient quantity. An argument is developed suggesting that cost-benefit analysis suffers from fewer deficiencies than often is claimed. The conclusion is reached that cost-benefit analysis' greatest potential lies in internal analysis of programs rather than in straightforward comparisons between different programs.

2

Vocational Education
in Secondary Schools

Vocational education in secondary and post-secondary schools poses fewer methodological problems for cost-benefit analysis than any other manpower program to which such analysis has been applied. This is so for four reasons. First, cost data, while imperfect, are kept on a more consistent basis in schools than in most out-of-school programs. Second, non-vocational high school graduates and high school graduates not attending post–secondary schools serve as ready-made control groups. Third, there appears to be general agreement on treating opportunity costs. At the secondary level such costs usually are regarded as zero on the reasoning that the alternative to high school vocational education – a general education – is institutionally imposed.[a] At the post–high school level, opportunity costs are considered to be the earnings differential between students who did not attend a post–secondary school and those who did during the period such a school was attended. Finally, data on personal characteristics of students usually are fairly complete, with information on family background, I.Q., and past school achievement readily available. Analysis of cost-benefit studies suggests that vocational education at the high school level yields a benefit-cost ratio in the neighborhood of four, but that a significant portion of vocational education – that conducted in comprehensive high schools – has yet to be studied.

Vocational Education in Worcester,
Massachusetts

Arthur Corazzini has examined comparative costs of vocational high school and academic high schools in Worcester, Massachusetts, for 1963-1964.[1] Cost data for his study came from school records. Benefit data came from a sampling of starting wages at twelve large manufacturing firms in the Worcester labor market.

Costs of schooling computed by Corazzini appear in Table 2-1. His cost calculations include current operating expenses of the schools, costs borne by students, foregone earnings (opportunity costs), and an adjustment for property

---

[a]One case in which this is not true, and opportunity costs should be included, is a study of high school vocational education as a dropout-prevention program. In this case, the income foregone by staying in school is rightly included.

taxes not paid by the schools. Total annual social costs per student in the vocational schools exceed those in the academic schools by $678. Over a four-year period, then, (undiscounted) additional costs of vocational high schools over regular high schools are $2,712.

More detailed analysis by Corazzini suggests that much of the higher costs in the vocational schools is the result of underutilization of facilities. The student-teacher ratio in general high schools is around 20 to 1; that for vocational schools 12.6 to 1.[b] Average salaries of instructors in the vocational schools are higher ($7,800 vs. $6,000), but it is not clear whether this is due to greater training of vocational teachers or a greater average seniority.[2] The net result probably is that marginal costs of operating the vocational schools are less than average costs computed by Corazzini, so expansion of vocational enrollments would not add an additional $678 per student (Corazzini notes this).

The nonrandom wage survey conducted by Corazzini indicates that graduates of male vocational high schools were being placed with a wage advantage over graduates of general high schools of from $.04 to $.28 per hour. Based on a forty-hour work week over fifty weeks (2,000 hours per year), and ignoring any differences in unemployment experiences, vocational high school graduates could be expected to earn from $80 to $560 a year more than graduates from general high schools.

Corazzini does not calculate benefit-cost ratios, but he does calculate "pay-back periods," or the length of time it would take graduates from vocational schools to earn back the additional costs of their vocational education. The present value of vocational graduates' increased earnings never will equal the present value of additional costs if the wage differential remains at $80 per year at either a 5 or 10 percent rate of discount. At the largest wage differential ($560 a year) it takes more than six years for increased earnings to equal additional costs if the discount rate is 5 percent. The time required increases to ten years if a 10 percent rate of discount is used.

Benefit-cost ratios can be estimated from the above data. Depending on assumptions concerning the size of the earnings differential, discount rate, and time horizon, the calculated ratios range from .6 to 2.6 (Table 2-2). At an assumed earning advantage of $500 and using a 5 percent discount rate, the benefit-cost ratio equals 1.3 over ten years, and reaches 2.6 if the time horizon is extended to thirty years. If the annual earnings differential is assumed to be an unweighted average of the range observed by Corazzini ($320), benefit-cost ratios are somewhat lower, although extending the time horizon beyond ten years will result in ratios exceeding unity. If the discount rate is 10

---

[b]Not all this difference can be ascribed to the nature of vocational education versus general education, because the student-teacher ratio in the female vocational school was also 12.6 to 1. Presumably, the girls' vocational school would have a higher proportion of office skills courses which generally do not necessitate small classes. Additionally, the vocational high school curriculum includes nonvocational courses.

Table 2-1
Annual Social Costs of Vocational and Academic High Schools in Worcester, Massachusetts, 1963–1964

	General High School Costs (per pupil) (Col. 1)	Male Vocational High School Costs (per pupil) (Col. 2)	Difference Col. 2 – Col. 1
Current Operating Costs	$ 452	$ 964	$512
Implicit Rent (depreciation)	59	165	106
Property Tax Imputation	21	81	60
Costs Borne by Students	56	56	—
Foregone Earnings	1,120	1,120	—
Total	$1,708	$2,386	$678

Source: Arthur J. Corazzini, "The Decision to Invest in Vocational Education: An Analysis of Costs and Benefits," *Journal of Human Resources* vol. 3 (Supp. 1968): table 4, p. 102.

Table 2-2
Benefit-Cost Ratios of Vocational High Schools in Worcester, Massachusetts, 1963–1964

Earnings Differential	5% Discount Rate		10% Discount Rate	
	10-Year Time Horizon	30-Year Time Horizon	10-Year Time Horizon	30-Year Time Horizon
$320	.9	1.7	.6	1.0
$500	1.3	2.6	1.0	1.5

Source: Arthur J. Corazzini, "The Decision to Invest in Vocational Education: An Analysis of Costs and Benefits," *Journal of Human Resources,* vol. 3, (Supp. 1968), table 6, p. 106.

percent, benefit-cost ratios generally are less than unity. However, if favorable earnings assumptions are made, and the time horizon extended to thirty years, the ratio equals 1.0.

Data developed by Corazzini indicate that vocational education in Worcester has not been especially valuable in terms of economic payoff, and he concludes that some alternative programs need to be developed in order to serve students' needs in a less expensive way.[3] According to Corazzini, many vocational programs have served only to indicate a career choice; they have not served to enhance students' economic futures.[4] These conclusions, however, must be interpreted with the five following observations kept in mind.

First, Corazzini notes that he probably has overestimated costs of increasing enrollments in the vocational high schools, because they appeared to be underutilized. Second, he has not examined employment experiences of the vocational high school graduates — the second half of the wage rate-employment equation that determines earnings. Third, potential advantages of vocational education not measured by earnings have not been investigated. Fourth, calculated costs include capital expenses and an adjustment for taxes. Last, earnings estimates rely on entry-level wage rates of graduates employed in a few large industrial firms. Thus, his conclusions concerning the efficiency of vocational-technical schools must be examined carefully.

Recalculations of benefit-cost ratios, starting with data presented by Corazzini and modifying his calculations to make the methodology parallel more common practice, result in substantially different conclusions than those Corazzini has reached. Taking cost data developed by him, and subtracting additions he makes for implicit rent and tax imputations results in vocational high school costing $512 more a year per student than general high schools rather than the $678 originally calculated by Corazzini. The unweighted average starting pay of vocational high school graduates was $1.93 per hour; that of general high school graduates $1.75. Using this $.18 per hour differential as an estimate of the wage advantage of vocational graduates and Max Eninger's nation-wide data for relative employment experiences of vocational and academic high school graduates between 1953 and 1962,[5] results in an estimated earnings advantage for vocational graduates of $273 per year.

Benefit-cost ratios calculated on this data appear in Table 2–3. Using the relatively conservative assumptions of a 10 percent discount rate and a ten-year time horizon, the benefit-cost ratio is 1.3. With more liberal assumptions, a ratio as high as 3.3 results. These estimates probably are closer to actual economic results than those presented by Corazzini, and suggest that vocational high schools have returned economic benefits in excess of costs. These results should not be interpreted to mean that more funds should be allocated to vocational high schools — alternative methods of preparing youth for entry into occupations may be still more efficient. They do suggest, however, that vocational high schools may be doing more than simply indicating students' career choices.

Table 2-3
Recalculated Benefit-Cost Ratios of Vocational High Schools in
Worcester, Massachusetts, 1963-1964[a]

Discount Rate	10-Year Time Horizon	30-Year Time Horizon
5 percent	1.7	3.3
10 percent	1.3	1.9

Source: Calculated from data developed by Arthur J. Corazzini, "The Decision to Invest in Vocational Education: An Analysis of Costs and Benefits," Journal of Human Resources, vol. 3, (Supp., 1968), pp. 88-120; and Max U. Eninger, The Process and Product of T. & I. High School Level Vocational Education in the United States: The Product (Pittsburgh: American Institutes for Research, 1965).
[a]Cost differential $512 per year and earnings advantage $473 per year.

Vocational Education in Three Pennsylvania Cities

An extremely detailed study of costs and benefits of vocational education in three Pennsylvania cities has been made by Jacob J. Kaufman, Teh-wei Hu, Maw Lin Lee, and Ernst W. Stromsdorfer[c] (referred to hereafter as Kaufman et al.).[6] Kaufman et al. use cross-sectional data over a five-year period between 1956 and 1960 to calculate the marginal costs (additional costs) of educating students in vocational and in comprehensive high schools (Table 2-4).

In both cities, comprehensive high schools were less expensive to operate than vocational schools. Between 1956 and 1960, marginal costs of vocational schools in City A were $156 above comprehensive schools. In City C, they were $116 above comprehensive schools. Marginal costs of both types of schools were lower in City C than in City A.

Kaufman et al. utilize equations developed from the cost data to estimate optimal enrollments of the high schools, i.e., school size where average costs per student would be minimized. Ignoring capital costs, optimal enrollment of comprehensive schools in City A is 2,957; in City C, 3,191 (Table 2-5). The optimal size of vocational schools in Cities A and C respectively is 2,295 and 3,339. When capital costs are included in City A, the optimal-sized comprehensive school increases and the optimal-sized vocational school decreases.[d]

---

[c]Cost data are available for only two of the three cities (A and C), so, while City B is included in the discussions of the results of vocational education, it is not included in calculations of benefit-cost ratios.
[d]Kaufman et al. note that these calculations are tentative, and should be interpreted carefully. The attempt to say something about the optimal-sized school relative to the actual size of those being utilized is important. By making such estimates, we can say something about the efficiency with which current schools are being operated. According to Robert S. Goldfarb ["The Evaluation of Government Programs: The Case of New Haven's Manpower Training Activities," Yale Economic Essays, vol. 9, no. 2 (Fall, 1969), pp. 59-104] the assumption made by most cost-benefit studies—that programs are being efficiently operated— is a major failing. To the extent that efficiency of the programs is discussed, then, this fault of cost-benefit analysis is avoided.

Table 2-4
Marginal Costs of Operating Schools in Cities A and C, for Fiscal Years 1955–1956 Through 1959–1960 Based on Average Daily Attendance (ADA)

| | City A | | | | City C | | | |
| | Comprehensive | | Vocational | | Comprehensive | | Vocational | |
Year	ADA	Marginal Costs	ADA	Marginal Costs	ADA	Marginal Costs	ADA	Marginal Costs
1956	1,834	$331	1,772	$408	2,232	$240	2,031	$432
1957	1,827	411	1,667	466	2,714	285	2,229	365
1958	1,820	325	1,254	476	2,513	289	2,294	194
1959	1,993	325	1,279	465	2,511	259	2,474	210
1960	2,126	313	1,303	540	2,458	329	2,428	279
1956–60	1,917	308	1,426	464	2,505	270	2,316	386

Source: Jacob J. Kaufman, Teh-wei Hu, Maw Lin Lee, and Ernst W. Stromsdorfer, "A Cost-Effectiveness Study of Vocational Education," *A Comparison of Vocational and Non-vocational Education in Secondary Schools* (University Park, Penn.: Institute for Research on Human Resources, Pennsylvania State University, March 1969), tables 20 and 21, pp. 123–24.

Table 2-5
School Enrollments that Would Minimize Average Student Costs
in Two Cities, 1956-1960

	Comprehensive	Vocational
City A	2,957	2,295
City A[a]	3,350	1,958
City C	3,191	3,339

Source: Jacob J. Kaufman, Teh-wei Hu, Maw Lin Lee, and Ernst W. Stromsdorfer, "A Cost-Effectiveness Study of Vocational Education," *A Comparison of Vocational and Non-vocational Education in Secondary Schools* (University Park, Penn.: Institute for Research on Human Resources, Pennsylvania State University, March 1969), p. 125.
[a]Including capital costs.

Economic benefits to society are measured by the earnings advantage of vocational high school graduates over comprehensive high school graduates during the first six years following graduation. The earnings advantage is controlled for differences in I.Q., race, marital status, and level of father's education. Average monthly earnings of graduates, when differences in personal characteristics have been controlled for, appear in Table 2-6. It is interesting to note that academic graduates earned less than graduates of any other curriculum.[e] First-year monthly earnings were $292, compared to $344, $349, and $354 for vocational-academic, vocational-comprehensive, and vocational-technical graduates, respectively. Graduates of the vocational-technical curriculum experienced highest earnings of all graduates in the first and sixth years ($354 and $491 respectively), although vocational-academic graduates averaged most during the entire period ($469). In each case, however (except for

---

[e]Kaufman et al. differentiate between graduates of five different curricula. All except vocational-technical graduates graduated from comprehensive high schools. The five types of curricula are described as follows:

"1, the academic curriculum for those who were college orientated;
2, the vocational-academic curriculum for those who had a dual qualification both as academic and vocational-technical graduates;
3, the general curriculum, whose curriculum was below the level of college preparatory and whose basic characteristic appears to be a lack of specific career orientation;
4, the vocational-comprehensive curriculum, which included those who took vocationally oriented courses but whose preparation was less concentrated than vocational-technical; and
5, the vocational-technical curriculum for those who concentrated their efforts in a coherent area of vocational or technical study."

[Jacob J. Kaufman, et al., "A Cost-Effectiveness Study of Vocational Education," *A Comparison of Vocational and Non-Vocational Education in Secondary Schools* (University Park, Penn.: Institute for Research on Human Resources, Pennsylvania State University, March, 1969), p. 133.] All of the earnings data refer only to those high school graduates who did not attend college.

Table 2-6

Average Monthly Earnings of Non-College-Bound High School
Graduates in a Six-Year Period Following Graduation[a]

| | Average Before-Tax Monthly Earnings | | |
Curriculum	First Year	Sixth Year	Six-Year Average
Academic	$292	$441	$415
Voc-Academic	344	486	469
Voc-Comp	349	463	451
General	322	454	433
Voc-Technical	354	491	463

Source: Jacob J. Kaufman, Teh-wei Hu, Maw Lin Lee, and Ernst W. Stromsdorfer,
"A Cost-Effectiveness Study of Vocational Education," A Comparison of Voca-
tional and Non-vocational Education in Secondary Schools (University Park,
Penn.: Institute for Research on Human Resources, Pennsylvania State University,
March 1969), table 27, p. 140.
[a]In 1960 prices.

vocational-academic), the earnings advantage of non–academic-curricula
graduates decreased over the six year period. Table 2-7, containing annual
earnings differentials, shows that in the first year after graduation, vocational-
comprehensive graduates earned $684 more than academic graduates. By
the sixth year they were earning only $288 more. Vocational-technical graduates
earned $744 more the first year, and $600 more the sixth. Over the six-year
period, vocational-technical graduates averaged $576 more than academic
graduates. Vocational-academic graduates (from comprehensive schools)
averaged $648 more over the six-year period.

Since differential cost data exist only for vocational-technical schools and
comprehensive schools as such, it is not possible to calculate benefit-cost
ratios for curricula other than vocational-technical. Kaufman et al. calculate
what seems (to this writer) to be very conservative benefit-cost ratios when
vocational-technical education is viewed as an alternative to the curricula in
comprehensive schools. The benefit-cost ratios in Table 2-8 are calculated with
the assumptions that benefits (earnings differentials) are constant and equal
to the six-year average over six years and then change to zero, and that total
marginal costs in the vocational-technical schools are the relevant costs for
computing the ratios. Even so, the lowest benefit-cost ratios in Cities A and C are
1.1 and 2.3 respectively. The data thus suggest that vocational-technical
schools, when viewed as an alternative to comprehensive schools taken as a whole
(including both academic and vocational education), return more in benefits
than they cost.

It is not clear, however, that Kaufman et al. calculated the benefit-cost

Table 2-7
Annual Earnings Advantage of Non-Academic Graduates Over Academic
Graduates in a Six-Year Period Following Graduation[a]

Curriculum	First Year	Sixth Year	Six-Year Average
Voc-Academic	$624	$600	$648
Voc-Comprehensive	684	288	432
Voc-Technical	744	600	576

Source: Table 2-6 above.
[a]In 1960 prices, gross of taxes.

Table 2-8
Benefit-Cost Ratios of Vocational-Technical vs. Comprehensive High
School Programs in Two Cities in Pennsylvania, 1956-1960

Discount Rate	B/C in City A	B/C in City C
6 percent	1.3	2.9
10 percent	1.1	2.3

Source: Jacob J. Kaufman, Teh-wei Hu, Maw Lin Lee, and Ernst W. Stromsdorfer,
"A Cost-Effectiveness Study of Vocational Education," A Comparison of Voca-
tional and Non-vocational Education in Secondary Schools (University Park,
Penn.: Institute for Research on Human Resources, Pennsylvania State University,
March 1969), table 43, p. 171.

ratios on correct cost data. The ratios are arrived at by use of the additional
benefits of vocational-technical schools over comprehensive schools, but
the additional costs over no school at all. More relevant costs are the differences
in marginal costs between vocational-technical schools and comprehensive
schools; or, the cost of transferring a student from a comprehensive school to a
vocational-technical school.[f] Ratios are calculated from these data in Kaufman
et al., but labeled "ratio of difference in marginal benefits to difference in
marginal costs" rather than "benefit-cost ratio."

Ratios based on the differences in marginal costs and benefits are larger than
those labeled "cost-benefit" ratios calculated by Kaufman et al. These ratios
appear in Table 2-9. With conservative assumptions (10 percent discount rate and
ten-year time horizon), benefit-cost ratios in Cities A and C respectively are
4.1 and 10.7. Favorable assumptions (5 percent discount rate and thirty-year
time horizon) yield respective ratios of 10.5 and 27.1.

One might be tempted to conclude that more money should be spent on
vocational-technical schools than presently is spent (at least in Cities A and C in

[f]This is the marginal cost concept.

Table 2–9
Restated Benefit-Cost Ratios of Vocational Technical vs.
Comprehensive High School Programs in Two cities in
Pennsylvania, 1956–1960[a]

	10-Year Time Horizon		30-Year Time Horizon	
Discount Rate	City A	City C	City A	City C
5 percent	5.4	13.9	10.5	27.1
10 percent	4.1	10.7	10.5	15.8

Source: Calculated from Jacob J. Kaufman, Teh-wei Hu, Maw Lin Lee, and
Ernst W. Stromsdorfer, "A Cost-Effectiveness Study of Vocational Education,"
A Comparison of Vocational and Non-vocational Education in Secondary Schools
(University Park, Penn.: Institute for Research on Human Resources, Pennsylvania
State University, March 1969), table 43, p. 171; and table 41, p. 168.

Note: Kaufman et al. limit their calculations to a six-year period on the justification that there is a convergence of earnings by the sixth year of the two groups,
and no earnings data are available after that. Data of earning differentials in
table 43 of that study, however, do not show this convergence. Thus I have
extended the period of observation to make these ratios more comparable to
others presented in this book on the justification that the earnings do not
necessarily converge.

[a]Based on "ratio of difference in marginal benefits to difference in marginal cost."

Pennsylvania). But this is not a safe conclusion to reach for the following
reason. The calculated ratios compare costs and benefits of graduates from
vocational-technical schools against *all* graduates of comprehensive schools (who
did not attend college), *including vocational graduates from those schools*.
We have learned nothing about the relative efficiency of offering vocational
education in a vocational-technical school versus offering it in a comprehensive
school, an important failing if a policy commitment has been made to offer
vocational education. Nor have we learned anything about the efficiency of
vocational education in a comprehensive school versus academic education.

The Kaufman et al. study is a "gold mine" of information concerning
relative experiences of vocational and nonvocational graduates, and the
experiences of vocational graduates with different characteristics. A few of these
observations are presented below.

Earnings experiences of vocational-technical graduates varied considerably
depending on these students' courses. The first year following graduation,
those taking agriculture and horticulture courses earned least of these graduates;
$108 a month less than those taking commercial courses. Graduates in tool
design earned most – $94 a month more than commercial course graduates. By
the sixth year, building trade graduates were earning $166 a month less than
commercial graduates, who in turn were earning $140 a month less than
graduates in agriculture and horticulture. The low income of building trades

Table 2-10

Relative Average Before-Tax Monthly Earnings Experiences of
Vocational-Technical Graduates in Pennsylvania[a]

Course	First Year Following Graduation	Sixth Year Following Graduation	Six-Year Average
Commercial	$ –	$ –	$ –
Food Service	– 70	– 16	–21
Building Trades	– 36	–166	–87
Mechanical and Repair	– 58	45	4
Tool Design	94	110	98
Wood Working Occupations	– 21	69	51
Electrical & Electronics	0	8	8
Ag. & Horticulture	–108	140	34
Professional Occupations	– 30	79	26
Distributive Education	3	– 71	–49
Personal Services	– 75	– 84	–85
Clothing & Fabrics	11	– 49	–23

Source: Jacob J. Kaufman, Teh-wei Hu, Maw Lin Lee, and Ernst W. Stromsdorfer, "A Cost-Effectiveness Study of Vocational Education," *A Comparison of Vocational and Non-vocational Education in Secondary Schools* (University Park, Penn.: Institute for Research on Human Resources, Pennsylvania State University, March 1969), table 39, p. 162.

[a]Measured as earnings relative to graduates in Commercial courses.

graduates is difficult to understand, unless a high percentage of these graduates was unable to find work in the trades and took jobs in occupations other than those trained for.

Occupational classifications with minus signs beside the earnings figures in Table 2-10 might be regarded as lower wage occupations (relatively), and those with positive amounts as higher wage occupations. Except for building trades, the occupations with minus signs follow most preconceived expectations. Food services, distributive education, personal services, and clothing and fabrics are often regarded as lower paying occupations. Graduates of these curricula earned from $21 to $85 a month less than commercial graduates over the first six years following graduation. Mechanical and repair, tool design, wood working, electrical and electronics, agriculture and horticulture, and professional occupations often are regarded as higher paying occupations. Graduates with these skills did in fact earn more than the average vocational-technical student.

On the other hand, these earnings figures reflect the effects of withdrawals from the labor force and unemployment. Occupations for which a relatively large number of women are trained, even if higher paying occupations, will show lower than average earnings if a large number of women marry and withdraw from the labor force. Likewise graduates in occupations characterized by relatively high unemployment rates will earn less than their wage rates would suggest. While these influences make net earnings a less reliable indicator of relative welfare levels, earnings can be an important consideration. To the extent that we are interested in increasing future incomes as much as possible with current expenditures, we will want to train persons in occupations characterized by high earnings, giving preference in training to those most likely to remain in the labor force and fully employed.

Additional findings:

1. Vocational-technical graduates in training-related jobs earned $648 more the first year following graduation than those with jobs in non-training-related occupations. By the sixth year this earnings difference had disappeared.
2. In the short run, those who completed some type of post–high school training earned less (as expected) than those who worked. Six years after graduation, however, they were earning $33 a month more than those without additional formal training.
3. Males earned more than females, and the differential increased over the six-year period.
4. I.Q. was related positively to earnings, but affected earnings very little.
5. The father's educational level did not affect earnings of graduates.
6. No significant differences showed in vocational-technical students' earnings in the three cities studied. This means that the substantial difference in benefit-cost ratios between Cities A and C (Table 2-9) was due partly to lower earnings of academic graduates as well as to slightly lower costs of education in City C (relative to City A).
7. Academic graduates experienced the highest unemployment of all graduates the first year following graduation. They were unemployed 1.8 months longer than vocational-technical graduates, 1.7 months longer than vocational-comprehensive graduates, and 1.5 and 1.1 months longer than vocational-academic and general graduates, respectively.
8. Academic graduates took longer to find first jobs following graduation than other types of graduates.
9. During the sixth year following graduation, vocational-technical graduates were still experiencing significantly less unemployment than academic graduates in spite of the fact that after six years, occupation was not related to type of graduate.
10. Dropouts from vocational-technical schools fared better than dropouts from comprehensive schools. (Since there might be significant differences in characteristics of students entering these programs, this observation must be interpreted with care.)

11. Vocational-technical graduates obtained more jobs in areas of their career interests than non-vocational-technical graduates. Thus vocational-technical graduates were able to pursue their interests more closely than other types of graduates.
12. No difference in frequency of voting existed between graduates of different curricula.
13. No differences showed in the aspiration levels of students among the various curricula (measured by questionnaire).
14. Vocational-technical graduates required an average of about three months less on-the-job training than graduates of other curricula and earned $245 more during that training period.
15. Race did not affect earnings.[7]

These observations indicate that vocational-technical graduates experience benefits other than those measured by relative earnings. On the other hand, to the extent that voting behavior is an indication of good citizenship, vocational training does not make them better citizens. Kaufman et al. reach a predictable conclusion from the above analysis.

This study has indicated that further investment in vocational-technical education is worthwhile. It does not necessarily follow that all alternative investments are not more worthwhile. Further studies are required to evaluate alternative programs of vocational or occupational education.[8]

Vocational Education in One Pennsylvania City

A study closely associated with that performed by Kaufman et al. has been conducted by Kaufman and Lewis.[9] Like the Kaufman et al. study, Kaufman and Lewis (referred to hereafter as the Kaufman study) are interested in vocational education in Pennsylvania. They are interested in a broader evaluation of the vocational education process than Kaufman et al., but they also examine the employment and earnings experiences of vocational graduates, and compute benefit-cost ratios. Kaufman utilizes some of the cost data developed by Kaufman et al., but examines the experiences of 1960 and 1962 graduates through 1964.

Kaufman uses cost data from school records in one large city. Data on graduates were collected through mailed questionnaires. Per-student costs of vocational education were estimated to be $553 per year ($2,212 undiscounted over four years). Per-year average benefits were $838 (as measured by the vocational-nonvocational earnings differential) over the four-year period following graduation (two years for the 1962 graduates). Kaufman controls for sex, race, I.Q., occupation, father's educational level, post-high school training, and training relatedness of employment. On the assumption that benefits would remain constant over the entire working life of the graduates (estimated to be forty-seven years), the following benefit-cost ratios appear in Table 2-11. With a discount rate of 5 percent and a ten-year time horizon, the benefit-cost ratio is 2.8. If the time horizon is extended to thirty years the ratio increases to 5.4. Even at the relatively high discount rate of 10 percent the respective ratios for the two time horizons are 2.1 and 3.1. We may conclude that cost-benefit analysis suggests that vocational education in Pennsylvania has been returning more in benefits than it cost.

It is important to note that the earnings advantage experienced by vocational graduates in the one Pennsylvania city was due to their more regular employment as well as higher wage rates. The average weekly starting pay of both academic (used in the same sense as by Kaufman et al.) and vocational graduates was $58. Vocational graduates earned more than academic graduates because they were employed about 6 percent more of the time, and because their wages increased faster.[10] These advantages, according to Kaufman

. . . appeared to be associated with obtaining a job which was related to their preparation. The employment stability and average monthly earnings indices were significantly higher for those graduates whose first jobs were highly related to their training.[11]

The observation that more regular employment is associated with training-relatedness of jobs becomes more significant when Kaufman finds that even when only a modest number of vocational graduates entered the labor market each year, many could not find jobs closely related to their training.

As Table 2-12 shows, architectural drafting graduates were most successful in finding jobs closely related to their training, with 80 percent finding such jobs. Next "best" area of study was in the business education curriculum with 78 percent. Auto body repair (64 percent) and sheet metal work (62 percent) ran a somewhat distant third and fourth. The relatively small success of graduates of some of the building trades skills in finding training-related jobs (and the earnings disadvantage experienced in jobs unrelated to training) is consistent with findings of Kaufman et al. that many vocational-technical students in building trades courses earn less than the average vocational-technical graduate.

Part of the difficulty vocational graduates experienced in finding training-related jobs may lie with poor school placement services. Kaufman reports that only about 20 percent of graduates' initial jobs resulted from school placement efforts.[12] Kaufman feels, however, that a large part of the problem lies in schools' efforts to turn out vocational graduates with too specialized skills. He feels that vocational schools would do well to offer fewer, but broader, courses of study.[13]

Table 2-11

Benefit-Cost Ratios of Vocational Education in One Pennsylvania
City, 1960-1964

Discount Rate	10-Year Time Horizon	30-Year Time Horizon
5 percent	2.8	5.4
10 percent	2.1	3.1

Source: Calculated from Jacob J. Kaufman and Morgan V. Lewis, *The Potential of Vocational Education: Observations and Conclusions* (University Park, Penn.: Institute for Research on Human Resources, Pennsylvania State University, 1968), pp. 142-45.

Table 2-12

Percentage of Vocational High School Graduates from One
Pennsylvania City Finding Initial Jobs Identical to, or Highly Related
to Their Training

Program	Percent Finding Jobs for Which They Were Trained
Business Education	78
Trade and Industrial	
Sheet Metal	62
Auto Body	64
Printing	58
Plumbing	54
Machine Shop	54
Carpentry	40
Auto Mechanics	44
Bricklaying	29
Welding	38
Cabinet Making	28
Technical	
Architectural Drafting	80
Mechanical Drawing	54
Electronics	31
Industrial Chemistry	40

Source: Jacob J. Kaufman and Morgan V. Lewis, *The Potential of Vocational Education: Observations and Conclusions* (University Park, Penn.: Institute for Research on Human Resources, Pennsylvania State University, 1968), table 48, p. 92, and table 49, p. 93.

Kaufman makes several other observations in evaluating experiences of vocational graduates. First, self-evaluation by vocational and nonvocational graduates indicated that vocational students felt better prepared for their first jobs than did nonvocational graduates. But supervisors felt just the reverse — that non-vocational graduates performed better on their first jobs than vocational graduates.[14] No clear explanation for this appears. Last, when graduates were asked to rate their first jobs with respect to satisfaction in type of work, pay and promotion opportunities, no differences in ratings emerge between vocational and nonvocational graduates.[15] Thus vocational graduates apparently were deriving no more satisfaction from their first jobs than non-vocational graduates.

Kaufman's study suggests that investment in vocational education as conducted in the Pennsylvania city was worthwhile insofar as it returned more in economic benefits than it cost. On the other hand, vocational programs were not accomplishing much when measured by their students' job performance or job satisfaction.

Kaufman refuses to suggest that his study results indicate that more funds should be shifted into vocational education as it has been conducted in the past. He suggests, rather, that programs should be reorganized to make them less job specific and more meaningful and relevant to students with various disadvantages.[16]

Vocational Education in New York City

In his analysis of vocational education in New York City, Michael Taussig [17] reaches a different conclusion concerning the economic efficiency of vocational education from the authors of the three previous studies examined.[18][g] Taussig's study was prompted by the New York City School Board's decision to move away from a system of separate academic and vocational high schools toward a system of comprehensive high schools.

According to Taussig, this decision was influenced by civil rights groups which objected to a separate school system comprised of large numbers of minority groups. Additionally, both research and casual observation suggested that vocational schools were not effective in preparing students for problems they would have to face when they left school. If true, little justification could be found for the higher per-student costs of vocational-technical schools. Finally, educators had suggested comprehensive high schools as an alternative to separate vocational schools. Taussig has attempted to discover if vocational high schools were more effective than academic high schools in preparing students for the labor market, and if so, were effective enough to justify their additional costs.

In 1965 New York City's school system included sixty academic high schools and twenty-nine vocational high schools with respective total enrollments

---

[g]While Corazzini agrees with Taussig concerning the apparent low economic returns of vocational education, it should be recalled that "reasonable" manipulation of Corazzini's data resulted in benefit-cost ratios exceeding one. The same thing happens with Taussig's data.

Table 2-13

Annual Per-Student Costs of Vocational High Schools in New York City, 1964-1965

	Academic High Schools	Vocational High Schools	Differential
Current Costs	$ 974	$1,391	$417
Capital Costs	214	306	92
Total Costs	$1,188	$1,697	$509

Source: Michael K. Taussig, "An Economic Analysis of Vocational Education in the New York City High Schools," Journal of Human Resources vol. 3 (Supp. 1968), table 2, p. 78, citing New York City Board of Education, Office of Business Affairs, Bureau of Finance, Annual Financial and Statistical Report, 1964-65, p. 18.

of 200,000 and 40,000. Of the twenty-nine vocational schools, twenty-four were "multi-trade" schools. The other five offered individual trades in art and design, automotive trades, aviation, fashion industries and printing and generally were considered to be better than multi-trade schools.[19]

Taussig uses cost data collected by the schools, and estimates that current annual costs per student were $974 and $1,391 in the academic and vocational schools respectively (Table 2-13). Respective per-student capital costs were estimated at $214 and $306. The total annual per-student costs of vocational schools exceeded those of academic schools by $509. Taussig notes two factors that suggest actual costs of increasing enrollments in vocational schools were less than this amount. First, there is good evidence that the vocational schools were underutilized, so that transferring additional students to them from academic schools would not add an additional $519 per student. Second, some vocational school facilities were utilized for evening classes, ". . . so that the higher capital costs of the vocational programs are overstated to some unknown extent."[20] On the other hand, Taussig feels actual capital costs probably have been underestimated in vocational schools because the original estimate did not allow for replacement of equipment. Also, if the alternative of vocational school students is considered to be a general academic curriculum rather than college preparatory, academic high school costs probably have been overstated. Taussig concludes that he is not sure of the net direction of the bias.[21]

Questionnaires mailed to students by the schools were the source of benefit data. Table 2-14 contains postgraduation employment experiences of the high school graduates. The short-run nature of the figures makes them merely suggestive, but they do indicate that vocational high school graduates experience less unemployment following graduation than graduates of academic high schools. This difference is especially noticeable for males. Male graduates from academic high schools were unemployed 25.5 percent of the time after

Table 2–14

Percentage of Time Unemployed Following Graduation Experienced by Vocational and Non-Vocational High School Graduates in New York City, 1964–1965

	Academic Graduates	Vocational Graduates
Average Experience	17.6	10.5
Males	25.5	10.8

Source: Michael K. Taussig, "An Economic Analysis of Vocational Education in the New York City High Schools," *Journal of Human Resources*, vol. 3, (Supp. 1968), p. 70.

graduation, while graduates from the vocational high schools were "only" unemployed 10.8 percent of the time. Taussig notes, however, that academic high school graduates are not necessarily a good control group because some vocational schools screen entering students, more academic school graduates are likely to enter the armed forces, and race has not been controlled for.[22]

While vocational school graduates were employed more of the time than academic school graduates, it is not clear that they earned a wage premium. For example, salaries of graduates from the seven all-female vocational schools about equaled median entrance salaries for inexperienced typists in New York City — $1.50 per hour for the former group as compared to $62 to $65 per week for the latter.[23] Additionally, Taussig cites a follow-up study conducted in a suburban county near New York City of earnings of vocational and nonvocational graduates immediately following graduation, and after six years. It detected no significant difference between earnings of the two types of graduates.[24] Thus Taussig cannot find firm evidence that the vocational curriculum offers an economic advantage to students over the nonvocational curriculum.

Two other aspects of the ability of vocational education to increase earnings are examined. First, Taussig hypothesizes that vocational students placed in training-related jobs should earn more than vocational students not so placed. A 12-cent differential prevailed in favor of such male graduates ($1.48 per hour vs. $1.36 per hour), but not for female graduates. Second, he hypothesizes that vocational school graduates should earn more than vocational school dropouts. However, a 1965 survey of 1962 graduates from the School of Printing indicates that ". . . earnings differentials between its graduates and its dropouts averaged only $1.00 per week, both immediately after graduation and again after 2 years." [25] The main cause for this, according to Taussig, is probably the apprenticeship program graduates of the School of Printing must go through after they graduate. High school training apparently does not decrease the time the graduates must spend as apprentices.

Taussig suggests that employers simply use vocational schools as a screening device in a labor market characterized by excess supplies of labor, and that they increasingly tend to hire only at entry-level jobs and promote internally. The burden of unemployment, then, is merely shifted from vocational graduates to academic graduates, with no net effect on total employment or earnings.[26] This probable shifting of unemployment, combined with inflexible apprenticeship programs, tends to limit the wage-advantage possibilities of vocational graduates.

Taussig declines to calculate a specific benefit-cost ratio for vocational high schools in New York City because it ". . . would give a false precision to the incomplete evidence available. . ."[27] He concludes, however, that he cannot find firm evidence that vocational schools in New York City yield positive economic benefits. The evident lack of economic benefits could go unnoticed by those operating the city's education program because Taussig feels the vocational schools themselves did not have goals that would indicate whether vocational training brought positive economic benefits. Three implicit criteria used in evaluating past programs — (1) good conditions within the schools, (2) placement in training-related jobs, (3) satisfied employers — could all be satisfied in the absence of economic benefits.[28]

Noneconomic benefits may exist though, and Taussig also considers the possibility that vocational programs may serve as a dropout-prevention program.[h] Not enough data are available to test this possibility. Students in vocational schools also may receive high consumption benefits. Study of the subject matter itself might be highly valued by many students and deliver unmeasured benefits.

Taussig insists that the displacement effect is going to be strong unless vocational graduates earn a wage premium over nonvocational graduates (demonstrating that they are recognized by employers as being more productive and capable of performing jobs which are not suitable for nonvocational graduates). This insistence that the displacement effect occurs in the absence of a demonstrated wage-rate differential appears prudent. Unfortunately, no one yet has demonstrated that displacement does not occur even if a wage differential exists. The differential simply may represent part of the costs faced by employers of training non–vocational school graduates.[i] Employers would then prefer to hire vocational graduates when available even at higher wages, and hire nonvocational graduates at lower wages only when vocational graduates are not available. Displacement of nonvocational graduates occurs in either case.

---

[h]This possibility is reasonable in light of a survey cited by Thomas I. Ribich [*Education and Poverty* (Washington, D.C.: The Brookings Institution, 1968), p. 60.] revealing that the prime reason students give for dropping out of school is lack of interest in subject matter. Economic reasons are given less frequently. Hopefully, a student could find something of interest in a multi-skill vocational school.

[i]This suggestion is consistent with findings of Kaufman et al. that vocational-technical graduates received three months less on-the-job training than academic graduates.

Even if we could insist on finding a wage rate advantage for vocational graduates before concluding that vocational education yields positive economic benefits, Taussig's data are too fragmentary to allow any firm conclusion either way. Additionally, he does not control for differences in personal characteristics between vocational and academic graduates. But since Corazzini[29] has reached conclusions similar to Taussig with no better data, Taussig's data just as legitimately (sic) can be adjusted in the same manner as Corazzini's.

If the cost data are adjusted to ignore capital costs (common practice), and if the wage and employment experiences of New York City graduates mirror those of the national sample of vocational graduates collected by Eninger (see Table 2-21),[j] earnings of vocational high school graduates exceed those of academic graduates by a sufficient amount to achieve benefit-cost ratios that all exceed one. As Table 2-15 indicates, the lowest ratio (with a ten-year time horizon and a 10 percent rate of discount) is 1.7. Liberalizing the assumptions to a lower discount rate and a longer time horizon increases the calculated ratio to 4.3. The cautious conclusion then might be reached that vocational education in New York City does yield significant net economic benefits.

Experiences of a National Sampling of Vocational Graduates

The most comprehensive data concerning the economic impact of secondary vocational education on its graduates was compiled by Max Eninger in 1965.[30] While his is not a cost-benefit study, not being concerned with the costs of vocational education, its broad coverage provides a kind of "check" on the two local studies examined earlier in which Kaufman participated. Eninger drew his data from a nationwide sample of 10,000 male high school graduates stratified by geographic area, school enrollment, and type of school. This 1965 sample included graduates of 1953, 1958, and 1962 from 100 high schools (50 comprehensive and 50 vocational-technical) in thirty-eight states. The study indicates that graduates of vocational curricula who do not go on to college consistently earn higher incomes and are employed more regularly than nonvocational graduates of comprehensive high schools who also do not attend college.

A vocational graduate's first benefit was a shortened period between graduation and first job. Table 2-16 illustrates this. In 1953, vocational graduates

---

[j]Actually, the national experience of vocational-technical graduates is substantially better than the average vocational graduate's (including those from comprehensive schools), so the assumption underlying the adjustment is that vocational-technical graduates fared somewhat worse in New York City than they did nationally.

Table 2-15
Benefit-Cost Ratios of Vocational-Technical High Schools in New York City, 1964–1965

Discount Rate	10-Year Time Horizon	30-Year Time Horizon
5 percent	2.2	4.3
10 percent	1.7	2.5

Source: Calculated from Max U. Eninger, *The Process and Product of T. & I. High School Level Vocational Education in the United States: The Product* (Pittsburgh: American Institutes for Research, 1965); and Michael K. Taussig, "An Economic Analysis of Vocational Education in the New York City High Schools," *Journal of Human Resources*, vol. 3, (Supp. 1968), pp. 59–87.

Table 2-16
Number of Months Between Graduation and First Job for a National Sample of High School Graduates in 1953, 1958, and 1962

Year of Graduation	Vocational Graduates	Academic Graduates
1953	1.3	2.6
1958	2.3	4.0
1962	1.7	2.8
Average	1.8	3.2

Source: Max U. Eninger, *The Process and Product of T. & I. High School Level Vocational Education in the United States: The Product* (Pittsburgh: American Institutes for Research, 1965), table 54, p. 5–8.

averaged 1.3 months between graduation and their first jobs, while academic graduates required 2.6 months to find employment. In 1958, a recession year, vocational graduates spent more time seeking first jobs than in either 1953 or 1962 (2.3 months vs. 1.3 and 1.7 months respectively, but the recession lengthened even further the initial unemployment time for academic graduates (4.0 months vs. 2.6 and 2.8 months respectively). One reason for this may lie in the vocational graduates' greater preparation for employment. Another probably lies in the placement efforts of vocational schools. Eninger reports that 37.7 percent of vocational graduates found first jobs as a direct result of assistance from their schools, while only 5.6 percent of academic graduates found jobs through such assistance. Academic graduates tended to rely more heavily on aid from relatives and friends than did vocational graduates, as 50.9 percent of academic graduates and 31.9 percent of vocational graduates found initial employment through this method.[31]

Table 2-17

Hourly Wage Rates in Initial Jobs of 1953, 1958 and 1962 Vocational
and Academic High School Graduates[a]

Year	Graduate	Initial W/hr	Differential[b]	Current W/hr[c]	Differential[b]
1953	Vocational	$1.31	-.13	$3.02	-.04
	Academic	1.44		3.06	
1958	Vocational	1.46	-.02	2.46	.11
	Academic	1.48		2.35	
1962	Vocational	1.46	.02	2.01	.14
	Academic	1.44		1.87	

Source: Max U. Eninger, *The Process and Product of T. & I. High School Level
Vocational Education in the United States: The Product* (Pittsburgh: American
Institutes for Research, 1965), table 148, p. 9–44, and table 154, p. 9–53.
[a]Students who subsequently did not attend college.
[b]Hourly wage of vocational graduate less hourly wage of academic graduate.
[c]1964.

While vocational graduates were able to find initial jobs more rapidly than
nonvocational graduates, the wage rates received on those jobs are less gratifying
(see Table 2-17). The 1953 graduates of vocational programs actually earned
$.13 an hour *less* than academic graduates ($1.31 per hour vs. $1.44), while the
1958 graduates of vocational programs earned $.02 an hour less than academic
graduates on first jobs. In 1962, however, vocational graduates reversed
this relationship and began their first jobs with an $.02 wage-rate advantage over
nonvocational graduates. One might conclude from this that the quality of
vocational education relative to general education has been increasing between
1953 and 1962.[k] An interesting observation is that academic graduates began
at $1.44 an hour in 1962 as well as in 1953. Their average beginning wage
did not change. At the same time, entry wages of vocational graduates increased
by $.15 an hour from $1.31 to $1.46.

Although vocational graduates were not faring as well with respect to entry
wages as other graduates in 1953 and 1958, they were receiving more rapid
wage increases from employers. As a result, by 1964 the 1953 vocational
graduates were earning only $.04 an hour less than other graduates. The 1958
vocational graduates experienced a change in wages relative to nonvocational
graduates from $.02 an hour less in 1958 to $.11 an hour more in 1964.
In only two years (between 1962 and 1964) the 1962 graduates increased their
wage advantage from $.02 to $.14 an hour. The evidence is clear and consistent.

----

[k]More accurately, vocational education probably improved relative to academic
education between the classes attending 1949–1953 and 1958–1962.

Table 2-18

Percentage of Time Employed by 1953, 1958 and 1962 Vocational and Academic Graduates from Graduation Until 1964

Year of Graduation	Type of Graduate	Percentage of Time Employed	Difference Between the Two Types of Graduates
1953	Vocational	93.5	
	Academic	89.6	3.9
1958	Vocational	88.0	
	Academic	83.2	4.8
1962	Vocational	85.0	
	Academic	76.2	8.8

Source: Max U. Eninger, *The Process and Product of T. & I. High School Level Vocational Education in the United States: The Product* (Pittsburgh: American Institutes for Research, 1965), table 121, p. 9–10.

Graduates of vocational programs receive wage increases more rapidly than other types of high school graduates.[1]

Vocational graduates of 1953 and 1958 may have started at lower wages than their nonvocational contemporaries, but as Table 2-18 shows, along with the 1962 vocational graduates, they consistently experienced less unemployment than academic graduates. Between 1953 and 1964, the 1953 vocational graduates were employed 93.5 percent of the time, 3.9 percentage points more than academic graduates of that year. The 1958 graduates of vocational programs were employed 4.8 more percentage points, and the 1962 graduates 8.8 more percentage points than academic graduates. Apparently, then, vocational graduates are more successful in their employment experiences than academic graduates. They are receiving more rapid wage increases and experiencing less unemployment. In addition, their entry wage rates may now be higher.

From the above information it is possible to estimate the value of vocational education to society (relative to non-college bound academic graduates) at the time of graduation of the 1953, 1958 and 1962 vocational graduates. These estimates will be based on the relatively conservative assumption that the

---

[1]It must be remembered that the comparisons are between vocational high school graduates who do not receive post–high school education and nonvocational graduates who also do not go on to school. To the extent that a vocational education in high school reduces the probability that a student will attend a two- or four-year college, the advantage in earnings observed above tends to overstate the actual advantage of vocational education. Additionally, Eninger has not controlled for personal differences between vocational and nonvocational graduates. The bias this introduces is unknown. However, earnings projections in Table 2-23 from Eninger's benefit data are lower than those from Kaufman, et al., who *did* control such differences.

wage rate advantage (or disadvantage) of vocational graduates may be estimated by averaging wage-rate differentials in Table 2-17 and that this differential will remain constant throughout the time period being considered; and on the assumption that the relative unemployment experiences of vocational and academic graduates of the various years, as presented in Table 2-18, will remain unchanged in the future.

Values in Table 2-19 can be interpreted as estimates of what society might be willing to pay to provide vocational education (given current educational mix and institutional framework) in lieu of a general education in order just to break even.[m] The value of vocational education to society (as measured by increased earnings) in 1953 for 1953 graduates was quite modest; only several hundred dollars. Earnings of the 1958 vocational graduates increased rapidly enough to make the value of their future earnings in 1958 equal to several thousand dollars. The 1962 graduates' vocational education was worth even more – an average of $6,500 (when a 5 percent discount rate and thirty-year time horizon are used). Thus, under liberal discount rate and time horizon assumptions, if the average high school vocational graduate's education costs in 1962 exceeded the non-college bound academic graduate by less than $6,500, society was receiving a net benefit.

Remember that vocational graduates may come from both vocational-technical and comprehensive high schools. One question not investigated by the empirical studies examined earlier is how graduates of vocational-technical high schools fare relative to vocational graduates of comprehensive high schools. Additional data presented by Eninger throw some light on this question, and suggest that graduates from vocational-technical schools fare a little better than their counterparts from comprehensive high schools in subsequent employment experience. They start at slightly higher wages, receive wage increases a little faster (with the exception of 1953 graduates), and probably are unemployed less.

These data are contained in Tables 2-20 and 2-21. As indicated in Table 2-20, vocational graduates from vocational-technical schools received entry wage rates exceeding vocational graduates from comprehensive schools by $.02 an hour in 1953, $.10 an hour in 1958 and $.04 an hour in 1962. With the passage of time, the 1953 vocational graduates from comprehensive schools received more rapid wage increases, and by 1964 were earning $.06 an hour more than other vocational graduates. This was not the case with the 1958 and 1962 graduating classes. Not only did vocational-technical graduates begin with higher wages, they also received more rapid wage-rate increases.

In general, vocational-technical graduates also have had more regular

---

[m]Another interpretation would be to view these amounts as the maximum it can cost to furnish vocational education and still achieve a benefit-cost ratio of unity. Of course, using lower discount rates and extending the time horizon will raise these values.

Table 2-19
Value of Vocational Education Relative to Non-Vocational Education at the High School Level at the Time of Graduation for
1953, 1958 and 1962 Graduates[a]

Year of Graduation	10-Year Time Horizon		30-Year Time Horizon	
	5 Percent Discount Rate	10 Percent Discount Rate	5 Percent Discount Rate	10 Percent Discount Rate
1953	$ 127	$ 101	$ 254	$ 155
1958	2,015	1,604	4,012	2,456
1962	3,300	2,626	6,563	4,005

Source: Calculated from tables 2–17 and 2–18.
[a]Includes vocational education in comprehensive and vocational-technical high schools.

Table 2-20
Initial and 1964 Hourly Wage Rates of 1953, 1958 and 1962
Vocational Graduates by Type of School[a]

Year	Type of School	Initial W/hr	Differential[b]	Current W/hr[c]	Differential[b]
1953	Vocational	$1.38	$ .02	$2.97	$-.06
	Comprehensive	1.36		3.03	
1958	Vocational	1.54	.10	2.45	.12
	Comprehensive	1.44		2.33	
1962	Vocational	1.48	.04	1.97	.09
	Comprehensive	1.44		1.88	

Source: Max U. Eninger, *The Process and Product of T. & I. High School Level Vocational Education in the United States: The Product* (Pittsburgh: American Institutes for Research, 1965), table 144, p. 9–41; and table 150, p. 9–49.
[a]These wage rates are not comparable to those of vocational graduates presented in table 2-17.
[b]Wage rate of the vocational graduate less the wage rate of the comprehensive graduate.
[c]1964.

Table 2-21
Percentage of Time Employed by 1953, 1958 and 1962 Vocational
Graduates by Type of School from Graduation Until 1964

Year of Graduation	Type of School	Percentage of Time Employed[a]	Differential[b]
1953	Vocational	93.6	2.4
	Comprehensive	91.2	
1958	Vocational	87.2	-.3
	Comprehensive	87.5	
1962	Vocational	85.2	3.0
	Comprehensive	82.2	

Source: Max U. Eninger, *The Process and Product of T. & I. High School Level Vocational Education in the United States: The Product* (Pittsburgh: American Institutes for Research, 1965), table 117, p. 9-6.
[a]From time of graduation until 1964.
[b]The percentage of time vocational graduates were employed less the percent of time comprehensive graduates were employed.

employment experience than "comprehensive" vocational graduates, although the data are hard to interpret. Members of the former group who graduated in 1953 and 1962 were employed 2.4 and 3.0 percentage points more between the time they graduated and 1964 than the latter group. The 1958 graduates have experienced no such employment advantage. The reason is not clear.

These general observations of relative wage and employment experiences suggest that economic benefits of vocational education are greater in vocational-technical schools than in comprehensive schools. This result would be hoped for because vocational-technical schools are considered a more expensive way of providing vocational education. It is comforting to know that the gross returns may be greater. Whether they are enough greater to justify the additional costs of vocational-technical schools over comprehensive schools is unknown. Research comparing relative costs of the two approaches to vocational education has not been conducted.

Conclusions

Authors of two of the cost-benefit studies examined in this section (Kaufman et al. and Kaufman) conclude that when vocational education in vocational-technical high schools is considered as an alternative to a general education, the gain in benefits exceeds the increase in costs. However, two other researchers, Corazzini and Taussig, have reached conclusions that such education cannot be regarded as having economic benefits that exceed costs. Further examination of the latter two studies reveals that differences in the conclusions probably are due more to differences in methodologies than program experiences. Recalculations of these studies' data based on more uniform methodology result in benefit-cost ratios that exceed one in every case. These results are summarized in Table 2–22. Two benefit-cost ratios are presented in each case (excepting that of Kaufman et al.); one based on the relatively liberal assumptions of a 5 percent discount rate and thirty-year time horizon, and the other on the relatively strict assumptions of a 10 percent discount rate and a ten-year time horizon. In no case does a benefit-cost ratio less than one result. Lowest, estimated for New York City from Taussig's data, is 1.3. The highest ratio, 27.1, results from Kaufman et al.'s data using a 5 percent discount rate and a thirty-year time horizon. The high ratio results from a combination of lower education costs and relatively successful employment experiences of vocational-technical graduates in City C in Pennsylvania. In other studies, the more generous assumptions for calculating the benefit-cost ratios give us ratios ranging from a high of 5.4 to a low of 3.3.

These favorable benefit-cost ratios calculated for each of the four case studies are generally consistent with Eninger's nationwide sampling of the earnings advantage enjoyed by high school vocational graduates over comprehensive high school graduates. The economic value of such an education to 1962 vocational graduates at the time they graduated was probably somewhere between $2,500 and $6,500. As long as additional costs of providing vocational education were less than these values, vocational-technical education could be tentatively regarded as having economic justification.

However, none of the authors would consider justifying an expansion or curtailment of vocational education solely on a benefit-cost ratio. This is

Table 2-22
Summary of Benefit-Cost Ratios of Vocational-Technical Education
as an Alternative to General High School Education[a]

Researcher	10-Year Time Horizon	30-Year Time Horizon
Corazzini		
5 percent discount rate	–	3.3
10 percent discount rate	1.3	–
Kaufman et al.		
5 percent discount rate	–	10.5[b]–27.1[c]
10 percent discount rate	4.1[b]–10.7[c]	–
Kaufman		
5 percent discount rate	–	5.4
10 percent discount rate	2.1	–
Taussig		
5 percent discount rate	–	4.3
10 percent discount rate	1.7	–
Unweighted Average	4.0	10.3

[a]Ignoring capital costs.
[b]City A.
[c]City C.

as it should be for two reasons. First, discussions in Chapter 1 indicated that at best the benefit-cost calculation is a partial representation of the economic impact of activities being examined. At its worst it distorts these consequences, and unduly focuses attention on one of what may be several important performance criteria. Consequently, the analyses by Kaufman et al. and Kaufman of the employment stability experienced by vocational graduates, graduates' views concerning how well they were prepared by their training for their occupations, the satisfaction such graduates have with their jobs, etc. are an important part of the analysis. Emphasizing these types of consequences, however, and failing to compare benefits and costs (as is often the case in educational research), tends to stifle the search for more efficient ways to accomplish the same goals.

Second, none of the four studies examined was concerned with comparing the efficiency of offering vocational education in vocational-technical schools as opposed to offering it in comprehensive schools. Thus even if cost-benefit analysis were to be used as the sole criterion in program choice, not enough alternatives were examined to permit administrators to choose between the settings in which occupational education can be offered. This is an unfortunate deficiency, because the setting in which vocational education is to be offered is one of the major decisions education administrators must make, and one of the more difficult to reverse.

Although none of the studies was interested directly in the type of school in which vocational education is offered, it is possible to make a general inference concerning overall relative efficiency of the two approaches to high school vocational education. The following figures are no more than a suggestion of the relative values of vocational education in a vocational-technical school and in a comprehensive school, and should be interpreted as such. Calculations from data developed by Eninger suggest that in 1962 the value (at time of graduation) of vocational education in a comprehensive school relative to nonvocational education was $1,481 if a high discount rate and a short time horizon are used, and $3,704 if these assumptions are liberalized (Table 2-23). Similar calculations using data of Kaufman et al. suggest relative benefits of $1,991 and $4,980.

Chester Swanson calculated costs (relative to academic curricula) of low-, median- and high-cost vocational programs in the Stockton, California, Unified High School District.[32] Annual additional costs in low-, median- and high-cost programs were $55, $80, and $409, respectively. Three-year costs, including interest, also are in Table 2-23. The resulting benefit-cost ratios appear in Table 2-24. Widely differing ratios are calculated depending on how expensive vocational programs were and which discount-rate time-horizon assumptions are made. With a 10 percent discount rate and ten-year time horizon, low-, median- and high-cost programs achieve ratios of 8.1, 5.6 and 1.1 respectively (using Eninger's earnings data). The more liberal assumptions for discount rate and time horizon increase these nearly three times.

Table 2-23
Estimated Costs and Benefits of Vocational Education in Comprehensive High Schools[a]

	5 Percent Discount Rate	10 Percent Discount Rate
Benefits		
Eninger's data	$1,481[b]	$3,704[c]
Kaufman et al. data	1,991[b]	4,980[c]
Costs		
Low-Cost Program	$ 182	$ 173
Median-Cost Program	265	252
High-Cost Program	1,354	1,289

Source: Calculated from Max U. Eninger, *The Process and Product of T. & I. High School Level Vocational Education in the United States: The Product* (Pittsburgh: American Institutes for Research, 1965), table 117, p. 9-6; table 150, p. 9-49; and table 154, p. 9-53; and Chester J. Swanson, *Leadership Role, Functions, Procedures and Administration of Vocational-Technical Education Agencies at the State Level: Program-Cost Analyses of a Vocational-Technical Education in a Junior College and in a Unified School District*, 3 vols. (Berkeley, Calif.: School of Education, University of California, March 1969), vol. 3, table 15, p. 40.

[a]Of three schools included in the study, one is a vocational school. Consequently, these costs are probably overstated.

[b]10-year time horizon.

[c]30-year time horizon.

Table 2-24
Estimated Benefit-Cost Ratios for Vocational Education in
Comprehensive High Schools

	10 Percent Discount Rate 10-Year Time Horizon	5 Percent Discount Rate 30-Year Time Horizon
Low-Cost Program	8.1	21.4
Median-Cost Program		
Eninger's Benefit Data	5.6	14.7
Kaufman et al. Benefit Data	7.5	19.8
High-Cost Program	1.1	2.9

Source: Calculated from table 2-23.

Note: Ratios for all but median-cost program use earnings estimated from Eninger.

These ratios must be interpreted cautiously. Biases pulling in both directions are reflected in the overall magnitudes of the ratios. Costs for a vocational school are included with those of comprehensive schools, probably raising stated average costs of vocational education in comprehensive schools. Also, costs are measured in 1967–1968, five years following the fiscal year of graduation (1961–1962) of students whose earnings are measured in 1964. Inflation alone would have increased costs about 15 percent over their 1961–1962 levels. These biases tend to understate actual ratios. On the other hand, Eninger's data indicate that most of the earnings advantage of comprehensive school vocational graduates over academic graduates comes from an employment advantage rather than higher wage rates. While this is not the case in Kaufman et al. data (after the first year), the long-run employment advantage of vocational graduates will be less than the short-run advantage contributing to the measured income differential. The result is an overstatement of benefits in Table 2-24. The net effect of these biases is unknown.

Additionally, the relationship between ratios for low-, median- and high-cost programs is distorted because a constant earnings estimate is used for all programs. Modifying this procedure with relative earnings observed by Kaufman et al. suggests that ratios for low-cost programs are understated, those for median-cost programs are about "right," and those for high-cost programs are overstated. Table 2-25 indicates how these conclusions were reached. Programs included in Swanson's study are grouped into low-, median- and high-cost categories. Six-year average earnings from the Kaufman et al. study for programs which seem relatively comparable also are grouped into low, median and high categories.

Table 2-25
Comprehensive Vocational Programs Categorized by Broad Cost Levels
and Earnings of Their Graduates

	Earnings Category		
	Low	Average	High
Low-Cost Programs			
Business Education		x	
Food Service	x		
Wood Working			x
Median-Cost Programs			
Electronics		x	
Mechanical Drawing			x
Auto Mechanics		x	
Cosmetology	x		
High-Cost Programs			
Bus-Boys and Waiters	x		
Food Ed. and Service Trng.	x		
Electronic Repair		x	
Typewriter Technology		x	

Source: Jacob J. Kaufman, Teh-wei Hu, Maw Lin Lee, and Ernst W. Stromsdorfer,
"A Cost-Effectiveness Study of Vocational Education," *A Comparison of Vocational and Non-vocational Education in Secondary Schools* (University Park,
Penn.: Institute for Research on Human Resources, Pennsylvania State University,
March 1969), table 39, p. 162; and Chester J. Swanson, *Leadership Role, Functions, Procedures and Administration of Vocational-Technical Education Agencies
at the State Level: Program Cost Analyses of Vocational-Technical Education in a
Junior College and in a Unified School District*, 3 vols. (Berkeley, Calif,: School
of Education, University of California, March 1969), vol. 3, table 4, p. 22.

As Table 2-25 indicates, business education, food service, and wood
working make up the low-cost vocational programs, and are associated with
average, low and high earnings respectively. High and low earnings of wood
working and food service graduates offset each other. Given the low costs and
generally average earnings levels, benefit-cost ratios in Table 2-24 for these low-
cost programs probably are understated. Similar observations indicate that
median-cost program graduates earn average incomes, as do high-cost program
graduates; suggesting that no adjustment in ratios is required in former
programs while those of latter programs should be adjusted downward (relative
to median- and low-cost programs).

Although the general benefit-cost ratios for vocational education in
comprehensive high schools have been calculated with data from diverse sources,
substituting earnings data from the Kaufman et al. study for those from
Eninger's study result in similar ratios. For the median-cost program only, such
a substitution (utilizing Swanson's cost data) results in ratios of 7.5 and 19.8

compared to 5.6 and 14.7 (Table 2-24). Both sets of ratios are greater than those calculated for vocational education in vocational high schools (Table 2-22). We tentatively might conclude, then, that while vocational education in vocational-technical schools may yield benefit-cost ratios of four even under severe discount rate and time horizon assumptions, similar education in comprehensive high schools may utilize resources even more efficiently. Clearly, more research in this direction is indicated.

3

Vocational Education
in Post-Secondary Schools

Up to this point only studies of vocational education at the high school level have been considered. While few researchers have examined economic returns to vocational education at the post-secondary level, two studies may shed light on this question. The first, by Arthur Corazzini, [1] examines the economic returns of vocational education at a junior college in Worcester, Massachusetts. The second, by Adger Carroll and Loren Ihnen, [2] computes the returns to society of two years of training at Gaston Technical Institute in Gastonia, North Carolina. Corazzini suggests that vocational education at the post-secondary level yields economic returns less than its economic costs. Carroll and Ihnen reach the opposite conclusion in their study. The differences in these conclusions can be found largely in the differing methodologies of the two studies.[a]

Post-Secondary Vocational Education in
Worcester, Massachusetts

Corazzini computes costs of post-secondary vocational education by adding current costs of school operations, imputed rent of capital facilities, a tax adjustment for unpaid property taxes, value of foregone earnings of the students (opportunity costs), and additional out-of-pocket costs borne by students attributable to attending school. These are contained in Table 3-1. Foregone earnings were the largest single component of costs ($2,423 a year), and current operating costs made up most of the rest. Ignoring interest, total two-year costs were $7,548. Ignoring capital costs and the tax adjustment, total two-year costs were $7,056.

Corazzini finds that if a graduate of an academic high school completed a program in junior college that was available in a vocational high school, the post–high school training paid a very small premium over what the student would

---

[a]A third study [Richard H. P. Kraft, *Cost/Effectiveness Analysis of Vocational-Technical Education Programs* (Tallahassee, Florida: Department of Educational Administration, Educational Systems and Planning Center, The Florida State University, 1969)], which develops a methodology for computing costs by occupational category, contains too many methodological and conceptual difficulties to be useful in this paper. For a discussion of that study see Steve L. Barsby, *An Analysis of Data Requirements for Cost-Effectiveness and Cost-Benefit Analysis,* Report to the Arizona Research Coordinating Unit, Arizona, January, 1970, mimeo.

Table 3–1
Annual Per-Student Costs of a Post-Secondary Vocational School in
Worcester, Massachusetts, 1963–1964

Current Operating Costs	$ 984
Implicit Rent	165
Property Tax Adjustment	81
School-Related Private Costs	121
Foregone Earnings	2,423
Total Annual Costs	$3,774

Source: Arthur J. Corazzini, "When Should Vocational Education Begin?"
Journal of Human Resources 2, no. 1 (Winter 1967), table 1, p. 47.

Table 3–2
Benefit-Cost Ratios of Post–High School Vocational Training in
Worcester, Massachusetts, 1963–1964[a]

Discount Rate	Ratios for Courses Available in Vocational High Schools		Ratios for Courses Not Available in Vocational High Schools	
	10-Year Time Horizon	30-Year Time Horizon	10-Year Time Horizon	30-Year Time Horizon
5 percent	.2	.3	.4	.8
10 percent	.1	.2	.3	.4

Source: Calculated from Arthur J. Corazzini, "When Should Vocational Education Begin?" *Journal of Human Resources* 2, no. 1 (Winter, 1967), pp. 45–47.

[a]Ignoring imputed capital costs and unpaid property taxes, and assuming the entry-wage differential remains constant at $.08 (when courses are available in vocational high schools) and $.19 (when courses are not available in vocational high schools) per hour, and that each group works 2,000 hours per year.

have received had he attended vocational high school. Based on initial placement wage rates, Corazzini finds that out of eleven trade areas available in both the vocational high school and the junior college, junior college graduates received less than vocational high school graduates in two areas, the same amount in three areas, and more in the remaining six areas.[3] He also found that

The average starting wage for post–high school graduates who took one of the 11 trade courses offered [vocational] high school students was $1.84 per hour; the average starting wage for the vocational high school graduates was $1.76 per hour. Hence, over-all the average premium paid post–high school graduates was a mere 8 cents per hour — $3.20 per week or $160 annually.[4]

On the other hand, if the academic graduate pursued a technical course of study in junior college that was not available in the vocational high school, the average premium earned over the vocational high school graduate was $.19 per hour, or nearly $400 a year.[5] The academic high school graduate who attended junior college was "better off" if he specialized in an occupational area not available at the high school level, i.e., if he used the additional training as a supplement to, rather than a substitute for his high school diploma.

Benefit-cost ratios for the two types of programs available in junior college can be computed (Table 3-2). As expected, the ratios are relatively low. Courses acting as a substitute for those in high school appear to offer little economic benefit for students completing them. The highest calculated benefit-cost ratio for these courses is 0.3. Courses acting as supplements to high school education also are associated with low benefit-cost ratios, except that by using a discount rate of 5 percent and a time horizon of thirty years, a ratio of .8 is achieved. All other ratios are less than this. Results from Corazzini's data suggest that post-secondary vocational education (at least in Worcester, Massachusetts), does not yield net economic returns to society.[b] One can argue, however, that Corazzini makes a conceptual error in comparing the sets of costs he selected. What Corazzini does in his paper is compare outcomes from the "time tracks" of two alternatives: (1) attending an academic high school and then entering junior college, and (2) attending a vocational high school and then going to work. The outcomes of these time tracks are the relative wages graduates of each received.

Direct costs of the time tracks include the costs of an academic high school education plus those of a two year post–high school for the first; and the additional cost of vocational high school for the second. In each case Corazzini leaves out the costs of high school. Since per-student costs in a vocational high school were $2,048 (ignoring interest) above those in an academic high school, he has overstated the net cost of following track number one (attending an academic high school and then going on to junior college). As a result, benefit-cost ratios of this alternative are all understated. Subtracting savings achieved by students attending academic, rather than vocational high school, reduces per-student costs from nearly $8,000 to under $5,000. These figures, along with the new benefit-cost ratios, appear in Table 3-3. Even with the large reduction in calculated costs, all but ratios computed with the most generous assumptions are still less than one.[c] Corazzini suggests that post-secondary students graduating with skills available at the secondary level receive the higher wage rates they do because they had graduated from an academic high school rather than from a vocational school. "Similarly, the potentially more lucrative

---

[b]Since the individual does not bear the full education costs, long enough time horizons and low enough discount rates can result in a private benefit-cost ratio slightly greater than one, a ratio still low relative to those for vocational education in the high school.

[c]Recall that benefits were calculated using only the differential starting wage rates of the various groups. Differences in employment experiences and in the rate at which wages increase could substantially alter these results.

Table 3-3

Total Costs and Recalculated Benefit-Cost Ratios for Post-High School
Vocational Training in Worcester, Massachusetts, 1963-1964

	Costs[a]	
	5 Percent	10 Percent
Calculated by		
Corazzini[b]	$7,737	$7,925
Recalculated[c]	4,799	4,534

	Cost-Benefit Ratios			
	Ratios for Courses Available in Vocational High Schools		Ratios for Courses not Available in Vocational High Schools	
Discount Rate	10-Year Time Horizon	30-Year Time Horizon	10-Year Time Horizon	30-Year Time Horizon
5 percent	.3	.5	.6	1.2
10 percent	.2	.3	.5	.8

Source: Calculated from Arthur J. Corazzini, "When Should Vocational Education Begin?" *Journal of Human Resources* 2, no. 1 (Winter 1967): 45-47.
[a]At time of graduation. Benefit data is unchanged from table 3-2.
[b]Costs incurred at the post-secondary level including capital factor and unpaid
taxes.
[c]Costs incurred at the secondary level exclusive of capital and unpaid taxes, less
savings from attending an academic, rather than a vocational, high school.

technical careers began with training which required high school graduation
as proof of ability." [6]

Alternative conclusions are possible. If post-high school training duplicates
that given at the high school level, employers have good reason for not paying
a large premium to these graduates — they have the same skills as vocational high
school graduates. The premium that does exist could then be attributed to
benefits accruing to the employer because of the greater maturity of post-high
school graduates. Similarly, graduates of technical post-high school programs not
available in high school receive more money because they have a level of
skill not attainable in high school *and* because they are more mature. These
conclusions are consistent with data presented by Max Eninger, Kaufman et al.
and Kaufman [7] (discussed in Chap. 2), which indicate that vocational
high school graduates receive consistent premiums over academic high school
graduates.

Had Corazzini compared starting wages of academic high school graduates
with those of vocational high school graduates after both groups completed
post-high school programs not available in vocational high schools, these

conflicting conclusions could be tested. If graduates of such programs with an academic background received more than those with a vocational background, Corazzini's conclusion that employers paid a premium to academic high school graduates would be supported. Contrary evidence would necessitate developing alternative hypotheses such as that suggested by me above.

Several less ambiguous conclusions *do* follow from the analysis. First, if a student knows he is interested in a career requiring vocational education, it is to his (and society's) advantage to take it in high school if possible. Good career counseling at the beginning of high school would probably result in a higher number of students following their occupational interests more closely than is now the case. Second, a vocational high school graduate who makes the decision to attend junior college should not specialize in a field available in high school and expect to earn substantially more than high school graduates with similar skills as a result.[d] Again the importance of counseling is emphasized. Last, Corazzini suggests that technical post-secondary vocational programs should be examined to see if a high school diploma is really a necessary prerequisite. If not, offering such programs in high school would be beneficial.[8] Also, the possibility of offering an accelerated high school program to capable students should not be ignored. Students in accelerated programs could complete high school and two years of post–high school in the twelve years normally required to graduate from high school.[9]

Post-Secondary Vocational Education at Gaston Tech, North Carolina

The study by Carroll and Ihnen contains more detail than Corazzini's. They have selected a sample of forty-five graduates of a two-year junior college in North Carolina who completed schooling in 1959 or 1960, and have compared their experiences with those of a carefully selected sample of high school students who graduated the same years. The high school sample was selected so that only students with characteristics similar to the junior college graduates were included. Thus, the control group included only those who did not receive formal post–high school education, who had academic records in high school similar to the junior college experimental group, who were members of the civilian labor force not self-employed or employed by a relative, who were not disabled, and who had not moved more than 200 miles from where they had graduated.[10] Carroll and Ihnen also controlled results of the analysis for differences in personal characteristics and experiences. The following variables were controlled for: (1) high school grade average, (2) age, (3) mother's

---

[d]Although there may be high noneconomic benefits if his career interests have changed which may negate this conclusion.

education, (4) residence during high school (urban vs. rural), (5) amount of military service, (6) migration from home, and (7) size of high school class.[11]

Costs of operating Gaston Tech were calculated using state budget data, and the results appear in Table 3–4. Calculated costs included expense of operating the school, student fees and supplies, and earnings foregone by students who attended junior college. No allocation of capital costs or unpaid taxes was made. Foregone earnings were estimated as the difference between earnings of Gaston Tech students while attending school and those of the high school control group. First- and second-year costs were estimated to be $3,551 and $3,874 respectively, per student. Ignoring interest, total costs for the two years amounted to $7,425 (as compared to $7,056 in Worcester, Massachusetts).

Earnings data were obtained through personal interviews in 1963 (four years following graduation). The first year following graduation junior college graduates earned an estimated $553 more than the high school graduate control group which already had been working for two years. By the end of the fourth year, junior college graduates were earning $1,036 a year more than high school graduates with six years of labor-market experience.[12] Based on these data, several sets of benefit-cost ratios can be calculated (Table 3–5). The first set is based on the assumption that the earnings advantage enjoyed by Gaston Tech graduates remains constant over the relevant time horizon. With this assumption, benefit-cost ratios range from .6 (10 percent discount rate and ten-year time horizon) to 1.5 (5 percent discount rate and thirty-year time horizon). Assuming that the earnings advantage would continue to grow at a rate suggested by 1960 census data (a slower rate than for the first four years), benefit-cost ratios are substantially higher. Those calculated using all but the most conservative combination of discount rate and time horizon exceed one.

Direct income benefits alone suggest that returns to technical education exceed costs. However, other job benefits accruing directly to Gaston Tech graduates are reported. Gaston Tech graduates were required to work 2.7 hours a week less than high school graduates, and were asked to work less overtime. They enjoyed longer paid vacations, more paid holidays, furnished less of their own equipment, and received more employer-paid insurance benefits.[13] Carroll and Ihnen have estimated that the value of additional leisure time available to Gaston Tech graduates was about $446 a year.[14] If this is added to the benefits in calculating benefit-cost ratios, they will be noticeably higher than those estimated above. In fact, the ratios developed under Assumption I will increase sufficiently so that none will be less than one.

Not emphasized by Carroll and Ihnen are the remarkably similar and low unemployment experiences of the two groups of graduates. "High school graduates had less than 0.3 percent unemployment and Gaston Tech graduates less than 0.2 percent unemployment."[15] This could result from the selective method used by Carroll and Ihnen to pick their samples; thus the numbers

Table 3-4
Annual Per-Student Cost at Gaston Tech, North Carolina, 1958-1960

	First Year	Second Year	Total
School Expenses	$1,001	$1,001	$2,002
Foregone Earnings	2,408	2,789	5,197
Student Fees and Supplies	142	84	226
Total Costs	$3,551	$3,874	$7,425

Source: A. B. Carroll and L. A. Ihnen, "Costs and Returns for Two Years of Post-Secondary Technical Schooling," *Journal of Political Economy* 75, no. 6 (December 1967), table 2, p. 866.

Table 3-5
Benefit-Cost Ratios of Technical Education at Gaston Tech, North Carolina, 1959-1960

Discount Rate	Time Horizon	
	10 Years	30 Years
Assumption I[a]		
5 percent	.8	1.5
10 percent	.6	.9
Assumption II[b]		
5 percent	1.1	4.2
10 percent	.8	2.2

Source: Calculated from A. B. Carroll and L. A. Ihnen, "Costs and Returns for Two Years of Post-Secondary Technical Schooling," *Journal of Political Economy* 75, no. 6 (December 1967), table 2, p. 866, and pp. 866-67.
[a]That the earnings differential remains at $1,038 a year after the fourth year.
[b]That the earnings differential increases at 2 percent a year as projected by the 1960 census.

themselves may have no special significance. On the other hand, since unemployment experiences of the two groups are so similar, the large difference in earnings is due almost entirely to differences in wage rates. (Recall that Eninger's nationwide study of vocational high school graduates indicates that most of the earnings advantage is due to differences in unemployment experiences rather than wage rates.)

Inclusion of variables other than graduation from a junior college in this study permits us to see the importance of these other variables on earnings. The most important factor on earnings was the technical education received by Gaston Tech graduates. The second factor (about half as important) was whether students attended high school in an urban or rural area. Students from urban high schools earned significantly more than those from rural schools.[e] The third was the age of students graduating from Gaston Tech. Students who had been employed in the civilian force or by the military prior to attending Gaston Tech, earned substantially more than students who went directly into Gaston Tech from high school.[f] The high school grade average of students was the fourth factor — about one-half as important as the type of residence (urban vs. rural) during high school, and a little over a third as important as the technical education received by Gaston Tech graduates. The student's mother's education was used to represent the socioeconomic environment experienced by the student at home. The higher the mother's education, the higher the student's starting wage. This factor ranked sixth. Surprisingly, a student's beginning wages were little affected by migration from his home community (limited to 200 miles).[16]

It is not surprising that factors other than whether a student attended Gaston Tech had an important impact on his earnings. These results emphasize, however, the importance of including personal characteristics such as those discussed above in a cost-benefit analysis. Their influence must be removed as much as possible in order to have any confidence that it was the schooling and not something else that caused any differences in observed earnings and employment experiences, or that differences in wage rates and employment were hidden by differences in personal characteristics. Failure to do this is one important shortcoming of both of Corazzini's studies.[17]

Conclusions drawn from this study are fairly obvious. Technical education in Gaston Tech appears to satisfy the economic test of success. Benefits as measured by increased earnings are greater than costs.[g] Graduates from Gaston Tech also have received significant non-wage benefits from employers.

---

[e]This does not necessarily mean that rural high school graduates are at an academic disadvantage to urban graduates. Since the sample of high school students came from all over the state, those from rural areas far from urban areas might have had fewer job opportunities. However, migration of 200 miles or less increases earnings very little, so unless a student graduates from a high school more than 200 miles from an urban area, he would have access to the same job markets as an urban high school graduate and one might then conclude that rural high school graduates are, in fact, at an academic disadvantage to urban graduates.

[f]These students would be older than those with no break between high school and junior college. Their earnings advantage relative to other vocational graduates is consistent with my suggestion on page 58 that Worcester junior college graduates who took a course of study offered in high school were being paid more than vocational high school graduates with those skills because of their increased maturity rather than because of their academic high school diploma. But the advantage also may have resulted from skills gained between high school graduation and enrollment at Gaston Tech.

[g]Carroll and Ihnen caution against generalizations concerning the value of post-secondary education. They indicate that Gaston Tech was the first such school in North Carolina and its graduates very well could have occupied extremely favorable positions in the job market. Since the study was made other junior colleges have been established, greatly expanding the number of such graduates available to employers.

Comparisons and Conclusions

Corazzini concluded that post-secondary vocational education in Worcester yielded cost-benefit ratios less than one. Carroll and Ihnen reached the apparently contrary conclusion that cost-benefit ratios associated with such education in Gastonia generally exceded one. These findings, however, do not contradict each other. Methodologies differ in several important respects. Carroll and Ihnen controlled for personal characteristics; Corazzini did not. Carroll and Ihnen measured earnings of graduates in a wide range of occupations, Corazzini did not. More importantly, the two studies utilized dissimilar control groups.

Corazzini compared junior college vocational graduates with high school vocational graduates. Carroll and Ihnen compared junior college vocational graduates with academic high school graduates. Earnings and cost comparisons in Corazzini's study were between graduates of different levels of vocational education; those of Carroll and Ihnen between academic graduates at one level and vocational education graduates at another. Consequently, Corazzini's conclusion that it is better to take vocational education in high school than to put it off until post–high school does not conflict with Carroll and Ihnen's conclusion that *given one has not taken vocational education in high school*, taking it at the post–high school level yields returns greater than costs.

Data from Corazzini's two studies can be combined to permit a rough comparison between experiences of post–high school vocational graduates and academic high school graduates in Worcester. The resulting benefit-cost ratios in Table 3–6 relate to groups similar to those used in the study by Carroll and Ihnen. Cost-benefit ratios in Worcester for curricula available in high school are nearly 60 percent lower than those calculated for education at Gaston Tech, but they are about double those comparing the two levels of vocational education in Worcester (Table 3–3). Ratios for curricula not available in high school equal those calculated for Gaston Tech programs under Assumption I.[h] In both cities, only the most liberal assumptions give benefit-cost ratios equal to, or greater than unity, although these results are achieved by both types of programs in Worcester.

Table 3–7 summarizes results of Corazzini's and Carroll and Ihnen's studies. In both studies, use of a 10 percent discount rate and ten-year time horizon yields benefit-cost ratios less than one. The non-technical curriculum in Worcester is lowest at .4, and (as expected) that of Assumption II in Gastonia the highest (.8). All ratios exceed one when the discount rate is reduced and time horizon extended. The lowest is 1.0, and the highest, 4.2.

---

[h]That earnings differentials remain constant after the first year. No ratio in table 3–6 is comparable to ratios developed under Assumption II for Gaston Tech graduates (that earnings differentials continue to increase throughout the relevant time horizon).

Table 3–6

Adjusted Benefit-Cost Ratios of Post–High School Vocational
Training in Worcester, Massachusetts, 1963–1964[a]

Discount Rate	Non-Technical Curriculum[b]		Technical Curriculum[c]	
	10-Year Time Horizon	30-Year Time Horizon	10-Year Time Horizon	30-Year Time Horizon
5 percent	.5	1.0	.8	1.5
10 percent	.4	.6	.6	.9

Source: Calculated from Arthur J. Corazzini, "When Should Vocational Education Begin?" *Journal of Human Resources* 2, no. 1 (Winter, 1967), 45–47.

[a]Developed on the assumption that the alternative to post-secondary vocational education was graduation from an academic high school and going immediately to work. Earnings data were calculated by taking the wage differential between post-secondary vocational graduates and vocational high school graduates, and adding to it the earnings differential between vocational and academic high school graduates. Annual earnings differentials for the two types of curricula thus were $480 for non-technical and $700 for technical.

[b]Available in high school.

[c]Not available in high school.

Table 3–7

Comparisons of Selected Benefit-Cost Ratios for Vocational Education
in Post-Secondary High Schools

Researcher	10-Year Time Horizon	30-Year Time Horizon
Corazzini		
Technical Curriculum[a]		
5 percent	–	1.5
10 percent	.6	–
Non-Technical Curriculum[b]		
5 percent	–	1.0
10 percent	.4	–
Carroll and Ihnen		
Assumption I[c]		
5 percent	–	1.5
10 percent	.6	–
Assumption II[d]		
5 percent	–	4.2
10 percent	.8	–

[a]Not available in high school.

[b]Available in high school.

[c]Earnings differential remains constant.

[d]Earnings differential increases at 2 percent a year.

The two studies of vocational education in post-high school institutions suggest that post-high school vocational education yields net returns to society at discount rates lower than 10 percent and time horizons longer than ten years. These returns may be greater when such programs offer skill training in occupations not available in vocational high schools. Substantial nonwage benefits also are seen to accrue to vocational graduates of post-high school programs.

It is now possible to compare results of cost-benefit studies of vocational education in high school to those of vocational education at the post-high school level. As Table 3-8 indicates, benefit-cost ratios for vocational high school

Table 3-8

Comparisons of Selected Benefit-Cost Ratios of Vocational Education in Vocational High Schools with Vocational Education in Post-High School Institutions, as Alternatives to a General High School Education

Part A – Vocational High Schools		
Researcher	10-Year Time Horizon	30-Year Time Horizon
Corazzini		
5 percent discount rate	–	4.8
10 percent discount rate	1.5	–
Hu		
5 percent discount rate		
City A	–	10.5
City C	–	27.1
10 percent discount rate		
City A	4.1	–
City C	10.7	–
Kaufman		
5 percent discount rate	–	5.4
10 percent discount rate	2.0	–
Taussig		
5 percent discount rate	–	3.6
10 percent discount rate	1.3	–
unweighted average	3.1	8.0

Part B – Vocational Education in Post-High School Institutions		
Corazzini[a]		
5 percent discount rate	–	1.5
10 percent discount rate	.6	–
Carroll and Ihnen[b]		
5 percent discount rate	–	1.5
10 percent discount rate	.6	–
unweighted average	.6	1.5

[a]Technical curriculum.
[b]Assumption I.

programs consistently exceed those for post–high school vocational programs. The unweighted average of vocational programs is five times greater at the high school, than at the post–high school level. None of the ratios in the four studies of vocational high schools is below one. The unweighted value of these ratios at a 10 percent discount rate and ten-year time horizon is 3.1 compared to .6 for those at the higher level. While these ratios must be interpreted carefully, they suggest that education in vocational high schools has a greater economic payoff than vocational education in post-secondary institutions when these activities are considered as alternatives to an academic high school education. Society loses if students delay participation in vocational programs until after high school graduation, and the benefit-cost ratios for vocational high schools exceed those for post–high school vocational education by a large enough margin to give some confidence to this conclusion. *But once the decision is delayed*, society may gain by financing post-secondary vocational education.

4 Institutional Out-of-School Retraining Under State and Federal Legislation

Introduction

Goals of the Manpower Development and Training Act (MDTA) of 1962 and its subsequent amendments may be summarized as increasing the efficiency with which the unemployed become employed, raising the average skill level of the labor force, supplying skilled persons in areas and occupations where there are labor shortages, increasing price stability, achieving a more equitable distribution of income, and altering established institutional arrangements.[1] While no one has attempted yet to measure the Act's contribution to reducing pressures on inflation, the success of the MDT Act and its predecessors (various state retraining acts and the Area Redevelopment Act) in aiding operation of the labor market and reducing poverty *has* been evaluated. The studies generally compare experiences of program participants following training with their experiences prior to receiving that training. Some studies utilized control groups so that program benefits could be separated from changes occurring elsewhere in trainees' environments, and some studies calculated benefit-cost ratios.

Every study examined in this chapter concludes that there were important differences between pre- and post-participation experiences of those aided by various retraining programs. Invariably, those who participated suffered less unemployment afterward than they had previously, and less than they would have experienced had they not participated in those programs (as measured by the experiences of control groups). Participants also earned more than before. Large benefits accrued to older and younger workers, as well as to those between the ages of twenty-one and thirty-five.

On the other hand, significant differences have shown up in other conclusions of these studies. Some studies, for example those by Rasmussen [2] (of a national sampling of urban training) and Trooboff [3] (of MDTA retraining in Atlanta, Georgia), concluded that nonwhites were helped more than whites. Michael Borus' study of retraining programs in Connecticut [4] indicated that race had little effect on the outcome of training. Glen Cain and Ernst Stromsdorfer, who examined retraining programs in West Virginia, [5] found that many females' labor market experiences were affected very much by training. Yet Borus concluded that sex was not an important factor in determining retraining success. A third conclusion was reached by Trooboff, and by Hardin and Borus [6] when they discovered that females actually did better than males.

When benefit-cost ratios were calculated, a wide range of answers emerged concerning the returns to society. Borus concluded that the overall benefit-cost ratio of retraining in Connecticut was about 97; Cain and Stromsdorfer said the average ratio in West Virginia was around 6. David Page found a benefit-cost ratio in Massachusetts of about 4.[7]

Clearly the differences in conclusions concerning how different groups participating in retraining programs fared is due to differences in methodologies employed by the various researchers as well as actual differences in the various groups' experiences. One significant conclusion reached in this chapter (as well as in others) is that calculation of a benefit-cost ratio is a sterile exercise unless accompanied by a detailed analysis of actual labor market experiences of program participants and reasons why any particular results were achieved.

Studies examined in this chapter have been divided between those evaluating training activities conducted under state legislation or under the Area Redevelopment Act, and more recent studies evaluating activities of the MDTA. The earlier studies are especially valuable for two reasons. First, they indicated that retraining activities are capable of increasing participants' incomes by more than the cost of the training. Although results of these studies were not available until after the MDTA was passed, they probably relieved the apprehension of a goodly number of legislators. Second, the efficacy of applying cost-benefit analysis to manpower activities was tested. Cost-benefit analysis yielded useful information. To the extent that outcomes of the early studies can be regarded as predictions of likely results of MDTA programs, the studies were successful. MDTA retraining programs also increased participants' incomes by more than the costs of increasing those incomes. The early studies suggested that a good portion of these benefits would be in the form of improved employment experiences, that women were likely to benefit less than men, that trainees benefitted even if they did not complete a training program, and that a wide variation of success would be observed among trainees prepared for various occupations. These results generally were substantiated by the later studies of MDTA programs.

State and Area Redevelopment Act–Sponsored Programs

Retraining in Connecticut

One of the early cost-benefit studies of manpower programs was published by Michael Borus in 1964.[8] He interviewed 373 persons who had participated in state-sponsored and Area Redevelopment Act (ARA) retraining courses in Connecticut between May 1961 and March 1962, in order to calculate relative costs and benefits to society, government, and the individuals participating in the programs. He also wanted to ascertain whether retraining programs were accomplishing stated goals of the subsequent MDT Act — (1) to increase the nation's output, (2) to reduce the unemployment level, (3) to reduce costs of income maintenance programs, and (4) to reduce burdens of unemployment on specific disadvantaged groups of the unemployed.[9]

Borus examined retraining courses that prepared men for employment as machinists, pipefitters and shipfitters. The machine shop course required eight weeks of instruction; the other courses four weeks. Costs of the retraining programs considered by Borus included additional costs borne by the U.S. Employment Service in selecting, testing, and placing trainees in the training programs, operating costs of the training programs, a portion of state and federal administration costs of overall ARA activities including forecasting and evaluation activities, and additional transfer payments made to trainees while participating in training. Capital costs of buildings and equipment utilized in retraining were ignored because Borus was interested in discovering marginal costs of retraining.[10] Opportunity costs to society of the participants' temporary withdrawal from the labor force were regarded as zero. Borus reasoned that since trainees were unskilled, any jobs they might have held during the retraining period could readily be filled by other persons who were unemployed but not participating in the program.[11][a]

Retraining courses examined by Borus were (to this writer) surprisingly inexpensive to conduct, even taking into account the omission of opportunity costs. Machine shop, an eight-week course, was the most expensive, costing $138.13 per student (Table 4-1). The other two courses (pipefitting and shipfitting), lasting four weeks each, cost about half as much as the machine shop course.

In order to estimate benefits of retraining, Borus utilized three control groups: (1) those who completed the training *but did not utilize that training in their first job*, (2) those who entered the program but failed to complete it *for reasons other than the offer of an immediate job*, and (3) those who qualified for the program but did not enter training *and did not have an immediate job prospect*.[12] Direct benefits of retraining programs were calculated on the basis of differences in earnings between those who completed training *and accepted a job utilizing the skills in which they were trained* (the experimental group), and the three control groups identified above. The assumption is made that if the trainee did not utilize his training in the job he accepted, the job could have been filled by a nontrainee, and earnings from the job could not be ascribed to training. Borus makes this assumption in an attempt to isolate the gains of training from those of placement; something that probably has yet to be done to anyone's satisfaction.

Those who completed training and utilized that training in their first job

---

[a]This is the so-called vacuum effect discussed above on p. 15.

Table 4-1

Average Per-Trainee Costs of Retraining Courses in
Connecticut, 1961–1962

Course	Cost Per Trainee
Machine Shop	$138.13
Pipefitting	67.75
Shipfitting	66.66

Source: Michael E. Borus, "A Benefit-Cost Analysis of the Economic Effectiveness
of Retraining the Unemployed," *Yale Economic Essays* 4, no. 2 (Fall 1964),
table 10, p. 409.

Table 4-2

Annual Earnings Advantage of Connecticut Trainees Who Utilized
Training in Jobs Over the Three Control Groups[a]

Control Group	Annual Earnings Advantage
Completed Training	$ 424
Dropped Out of Training	1,176
Did Not Report for Training	1,033

Source: Michael E. Borus, "A Benefit-Cost Analysis of the Economic Effectiveness
of Retraining the Unemployed," *Yale Economic Essays* 4, no. 2 (Fall 1964), p.
381.
[a]Controlled for differences in personal characteristics.

experienced consistently higher annual earnings the first year following training
than any of the three control groups. As Table 4-2 shows, the experimental
group earned $424 more than those who completed training but did not utilize
that training, $1,033 more than those who did not report for training for
reasons other than an immediate job opportunity, and $1,176 more than those
who dropped out of the retraining program without prospects for an immediate
job. Estimating the effects that differences in motivation might have on
overstating earnings gains, and weighting earnings gains based on relative sample
sizes, Borus placed the average gain at $500 a year.

These earnings advantages are sizable. Borus argues, however, that the
contribution to national income of additional trained workers employed
in occupations characterized by labor shortages is not just the increase in
earnings these workers experience over those not taking training or utilizing it
($500 as estimated by Borus in this case). Rather, it is the *total* value of
each newly-trained worker's annual output — $4,359.[13] His argument is based
on the assumption that the displacement effect is zero, i.e., that the jobs in
which trainees were placed would not have been filled by nontrainees. He

further argues that an income multiplier should be used when there is less than full employment, so that secondary effects of spending can be taken into account.[14][b]

Utilizing the assumptions discussed above, plus a discount rate of 5 percent, a ten-year time horizon, and the assumption that benefits of retraining are lost when trainees change their occupation to something other than that for which they were retrained, Borus computed benefit-cost ratios for society, the individuals participating in the retraining programs, and the government. Depending on characteristics of trainees and whether training was offered by the state or under ARA, benefit-cost ratios for society ranged from 73.7 to 114.1 for state-sponsored programs and 55.7 to 86.2 for federally-sponsored programs.

The average benefit-cost ratios for the state and federal programs were 96.9 and 73.3, respectively. In all programs, when the trainee had some type of disadvantage (age thirty or over, less than ten years of education, or thirteen or more weeks of unemployment prior to taking the aptitude test), benefit-cost ratios were lower than for workers without any of these disadvantages. Examination of the social benefit-cost ratios in Table 4–3 indicates that this variance in ratios between the several groups was larger in state-sponsored, than in federal-sponsored programs. Differences in ARA programs' ratios for trainee groups actually are not very large, considering the absolute magnitude of the ratios.

Benefit-cost ratios from the government's standpoint are somewhat lower than those for society. This is expected, because gains of retraining to the government are not total gains in income, but are increases in tax revenues and savings in transfer-payment programs resulting from that increased income. As before, groups with specific disadvantages yield lower returns than the so-called "cream of the crop." Returns to individuals taking training are lower still, but exceed one in every case. The average trainee gained back 4.4 times as much as it cost him (including lost earnings) to take the training. Those with specific disadvantages gained somewhat less.

The exceptionally high benefit-cost ratios of retraining in Connecticut calculated by Borus result from his assumption of the presence of the vacuum effect, so that total incomes of the experimental group are considered as benefits rather than the improvement attributable to training; and from his use of the income multiplier that magnifies the benefits attributed to training.

---

[b]This is the only study of institutional training programs that includes a multiplier (assumed to be two). Cain and Stromsdorfer [Glen G. Cain and Ernst W. Stromsdorfer, "An Economic Evaluation of Government Retraining Programs in West Virginia," *Retraining the Unemployed,* ed. Gerald G. Somers (Madison, Wis.; University of Wisconsin Press, 1968), pp. 333–335] set out conditions necessary for training programs to reduce aggregate unemployment, and note that such programs can succeed when an influx of money comes into a depressed area with high unemployment. West Virginia might well have satisfied these conditions, and the programs might have contributed to actual expansion of its economy.

Table 4-3

Benefit-Cost Ratios of Retraining Programs in Connecticut for Society,
Government, and Individuals

Basis for Calculation	State Sponsored	Federally Sponsored
Social		
Overall average	96.9	73.3
Age 30 and over	73.7	55.7
Less than 10 years education	48.8	59.6
Unemployed 13 weeks or more at time of aptitude test	84.5	63.9
Employed at time of aptitude test	114.1	86.2
Government		
Overall average	25.3	22.1
Age 30 and over	19.3	16.8
Less than 10 years education	20.6	18.0
Employed at time of aptitude test	29.8	26.0
Private Benefit-Cost Ratios		
Overall average	4.4	
Age 30 or over	2.3	
Less than 10 years education	3.5	
Unemployed more than 13 weeks at time of aptitude test	3.8	

Source: Michael E. Borus, "A Benefit-Cost Analysis of the Economic Effectiveness
of Retraining the Unemployed," *Yale Economic Essays* 4, no. 2 (Fall 1964), pp.
415-18.

Einar Hardin recalculates the overall benefit-cost ratio to society from Borus'
data using more common assumptions — that the vacuum effect is not operating,
and that the multiplier is zero.[15] With a 10 percent discount rate and a
ten-year time horizon, a benefit-cost ratio of 5.9 results. This more modest (but
still impressive) ratio is more comparable to other cost-benefit studies of
institutional MDTA and Area Redevelopment Act programs. This ratio should
be used as a benchmark when comparing Borus' study to others.

When Borus examined wage-employment experiences of the experimental
group with those of the three control groups, he found that the experimental
group's higher earnings the first year following training were due almost entirely
to differences in employment experiences rather than to differences in wage
rates. This occurred in spite of the fact that only the experimental group
completed training and took jobs in training-related occupations. Table 4-4
indicates that control group 1 (those who completed training but took jobs in
non-training-related occupations) earned $.10 an hour more than the experimen-
tal group. Only those who dropped out of training for a non-job-related reason
(e.g., poor health or discouragement) earned less at their initial job. Even this
group had made up the difference after a year, earning $2.13 per hour compared
to the experimental group's $2.01 per hour.

Table 4-4
Wage Rates of Workers Involved With Retraining
Programs in Connecticut

Time	Experimental Group	Control Group 1[a]	Control Group 2[b]	Control Group 3[c]
First Placement	$1.78	$1.88	$1.67	$1.81
After 6 Months	1.93	1.97	1.81	2.08
After 12 Months	2.01	1.97	2.13	2.04
Estimated Average[d]	1.91	1.94	1.87	1.98

Source: Michael E. Borus, "A Benefit-Cost Analysis of the Economic Effectiveness of Retraining the Unemployed," Yale Economic Essays 4, no. 2 (Fall 1964), p. 381, f.n. 4.
[a]Completed training but did not utilize skills learned.
[b]Dropped out of training without an immediate offer.
[c]Qualified for training, but did not report.
[d]Calculated as a simple average of the three reported wage rates.

Relative employment experiences of the four groups show a completely different picture. The experimental group had the best experience. Taking a non-training-related job, dropping out of training, and not reporting induced successively poorer employment experiences. Counting only the time the members of each of the groups were in the labor force (either employed or not employed and looking for work), the experimental group was employed 9.5, 12.5, and 13.3 percentage points more than control groups 1, 2, and 3 (as identified in Table 4-4), respectively.

Four years later Borus conducted a follow-up study to see if the earnings gains of those who went through retraining programs were maintained over time, or if the gains were temporary and disappeared as time passed.[16] Using social security data, Borus found that those who went through retraining not only maintained a sizable earnings advantage over nontrainees throughout the five-year period ($1,167 a year), but increased their earnings advantage from $1,070 in the first year to $1,350 in the fifth.[17]

Borus also discovered that long-term gains of brief training courses were not significantly influenced by sex, race, marital status, level of education, number of dependents, or level of earnings prior to enrolling in a training program.[18] [c] Age did not show up as an important determinant of earnings until the third year following training. Those aged thirty to thirty-five at the time they completed their training benefited most over the five-year period. Those aged

[c]David Taylor suggests that the small sample sizes of nonwhites and of certain educational levels could explain the failure of education and race to affect the outcome of training [Discussion of "Time Trends in the Benefits From Retraining in Connecticut," by Michael E. Borus, Proceedings of the Twentieth Annual Winter Meeting of the Industrial Relations Research Association (Madison, Wis., 1967), p. 58].

twenty-five to thirty and thirty-five to forty gained somewhat less, and those under twenty-five or over forty gained least.[19]

Several tentative conclusions can be drawn from these studies by Borus:

1. Since training courses in Connecticut were short, they clearly did not attempt to provide trainees with all the skills necessary to allow them to work efficiently in the occupations for which they were being trained. Rather, trainees were being familiarized with types of work they would be doing, and were brought up to a level where they could be trained effectively by a firm's own training program. The high benefit-cost ratio (5.9) to society achieved by training in Connecticut indicates that, from society's standpoint, firms have not been doing enough of this hiring and training voluntarily. That more training has not taken place in the private sector in the face of high benefit-cost ratios can be explained if society, rather than the firm, captures a good portion of benefits of retraining. Thus while it may be to society's advantage for the training to be undertaken, the firm understandably might be unwilling to bear the full costs. The implication is that training within the firm (OJT, if you wish) should be expanded — if necessary at the expense of society rather than the firm.[20]

2. Since characteristics of trainees had little impact on their subsequent long-run earnings patterns, trainees in future programs might be selected on the basis of almost any set of priorities determined by the government with the knowledge that successful training does not depend upon any specific set of trainee characteristics.[21] Thus, MDTA's "reduction of poverty" goal could be used as a criterion in selecting trainees without sacrificing the (possibly less important) "efficiency" criterion in use of resources.

3. Since age did not show up as an important variable until after three years, short-run studies based on one or two years of earnings and employment experience may miss important variables that could be used to direct policy.[22]

4. Since the earnings advantage of trainees placed in occupations for which they trained was due more to improved employment experience than to higher wages, doubts may be raised that training had anything to do with increased earnings of these trainees. It might be argued that wage rates measure a worker's productivity, and that unless training increases wage rates, there is no evidence that a trainee's productivity has been increased by that training, i.e., that his increased skills have made him a more attractive employee. Taussig argues this with respect to vocational training in New York.[23] If this argument is accepted, the benefit measured by Borus could be due entirely to placement efforts accompanying the program. Thus it is not clear that Borus successfully separated the benefits of training from those of placement in the selection of his special control groups.

5.   Since the earnings advantage of trainees did not disappear or decrease over a five-year period, less criticism can be leveled at the practice in cost-benefit analysis of extrapolating the measured earnings advantage beyond the year or two in which it usually is observed. Also, the apparent permanency of the earnings advantage suggests that retraining (and placement) programs of MDTA are having a lasting impact on groups the Act is attempting to aid.[d]

Retraining in West Virginia

In the summer of 1962, Glen Cain and Ernst Stromsdorfer interviewed 1,379 persons who had completed, or were participating in, training programs in West Virginia. The training programs they studied were funded by the Area Redevelopment Act (ARA) and by state funds under the Area Vocational Training Program of West Virginia. ARA courses generally were sixteen-week full-time courses, geared to specific employment opportunities in local areas. Courses sponsored by the state lasted six months to a year, but were less intensive. Both programs contained about the same total hours of instruction.[24] Furthermore, "The courses selected for analysis were representative of the types of courses which are being offered on a large scale throughout the country under the Manpower Development and Training Act."[25] and included training in riveting, clerical skills, auto repair, nurses aides, waitresses, construction trades, welding, electrical and maintenance repair, and machine tool operating and inspecting.[26]

A follow-up conducted in the spring of 1964 provided the benefit data for the study. Three periods of analysis were used: (1) first 18 months following training, (2) longest period available (included only trainees who had been out of the program for 27 months), and (3) last available quarter earnings (included trainees with post-training experiences of 18, 21, 24, and 27 months).

Training programs' costs were calculated by adding direct training costs, training and subsistence allowances granted during training period, increase in welfare and unemployment payments received by trainees during training, and opportunity costs of trainees.[27][e] Both private and social costs were calculated.

---

[d]As it turns out, the observed "continued earnings advantage" of trainees included two of the control groups (those who completed training but did not take a training-related job, and those who dropped out of training for a non-job related reason) of Borus' original study. The advantage of the *original* experimental group over these two other trainee categories disappeared. All trainees, whether they finished the program or utilized their training, were earning more than nontrainees. Taylor (p. 57.) takes this as additional evidence that placement may have been more important than training.

[e]The inclusion of subsistence payments as a social cost overstates the calculated total social costs. On the other hand, increases in administrative costs associated with training and placement are left out. This tends to understate the actual costs. The net effect is unknown.

Total social costs were $918 and $527 for male and female trainees respectively (Table 4-5), and respective private costs were $233 and $30 (Table 4-6).

Table 4-7 shows that when incomes of graduates of training programs were compared to incomes of a random sample of nontrainees unemployed at the time the training program began, the trainees, especially males, experienced substantially higher earnings than females. Following training, the first-year earnings advantage of males was $1,008; that of females, $192. Second-year income advantages were $996 and $180 respectively. The average trainee earned $736 more the first year and $724 more the second.

Comparisons of benefits with costs result in benefit-cost ratios that substantially exceed one for males, and exceed one for females by a much smaller amount (Table 4-8). Assuming a discount rate of 10 percent and a time horizon of ten years, the benefit-cost ratios for males and females respectively are 6.7 and 2.2. With a 5 percent discount rate the ratios are 8.4 and 2.7 respectively. Extending the time horizon to thirty years increases ratios for males to 16.8 and 10.2 with 5 percent and 10 percent discount rates respectively. Similar ratios for females are 5.4 and 3.3. The overall benefit-cost ratio with the severe assumptions of a 10 percent discount rate and a ten-year time horizon is 5.7.

Age category of males (under age thirty-five vs. thirty-five and over) and educational level (less than twelve years vs. twelve or more), had only a moderate effect on the earnings advantage of program graduates.[28] [f] On the other hand, famales aged thirty-five and over with twelve or more years of education gained substantially more than any other female groups. This was due possibly to the greater labor-force attachment of older women with fewer young children at home than younger women.[29] The generally poorer economic benefits accruing to females can be attributed mainly to the poorer attachment females traditionally have to the labor force and a higher propensity to train females for occupations with a high attrition rate, such as nurses aides.[30]

Table 4-9 indicates that the overall earnings advantage of male trainees over nontrainees decreased slightly ($1 a month) between the first and second years following training. Data in this table suggest that the reduction was due entirely to the experiences of trainees with twelve or more years of schooling. Male trainees under thirty-five with twelve or more years of education experienced a modest $1 a month (from $92 to $91) decline in relative earnings while those over thirty-five with the same education experienced a $53 a month (from $-5 to $-58) decline in their earnings advantage over nontrainees

---

[f]The exception to this involved males aged thirty-five and over with twelve or more years of education. In this category, trainees were at an earnings disadvantage. Cain and Stromsdorfer suggest it might have been due to the extremely small sample size of that group.

Table 4-5

Social Costs Per Trainee of Early Retraining Programs in
West Virginia

	Male	Female	Weighted Average
Direct Training Costs	$434	$298	—
Payments to Trainees	129	126	—
Opportunity Costs	355	103	—
Total Costs	$918	$527	$787

Source: Glen G. Cain and Ernst W. Stromsdorfer, "An Economic Evaluation of
Government Retraining Programs in West Virginia," in Gerald G. Somers, ed.
Retraining the Unemployed (Madison: The University of Wisconsin Press, © 1968
by the Regents of the University of Wisconsin), table IX.2, p. 313.

Table 4-6

Private Costs Per Trainee of Early Retraining Programs in West Virginia

	Male	Female
Payments to Trainees[a]	$-129	$-126
Opportunity Costs	362	156
Total Costs	$ 233	$ 30

Source: Glen G. Cain and Ernst W. Stromsdorfer, "An Economic Evaluation of
Government Retraining Programs in West Virginia," in Gerald G. Somers, ed.
Retraining the Unemployed (Madison: The University of Wisconsin Press, © 1968
by the Regents of the University of Wisconsin), table IX.2, p. 313.
[a]Payments to trainees represent income they would not otherwise have earned,
and can be regarded as negative costs.

Table 4-7

Annual Earnings Advantage of Trainees Over Non-Trainees
in West Virginia

	Males	Females	Weighted Average
First Year	$1,008	$192	$736
Second Year	996	180	724

Source: Glen G. Cain and Ernst W. Stromsdorfer, "An Economic Evaluation of
Government Retraining Programs in West Virginia," in Gerald G. Somers, editor
Retraining the Unemployed (Madison: The University of Wisconsin Press, © 1968
by the Regents of the University of Wisconsin), table IX.7, p. 324.

Table 4-8
Benefit-Cost Ratios of Early Retraining Programs in West Virginia[a]

| | 10-year Time Horizon | | 30-year Time Horizon | |
| | [Discount Rate (percent)] | | | |
	5	10	5	10
Males	8.4	6.7	16.8	10.2
Females	2.7	2.2	5.4	3.3
Average	7.2	5.7	14.3	8.7

Source: Calculated from table 4-5 and 4-7.

[a]Assuming benefits continue the trend established between the first and second year.

Table 4-9
Monthly Wage Advantage of Trainees Over Non-Trainees in
West Virginia

| | Under Age 35 | | Aged 35 and Over | |
	Less Than 12 Years Education	12 Years or More	Less Than 12 Years Education	12 Years or More
Males				
First 18 months following training	$ 99	$ 92	$ 98	$- 5
First Quarter, 1964	116	91	117	-58
Females				
First 18 months following training	8	0	48	9
First Quarter, 1964	- 1	-28	58	24

Source: Glen G. Cain and Ernst W. Stromsdorfer, "An Economic Evaluation of Government Retraining Programs in West Virginia," Retraining the Unemployed, ed. Gerald G. Somers (Madison, Wis.: University of Wisconsin Press, 1968), table IX.5, p. 317.

with similar characteristics. These trends were opposite those being experienced by male trainees with less than twelve years of education regardless of age group. Those with less education were experiencing substantial relative wage gains of $17 and $19 a month for the less than thirty-five and thirty-five and over age groups respectively. These results clearly suggest that training was more "successful" in cases where males had not graduated from high school.[g]

---

[g]While the information is not available, the poor relative showing of males with twelve or more years of schooling could have been due to the rapidly rising wages of nontrainees with the same amount of education, rather than a decline in, or slow growth of trainees' incomes.

A 1966 follow-up of this study by Somers and McKechnie indicated that employment experiences of nontrainees were gaining relative to those of trainees over a four to five year period following training. They also found that although training was still a significant variable in explaining regularity of employment of the two groups (trainees and nontrainees), it was decreasing in importance. Demographic variables were becoming more important. Age, sex, race and education were not important explanatory variables a year and a half following training, but became important (and statistically significant) after several more years had passed.[31]

Somers and McKechnie conclude from this that "There appears to be some indication, . . . that the advantages gained by retraining may begin to wash out after years of general employment expansion."[32] This probably is an unwarranted conclusion. A decrease in the *employment* advantage of trainees over time does not imply that the *earnings* advantage is similarly decreasing. Neither the original study nor its follow-up mentions relative wage rates.[33] However, enough has been presented to allow us to infer something about what most likely was happening to relative wages.

Somers and Stromsdorfer report that trainees were employed 7.6 months the first year following training, and nontrainees employed only 4.7 months during the same period.[34] [h] Trainees received special help in obtaining jobs and

In extreme cases, the trainees had practically guaranteed jobs. . . . In some instances the companies had been awarded defense contracts on a preferential basis in accordance with our national policy which created new jobs rather than to the training program as such.[35]

Consequently, a good portion of the first year's employment advantage (and earnings advantage) resulted from placement practices accompanying the programs. We would expect the advantage of initial placement to diminish as time passed, even possibly by the end of the second year. Yet it was reported that for most male trainees the earnings differential was larger in the second, than in the first year. The most likely explanation is that the wage rate advantage of trainees was increasing over time.[i] Thus, no conclusion concerning the trend in "advantages gained by retraining" can be made.

These conflicting interpretations of the same data reinforce the importance of researchers presenting relatively complete (even if summarized) data on the experiences of experimental and control groups following training. In this case, failure to present wage and employment information separately makes reasonable two opposing conclusions concerning permanency of benefits

---

[h]Somers and Stromsdorfer are making a summary report of the study performed by Cain and Stromsdorfer, so both sets of authors are talking about the same basic data.

[i]A conclusion consistent with findings of Borus [Michael E. Borus, "A Benefit-Cost Analysis of the Economic Effectiveness of Retraining the Unemployed," *Yale Economic Essays* vol. 4, no. 2 (Fall 1964), pp. 371–429].

of retraining. Given that cost-benefit analysis is concerned with future flows, knowledge about the probable shape of these flows is extremely important.

Other conclusions are less ambiguous. Incomes of males increased substantially more than those of females, due at least partially to greater labor force attachment of the former group. Men with less than twelve years of education experienced greater increases in earnings than those with twelve years or more. Men aged thirty-five or over (with less than twelve years of education) gained as much in earnings as younger men (at least in the short-run). Policy implications are clear. If the experiences in West Virginia are representative, economic gains to training can be maximized by orienting it toward men with less than twelve years of education, and toward women with a known labor force attachment. Age (within the very broad categories utilized by Cain and Stromsdorfer) should not be one of the more important screening devices. While placement effort was apparently an important part of the program, there is no way to estimate its relative importance to training. More recent studies of manpower programs also leave us in the dark about the relative importance of placement.

Retraining in Massachusetts

David Page has conducted a study of workers who participated in state-sponsored retraining programs in Massachusetts between 1958 and 1961. His sample was comprised of 618 men and 289 women who entered training during that period. Courses offered were in occupations in which, at least in New England, demand appeared to be in excess of supply. Over 50 percent of the trainees were trained as barbers or beauticians; 18 percent as draftsmen, technicians, office machine operators and mechanics; 4.4 percent in office occupations; and 4.6 percent as practical nurses.[36] Although the courses were offered under a Massachusetts program, Page felt that enough similarities existed between the type of training envisioned by MDTA and the training in Massachusetts to allow the Massachusetts' experience to indicate what might be expected under MDTA.

In calculating costs, Page included tuition fees and subsistence payments (less unemployment compensation). Administration costs were considered negligible since existing personnel was used for administering the programs.[37] Opportunity costs were ignored. (Results are in Table 4-10.) Average costs per trainee (entering the program) were $698.30. Of the original 907 trainees, 324 dropped out for various reasons, and 583 completed the program. Of the 583 who completed the program, 145 either had found jobs other than those for which they trained, or had withdrawn from the labor force.[38] Consequently, of the original 907 who entered training, only 438 completed the program and found training-related jobs. Based on the number of persons in this category, average costs per trainee were $1,453.

Benefits were calculated based on the earnings experience of these 438 trainees who completed the program and were placed in occupations for which they had trained as compared to incomes of a control group with personal characteristics similar to the trainees randomly selected from Employment Security Office files.[39] Annual incomes of trainees increased from $2,847 before training to $3,823 following training (Table 4-11). Since incomes of the control group also increased, only $891 of the $976 increase can be attributed to the training itself.

When benefits are compared to costs, resulting benefit-cost ratios range from a low of 3.8 up to 9.4 depending on specific assumptions concerning the discount rate and time horizon (Table 4-12). The earnings differential is assumed

Table 4-10
Costs of Training in Massachusetts 1958-1961

	Costs Per Trainee	Costs Per Trainee Who Utilized Skill
Tuition	$567.10	$1,180
Subsistence	131.20	273
Total	$698.30	$1,453

Source: Calculated from David A. Page, "Retraining Under the Manpower Development Act: A Cost-Benefit Analysis," Public Policy, ed. John D. Montgomery and Arthur Smithies (Cambridge, Mass.: Harvard University Press, 1964) vol. 13, exhibit 1, p. 261.

Table 4-11
Annual Income Gain and Gain Attributable to Training in Massachusetts

Earnings following training	$3,823
Earnings prior to training	2,847
Increase attributable to training	891

Source: David A. Page, "Retraining Under the Manpower Development Act: A Cost-Benefit Analysis," Public Policy, ed. John D. Montgomery and Arthur Smithies (Cambridge, Mass.: Harvard University Press, 1964), vol. 13, exhibit 2, p. 262.

Table 4-12
Benefit-Cost Ratios of Retraining in Massachusetts, 1958-1961

Discount Rate	10-Year Time Horizon	30-Year Time Horizon
5 percent	4.7	9.4
10 percent	3.8	5.7

Source: Calculated from tables 4-10 and 4-11.

to stay constant throughout the relevant periods.[j] These ratios are smaller than comparable ones developed by Borus and by Cain and Stromsdorfer in their studies of retraining programs in the first several years of the 1960s. However, the 3.8 benefit-cost ratio resulting from use of a 10 percent discount rate and ten-year time horizon (as compared to 5.9 from Borus and 5.7 from Cain and Stromsdorfer using similar assumptions) is still sizable.

To the extent that Page understates costs by neglecting opportunity costs, his benefit-cost ratios are overstated. On the other hand, he includes subsistence payments as a cost of training. Since most of these probably represent income transfers, costs are being overstated. Additionally, even though 907 persons entered training, he assumes that benefits were zero for all except those who completed training and found training-related jobs. Borus found that differences in incomes between this group and those who either dropped out of training or found jobs not requiring their newly-learned skills disappeared within five years. If this is true in Massachusetts as well as in Connecticut, benefits of the program are substantially understated. The net effect of these biases is unknown.[40]

Page concludes that retraining under MDTA will yield returns to society greater than its costs if trainees are carefully selected, and if training is offered in occupations for which labor shortages exist. "Properly administered, the federal program should produce national economic and social gains, and help reduce the functional and structural segment of 'normal' unemployment." [41] No details are presented indicating differences in post-training experiences caused by personal characteristics of trainees, so the only implication for policy that emerges from Page's study is the one quoted above — MDTA programs, run like the state-sponsored programs in Massachusetts, may yield greater benefits to society than they cost.

Retraining in Tennessee

Richard Solie has tested the effect of retraining on unemployment in depressed rural areas of northeast Tennessee.[42] Retraining took place between February and June of 1962, and was supported by ARA. Benefit data were collected through June 1964 by personal interviews with 217 workers. Solie's study is not a cost-benefit study because he does not attempt to calculate program costs or trainees' earnings. Goals of the study were to see if retrainees experienced significantly less unemployment following training than did three separate control groups, and to measure the program's ability to place its

[j]Recall that Borus ("Time Trends in the Benefits From Retraining in Connecticut," *Proceedings of the Twentieth Annual Winter Meeting of the Industrial Relations Research Association*) found that the incomes advantage of trainees over nontrainees actually increased slightly over a five-year period in Connecticut. Thus the assumption is not extreme.

trainees in training-related positions. Courses were offered in welding, machine
tooling, auto mechanics, radio-T.V. repair, and cabinetmaking.

Three control groups were used: persons accepted for retraining who either
did not show up or who dropped out; persons who applied but were rejected
for retraining; and persons selected at random who were unemployed at
the time training was offered, but who did not apply for retraining. Solie notes
that there are three main sources of labor-market benefits for workers who
completed training: (1) special placement efforts upon completion of the
program, (2) restoration of self-confidence through qualifying for and completing training, and (3) improved skills. Because trainees did not receive special
placement help and because nonqualified applicants were screened from the
training program, it is not certain how many of the benefits should be attributed
to training, and how much to screening and placement.[43]

Immediately following training, the employment experiences of those who
had completed training were no better than those of any of the three control
groups. Table 4-13 contains these details. "Completes" were experiencing
a 33.3 percent unemployment rate while "non-completes," "rejects," and non-
applicants were experiencing unemployment rates of 25.8, 35.0, and 42.5
percent, respectively. A year following training (June 1963) the four groups were
experiencing unemployment rates of 5.3, 14.8, 30.8, and 23.9 percent,
respectively. Thus, over a period of a year, the group completing training had
developed a substantial employment advantage over the other three groups.
During the second year following training, the employment advantage decreased.
Since the experimental group had reached a 5.3 percent unemployment
rate by June 1963, while the other three groups were averaging a little over 20
percent unemployment, the latter groups hardly could help but gain in continued
prosperity. Solie suggests that the decrease in employment advantage during

Table 4-13
Unemployment Rates of the Experimental Group and the Three
Control Groups in Tennessee July 1962–June 1964 (percentages)

| Date | Group | | | |
	Completes	Non-Completes	Rejects	Non-Applicants
June 1962	33.3	25.8	35.0	42.5
August 1962	25.0	22.6	30.0	34.7
September 1962	21.4	30.0	30.0	31.0
December 1962	16.3	30.0	36.8	38.0
June 1963	5.3	14.8	30.8	23.9
December 1963	2.9	16.7	20.0	25.4
June 1964	5.6	14.8	15.0	16.4

Source: Richard J. Solie, "Employment Effects of Retraining the Unemployed,"
Industrial and Labor Relations Review 21, no. 2 (January 1968), table 3, p. 216.

Table 4-14

Ability of Graduates of Different Courses to Find Employment in Training-Related Jobs in Tennessee

Course	Percentage Finding Training-Related Employment
Radio-T.V.	33
Auto Mechanics	92
Welding	67
Machine Tooling	61
Cabinet Making	68

Source: Richard J. Solie, "Employment Effects of Retraining the Unemployed," *Industrial and Labor Relations Review* 21, no. 2 (January 1968), p. 213, and f.n. 5, p. 213-14.

Note: "Some of these figures are slightly misleading, . . . since those for auto mechanics include a number of trainees who obtained work in service stations where they worked primarily as attendants but also did some mechanical work. In the case of the radio-T.V. class, placement was strongly affected by the closing (on the day the program ended) of a relatively large electronics plant in the immediate labor market area which had been expected to hire a number of trainees."

the second year might indicate that training merely helped trainees get jobs quicker through the placement services offered upon completion of training, and did not give trainees any *permanent* labor-market advantage.[44] This decreasing advantage also may be a partial reflection of the "rejects" greater tendency to withdraw from the labor force ("out of labor force" is not "unemployed").

When experiences of the four groups are controlled for demographic differences, the employment advantage of the experimental group is reduced anywhere from 27 to 58 percent. Controlling for age, education, skill level, previous labor-market experience and marital status, "completes" were unemployed 8.3 weeks, 5.0 weeks and 6.5 weeks less in those two years than were non-applicants, "non-completes" and "rejects." [45] [k] Even with this reduced estimate of employment advantage, it seems clear that workers participating in the complete program gained a distinct labor-market advantage over those who did not.[l]

Although no firms made advance commitments to hire graduates of the training programs (as was the case for many West Virginia trainees), 50 percent

---

[k]Only the difference in unemployment experiences between the "completes" and non-applicants is statistically significant.

[l]The problem, as Solie (and many others) notes earlier, is that he is not able to separate the screening and placement effects of the program from the training effects. According to Solie, no one has yet tested the importance of the complementary relationship between training and placement. He suggests this is a valid area of research.

of the trainees' first jobs were in the occupation for which they had trained. Two years later 45 percent of the employed trainees were still in these occupations. However, only 39 percent of the first jobs obtained by trainees actually required that training. The ability of 71 percent of the trainees to get jobs either in some occupation other than that for which they trained, or in occupations not requiring the skills they gained, indicates that many employers were offering jobs with relatively low skill requirements and were willing to hire trainees for training positions when additional skills had to be learned.[46]

There was a wide variance in the ability of trainees completing different courses to find jobs in their selected occupations. As Table 4–14 shows, only 33 percent of those graduating from the radio-T.V. class were successful, while 92 percent of those completing the auto mechanics course were successful. Three factors seem to be operative in determining success in finding training-related jobs: the manner of defining specific occupations, the adequacy of training relative to the skill requirements for job entry, and the relative availability of jobs.[47]

Summary

Evidence from four studies of early manpower programs indicates that MDTA programs could be expected to yield benefit-cost ratios greater than one. Borus' data suggest that training in Connecticut had a ratio of 5.9.[48] Cain and Stromsdorfer indicate that training in West Virginia yielded a ratio of 5.7. Page calculated a benefit-cost ratio for training in Massachusetts of 3.8. All these ratios are based on conservative assumptions of a 10 percent discount rate and a ten-year time horizon.

The several studies presenting some breakdown of comparative experiences of different groups of trainees (those by Borus, Cain and Stromsdorfer, and Solie), offer several (sometimes conflicting) policy guides:

1. Trainees over wide "age and education ranges" can benefit from retraining. Sometimes those with less education seem to do a little better than those with more, and sometimes the reverse is true. The explanation probably lies in types of training offered, length of training, and job opportunities available upon completion of training.
2. Both males and females can make large gains from retraining, but the degree of labor-force attachment is an important variable. Women with dependent children appear less able to stay in the labor market upon finishing training.
3. Race is not a good predictor of relative success.
4. All persons participating in a training program benefit. They do not have to finish training in order to experience increases in earnings relative to those not participating, nor do they have to find a job requiring the skills

they learned in the training courses. Satisfying all these conditions, however, generally results in a more regular employment experience following training.

5. Training programs need not be long to yield benefits. Borus, for example, finds that familiarization with working conditions and equipment is enough in many cases to induce firms to hire program participants.

6. More regular employment experience is an important source of program benefits. Every study that examined the relative employment experiences of the experimental and control groups made this finding.

7. Benefits from training are not transitory; they are long lasting. This is a significant finding, offering support both for the form and content of training programs, and for the methodology used in assessing their results.

Manpower Development and Training Act–Sponsored Programs

Surprisingly few "full-blown" cost-benefit studies have been conducted of institutional training activities pursued following passage of the MDTA. Svetozar Pejovich and William Sullivan conducted a cost-benefit study of institutional training in Michigan, but their study suffers from serious methodological proglems. [49] A national study by the Planning Research Corporation of both institutional and OJT programs also suffers from serious deficiencies. [50] Earl Main has studied the earnings and employment experiences of a national sample of MDTA trainees, [51] and although he does not calculate any benefit-cost ratios, it is possible to develop some suggestive ratios by combining his data with cost data presented by Garth Mangum. A recent study by Einar Hardin and Michael Borus of retraining in Michigan gives a detailed analysis of the programs as well as computes benefit-cost ratios. As predicted by the cost-benefit studies of pre-MDTA training activities, these studies indicate that institutional training programs offered under MDTA have resulted in benefits accruing to society in excess of the costs. Hardin and Borus calculate a benefit-cost ratio of 1.5. Data presented by Main also yield an estimated ratio of 1.5. Both of these ratios result from conservative assumptions.

A large number of non-benefit-cost evaluative studies of MDTA have been conducted. Some of these have been examined for this book, primarily because results of the two approaches of analysis can be shown to complement each other; the conclusions of each reinforcing those of the other.

Retraining in Michigan

Hardin and Borus have studied a wide range of retraining courses in Michigan offered between May 1962 and September 1964 under both ARA and MDTA. They wished to measure the effects of such training ". . . on the national product, the disposable income of trainees, and the expenditures and receipts of the government." [52] Their study included forty-nine classes in forty different occupations ranging from two to fifty-two weeks in length. Data for the study were gathered through interviews with trainees and from training institution and government records. Both the experimental group (persons who entered the program) and control group (persons who applied for and were qualified to enter training, but did not) were randomly selected. Of the 1,036 selected, inability to locate, nonsatisfactory interviews and other problems reduced the final sample size to 784 (503 trainees and 281 nontrainees). Multiple regression analysis was used throughout the study to control for differences in labor market conditions as well as in demographic characteristics.

Social costs of all sampled retraining programs were $1,272 per trainee (Table 4-15). Included were instructional outlays for classroom training of $493,[m] local, state and federal administration costs of $184, opportunity costs of $499, and additional expenses incurred by trainees of $95. Since course length varied substantially, costs by broad category of course length also appear in Table 4-15. Courses ranging from 60 to 200 hours cost $346 per trainee, while those lasting from 1,201 to 1,920 hours cost ten times as much – $3,293. Opportunity costs, which were a small part of costs in short courses ($47) increased substantially until they comprised over half of total costs in the longest courses ($1,838).

Benefits were calculated as the gain in earnings attributable to training measured over the first year immediately following training, relative to earnings the year immediately preceding. Here the importance of a control group is emphasized. Trainees' earnings increased $1,524 from the year before training to the year following training. At the same time, however, nontrainee earnings increased by $1,308; making the average trainee's net gain in income only $216. [53] Adjusting these figures for demographic and labor market characteristics increases the gain slightly to $252.

This average gain of $252 conceals what is the most startling finding of the study – *the net gains from training decrease as course length increases.* In fact, *they decrease so rapidly that all courses longer than 200 hours are associated with overall net losses in earnings.* As Table 4-16 shows, the income gain from the shortest courses (60-200 hours) is $976, while that associated with successively longer courses of 201-600, 601-1,200, and 1,201-1,920 hours is $-5, $-121, and $-136, respectively. Of course, trainees did receive greater incomes following training; but nontrainees were experiencing even greater increases. Hardin and Borus explore the possible reasons for the earnings disadvantage of trainees who participated in longer courses, and offer the

---

[m]This includes current purchases of equipment and ignores opportunity costs of buildings. Hardin and Borus recognize that the former overstates, and the latter understates, total costs [Einar Hardin and Michael E. Borus, *The Economic Benefits and Costs of Retraining* (Lexington, Mass.: D.C. Heath and Company, 1971), p. 213.] On the other hand, ignoring capital costs brings us closer to marginal costs.

Table 4–15
Per-Trainee Social Costs of ARA and MDTA Institutional Training Courses in Michigan, 1962–1964

Cost Category	All Courses	Courses by Hours of Instruction			
		60–200	201–600	601–1,200	1,201–1,920
Instruction	$ 493	$109	$412	$1,013	$ 969
Administration	184	175	182	191	205
Lost Earnings	499	47	229	816	1,838
Trainee Expenses	95	15	62	163	281
Total	$1,272	$346	$885	$2,183	$3,293

Source: Einar Hardin and Michael E. Borus, The Economic Benefits and Costs of Retraining (Lexington, Mass.: D. C. Heath and Company, 1971), table 12:2, p. 144.

Table 4-16

Annual Income Gains Per Trainee of ARA and MDTA Institutional
Training Courses in Michigan, 1962-1964[a]

Course Length by Hours of Instruction	Annual Income Gain
60–200	$ 976
201–600	– 5
601–1,200	–121
1,201–1,920	–136
All Courses	$ 251

Source: Einar Hardin and Michael E. Borus, *The Economic Benefits and Costs of Retraining* (Lexington, Mass.: D. C. Heath and Company, 1971), table 13:2, p. 262.

[a]Relative to control groups.

following possible explanations: (1) systematic unmeasured forces that acted with differing strength between short and long courses; (2) a wage advantage held by nontrainees who were able to work and gain experience while trainees were attending classes, an advantage that was maintained for at least a year; (3) a wage advantage held by nontrainees in occupations for which long courses were designed and characterized by low starting wages, but offering rapid increases; (4) a greater tendency for job vacancies to disappear by the time trainees completed long courses formed to fill those vacancies; and (5) the possible tendency for short courses to train persons for new occupations offering them substantially higher wage rates than they earned previously; and for long courses to give persons primarily increased skill levels *within* a broad occupational category, offering only moderate wage increases as rewards.[54] These possibilities are not explored in the study, but surely are suggestions which should be examined.

A number of benefit-cost ratios can be calculated. Table 4-17 contains average ratios for all programs examined, and ratios by broad course length. As Table 4-17 shows, average returns from all training programs included in those sampled by Hardin and Borus achieved ratios from 1.2 to 3.0 depending on the discount rate and time horizon assumptions.[n] When the sample results are adjusted to reflect the actual course-length combination of all courses in Michigan between 1962 and 1964, these overall ratios are increased to 1.5 and 3.8. The low total costs and high income gains associated with courses lasting from 60 to 200 hours resulted in ratios ranging from 17.3 to 43.3. These

[n]Hardin and Borus also calculated private and government ratios. Using a 10 percent discount rate and a ten-year time horizon, all courses sampled yielded a private benefit-cost ratio of 6.0 and a government ratio of .5 (table 14:1, p. 287 and table 15:2, p. 10).

Table 4-17

Benefit-Cost Ratios for ARA and MDTA Institutional Retraining in Michigan by Course Length, 1962-1964[a]

Course Length (hours)	Discount Rate (percent)	10-Year Time Horizon	30-Year Time Horizon
60–200	5	21.8	43.3
	10	17.3	26.5
All Others	5	a	a
	10	a	a
All Courses Sampled	5	1.5	3.0
	10	1.2	1.9
All Courses Sampled, Adjusted to Actual Experience	5	1.9	3.8
	10	1.5	2.3

Source: Einar Hardin and Michael E. Borus, *The Economic Benefits and Costs of Retraining* (Lexington, Mass.: D. C. Heath and Company, 1971), table 12:2, p. 144; and table 12:9, p. 155.

[a]Calculated ratios were negative.

extremely high benefit-cost ratios countered those which were actually negative for the longer courses by a sufficient amount to lift the average ratio for all courses over one.[o]

When characteristics of trainees were examined, Hardin and Borus found substantial differentials in benefits (and costs) depending on trainee's race, sex, and education; and unemployment compensation and welfare status prior to training. Benefits also were affected by the occupational area for which training was taken. Benefit-cost ratios are summarized for these details in Table 4-18. Ratios are higher for nonwhites than for whites, and for nonwhite females than for nonwhite males. Educational level made little difference in the ratios

[o]Negative benefit-cost ratios are difficult to interpret. It is clear that larger income gains by trainees would make the negative values of ratios smaller and eventually push the ratios to the positive side. We then might be led to prefer smaller negative ratios to larger negative ratios (taking the lesser of the evils). On the other hand, increasing program costs while leaving benefits unchanged also brings the negative ratios closer to zero; but this clearly is not preferred. The problem can be avoided by considering *all* earnings of non-trainees both during *and after* training as opportunity costs of participating in practice (i.e., adding these earnings to costs rather than subtracting some of them from benefits). With this approach, benefit-cost ratios would not be less than zero unless trainees experienced an actual deterioration of post-training earnings. Interpreted in this fashion, all Michigan training courses have positive benefit-cost ratios. Unfortunately, ratios resulting from this method of calculation could not be compared to those calculated in any other study (without adjusting their results) since common practice is to subtract control group earnings from those of the experimental group. The problem of negative benefit-cost ratios was discussed also in Ernst W. Stromsdorfer, "Discussion," *Cost-Benefit Analysis of Manpower Policies. Proceedings of a North American Conference,* ed. by G. G. Somers and W. D. Wood, (Ontario: Industrial Relations Centre, Queen's University at Kingston, 1969), pp. 157–159.

Table 4-18
Benefit-Cost Ratios for ARA and MDTA Institutional Retraining in Michigan by Trainee Characteristics, 1962–1964

	Courses of 60–200 Hours	Courses of 200–1,920 Hours[b]	
Trainee Characteristics	Benefit-Cost Ratio[a]	Trainee Characteristic	Benefit-Cost Ratio[a]
White		White	
Male	9.3	5–8 years education	.9
Female	24.6	9–11 years education	.6
5–8 years education	14.9	Non-White	
9–11 years education	13.4	9–11 years education	.2
12 and more years education	14.3		
Non-White			
Male	21.2		
Female	29.7		
5–8 years education	19.8		
9–11 years education	25.5		
12 and more years education	26.9		
Prior Earnings			
Up to $1,786	21.0		
Over $1,786	12.5		
Unemployment Benefits			
Recipient	10.5		
Non-recipient	20.0		
Welfare Benefits			
Recipient	18.4		
Non-recipient	17.1		
Occupational Area			
Factory	12.1		
Health Care	26.0		
Auto Repair	9.2		
Other[c]	30.0		

Source: Einar Hardin and Michael E. Borus, The Economic Benefits and Costs of Retraining (Lexington, Mass.: D. C. Heath and Company, 1971), tables 12:3–12:7, pp. 144–52.

[a] Using a 10 percent discount rate and 10-year time horizon.

[b] Includes only breakdowns yielding benefit-cost ratios exceeding zero.

[c] Does not include any office occupation. They all required more than 200 hours of instruction. Includes auto station operator, automobile painter, furniture upholsterer, nurses aide, waitress, and floral designer (inferred from Einar Hardin and Michael E. Borus, The Economic Benefits and Costs of Retraining (Lexington, Mass.: D. C. Heath and Company, 1971), table 4:1, pp. 70–71.

associated with whites (13.4 to 14.9), but did affect those for nonwhites (19.8 to 26.9). Benefit-cost ratios were highest for nonwhite high school graduates. The generally higher benefit-cost ratios for nonwhites, and the substantial difference in ratios between nonwhite high school graduates and nongraduates that was absent for whites, suggest that training in Michigan helped reduce job discrimination based on race and that it was most effective in reducing discrimination against nonwhite high school graduates.

Benefit-cost ratios for trainees with prior annual earnings under $1,786 were greater than those for trainees with earnings in excess of $1,786 (21.0 vs. 12.5). This leads one to suggest that larger income gains experienced by those with low "before" earnings resulted from unusually depressed earnings just prior to entering training. However, this possibility is contradicted by the relatively higher ratios associated with trainees who were not receiving unemployment compensation when they entered training compared to those who were receiving it at that time (20.0 vs. 10.5). The reverse would have had to be true to be consistent with the suggestion that high ratios resulted from depressed earnings prior to training.

Benefit-cost ratios for those receiving welfare benefits when training started were a little higher than those for nonwelfare recipients. This is significant, because it means that the retraining programs were successful in reducing participants' dependence on welfare. Welfare recipients who were trainees decreased their average welfare receipts from about $800 the year before entering training to around $340 the year following training. Persons on welfare who did not receive training only reduced their welfare receipts from around $800 to about $640 over the same periods.[55] While welfare recipients decreased their dependence on welfare benefits through participating in training, only about 10 of the 114 persons receiving welfare when they entered training did not receive some welfare the year following training. This is probably to be expected, since the range of problems faced by welfare recipients is not likely to be solved immediately by a short training course.

Benefit-cost ratios varied considerably among the broad occupational classifications utilized in the study. Auto repair occupations fared the worst (relatively) with a ratio of 9.2. "Other" occupations (miscellaneous service and sales) achieved the highest ratios of 30.0. The high ratio of 26.0 for health care occupations is surprising, since nurses aide was the dominant occupation, an occupation associated with substantially lower ratios in training programs offered in other states. No broad occupational area offered in the longer courses (200–1,920 hours) managed to achieve a benefit-cost ratio greater than zero. In fact, no group of trainees detailed in Table 4–18 which participated in these longer courses was given instruction that yielded a benefit-cost ratio greater than one.

Hardin and Borus conclude from this study that the benefit-cost ratios associated with institutional training in Michigan are large enough to justify continuing this type of training. They suggest, however, that the composition of training be altered toward the shorter courses. This would result in higher net benefits to society than has been the case in the past and would permit training larger numbers of persons for a given dollar outlay.

Based on the differences in the benefits associated with different types of participants, Hardin and Borus indicate that net benefits could be increased also by expanding course offerings for (1) women relative to men, (2) whites relative to nonwhites,[p] (3) those with less, relative to those with more, education, (4) those with low previous earnings relative to those with high previous earnings, (5) welfare recipients relative to nonwelfare recipients, and (6) health care, and sales and service occupations relative to factory work and auto repairs.[56]

The main shortcoming of this study is its failure to separate the effects of wage rates and employment regularity from income. This failure prevents an evaluation of the probable placement, from the training benefits, of the programs. This shortcoming is overshadowed by the many policy recommendations that do emerge.

Pejovich and Sullivan examined results of MDTA programs conducted in an area vocational school near Winona, Michigan, between 1960 and 1965. MDTA courses were offered in nine skill areas — auto mechanics, auto body repair, industrial electronics, highway technician, machine tool and die making, welding, general office clerk, practical nursing, and stenography. Their sample consisted of 190 students who had completed training and 169 still in the program.

Social costs of the program were estimated by adding direct educational expenditures, subsidies paid students during the program, opportunity costs, and an allocation for capital costs based on a 10 percent rate of depreciation.[57] Private costs included direct costs of the program to the student (fees, supplies, and transportation) and opportunity costs. Opportunity costs were measured in two ways. If a person was employed prior to entering the program, his earnings at that time were extrapolated through the period he was in the program under the assumption that he would have suffered no unemployment.[q] If

---

[p]This recommendation is made even though Table 4-18 suggests benefit-cost ratios for whites exceed those for nonwhites. Data from which Table 4-18 is built are nonstandardized. Standardized data suggest the reverse is true.

[q]Pejovich and Sullivan state that they deliberately overestimate costs and underestimate benefits so that " . . . the calculated rates of return in this study are either equal to or below the true rates of return on investment in education by the WATS (Winona Area Technical School)." [Svetozar Pejovich and William Sullivan, "The Role of Technical Schools in Improving the Skills and Earnings of Rural Manpower. A Case Study," Final Report to the Office of Manpower Policy, Evaluation and Research, U.S. Department of Labor (Washington, D.C.: G.P.O., September, 1966), p. 2.] The reader is aware, from earlier discussions of unmeasured benefits and costs and of inaccuracies that exist in those that are measured, that there is no guarantee (regardless of the methodology used) that calculated rates will be "equal to or below the true rates."

the person was unemployed at the time he entered the program, the opportunity
costs were estimated by extrapolating the ratio of median income in Winona
to median income in the U.S. (.85) multiplied by median income in the U.S. for
the appropriate age and education category of the worker.[58] [r]

Benefits of the program are calculated as the difference between the
trainees' postprogram and preprogram experiences. No control group is used,
nor any adjustment made for changes in economic conditions that might have
contributed to the improved labor-market experiences of trainees. The benefits
accruing to those still in the program were estimated by what the State
Employment Service stated they could expect to earn after graduating.[s] Based on
the methodology discussed above, a series of private and social median rates
of return have been calculated for each of the nine skill categories. They
appear in Table 4–19. Private rates of return generally are higher than social rates
of return, and range from 11 to 53 percent compared to a range of 9 to 35
percent for social rates of return. These results are difficult to interpret because
of methodological problems discussed earlier.

A more concise list of ways in which Pejovich and Sullivan's methodology
varies from that more often used and the likely bias introduced by each
includes:

1. use of before and after earnings to estimate benefits — tends to overstate
    benefits;
2. assumption of full employment for estimating opportunity costs — tends to
    overstate costs;
3. exclusion of subsidies received by program participants — tends to
    overstate private costs;
4. inclusion of the subsidy as a social cost — overstates social costs;
5. use of prior earnings estimates of those unemployed at the time they
    entered the program based on national data — probably overstates
    opportunity costs and understates benefits;
6. inclusion of capital costs of the Area Technical School as part of program
    costs — tends to overstate social costs.

The net effect of these on the calculated rates of return is unknown.

The results can be useful when used another way, however. If the
methodology employed was used consistently throughout the study, the
differences in rates of return from either the private or social standpoint may

---

[r]This overstates opportunity costs to the extent that estimated earnings based on the
experience of the median worker exceed those the MDTA participant could have earned.
The fact that these persons were unemployed when they entered the program suggests that
their experience would have been worse than the median experience of all workers.

[s]These types of estimates probably result in overstatement of benefits. The amount of
overstatement is unknown.

Table 4-19
Median Rates of Return for MDTA Programs Conducted in Winona,
Michigan, Between 1960 and 1965[a]

Course	Median Rates of Return (percent)	
	Private	Social
Auto Mechanics	20	19
Auto Body Repair	11	9
Machine Tool and Die	24	24
Highway Technician	36	17
Welding	53	19
Industrial Electronics	22	23
General Office	47	35
Stenography	42	22
Practical Nursing	20	18

Source: Svetozar Pejovich and William Sullivan, "The Role of Technical Schools
in Improving the Skills and Earnings of Rural Manpower, a Case Study," Final
Report to the Office of Manpower Policy, Evaluation and Research (Washington,
D.C.: U. S. Department of Labor, September 1966), pp. 10-17.
[a]Pejovich and Sullivan calculated a rate of return for each individual participating in
the program. Thus these figures represent the experiences of the median individual.

have some meaning. Thus, though we cannot be sure that the social rate of
return for auto mechanics was 19 percent, we may feel more confident that,
whatever it was, it was less than that for general office skills (calculated at 35
percent). *Rankings* of rates of return can be taken with more confidence
than absolute values. We might suggest, then, that from the social standpoint,
auto body repair, auto mechanics, highway technician, welding, and practical
nursing had lower returns as a group than machine tool and die, industrial
electronics, general office, and stenography. Further study of the characteristics
of those entering those occupations and of conditions in the relative labor
markets might have helped explain why returns were higher in some occupations
than others, and indicate guidelines that might be followed in future programs.

The study by Pejovich and Sullivan does suggest that there were significant
differences in rates of return for different occupational programs, but its
conceptual and methodological difficulties preclude justifying its conclusions
". . . that (1) the WATS has used resources allocated to it efficiently and
profitably, and (2) use of the same resources elsewhere could not, on the
average, be expected to provide the community with a higher rate of return." [59] High rates of return do not imply "efficient" use of resources unless
it can be shown that no changes could be made that would result in even
higher rates. Any one program cannot be extolled as the "best" program
available until the results of alternatives have been explored.

Retraining Nationwide

Earl Main has assessed the ability of institutional MDTA training to improve trainees' labor market experiences. In conducting his study, he built a stratified random sample of about 1,200 persons who had completed training at least a year before being interviewed to serve as the experimental group. He selected the control group from friends and relatives who were unemployed about the time participants entered training. (This is the "snowball" method discussed in chap. 1.)

Main found that females who completed training earned more than female nontrainees in their last reported full-time job, but he could not detect a similar difference in the wage rates of males with full-time jobs. To see what impact differences in personal characteristics between the experimental and control groups had on wage rates, he controlled for demographic characteristics — sex, education, age, race, previous unemployment, "main earner status," geographic region, marital status, number of unmarried children under eighteen, and the state-of-residence per capita income.

When controlling for the ten "background" variables simultaneously, MDTA training still had no statistically significant net effect on wages for [the] last full-time job since training. . . . Even when considering completers and dropouts separately, MDTA training had no effect on weekly wages for those who found full-time employment after training. [60]

Even though wage rates of those who participated in MDTA training and subsequently accepted full-time work were not significantly increased, Main found that incomes were (Table 4-20). Considering all the trainees together, their income advantage over nontrainees was $9.60 a week ($480 a year). Those completing training gained $10.08 a week ($504 a year). Dropouts made a small gain of $3.61 a week ($180 a year). Since full-time wage rates of those participating in MDTA programs were not increased, but their incomes were, the difference has to lie in their comparatively better employment experience.

Examination of employment experience since training verifies this. Program participants (all trainees) were employed 11–22 percent more than non-participants, and those completing training fared even better. While "completes" had substantially better employment experiences than those dropping out (13–23 percent vs. 7–19 percent), the difference is not statistically significant. Trainees who participated in longer courses had better employment experiences than those in shorter courses, and participants trained in skilled and semiskilled jobs had better employment experiences than those trained in service and clerical occupations. However, Main found that when he controlled for whether the person completed the course, and for their background characteristics,

Table 4-20
Weekly Family Income Advantage of MDTA Institutional Trainees
Over Non-Trainees at Least a Year Following Training[a]

	Weekly Income Advantage
All Trainees	$ 9.60
Completes	10.08
Dropouts	3.61[b]

Source: Earl D. Main, "Nationwide Evaluation of M.D.T.A. Institutional Job
Training," Journal of Human Resources 3, no. 2 (Spring 1968), p. 165 and f.n.
[a]Controlling for background characteristics and assuming that training status did
not affect the number of family workers.
[b]Not statistically significant.

Table 4-21
Employment Advantage of Institutional MDTA Trainees Over
Non-Trainees (percentage)

All Trainees	11–22
Completes	13–23
Dropouts	7–19

Source: Earl D. Main, "Nationwide Evaluation of M.D.T.A. Institutional Job
Training," Journal of Human Resources 3, no. 2 (Spring 1968), p. 167.
Note: The lower figure in each case takes into account that program participants
could be looking for their first jobs while still in training, so that no period of unemployment necessarily follows their leaving or finishing the program. The high
figure ignores this initial advantage. Main feels the true advantage is somewhere in
between the two extremes.

neither program length nor occupation had a statistically significant effect on
unemployment rates.

This raises some doubts about the effect of MDTA training on employment,
since it is mathematically possible – though unlikely – that it makes no
difference how much or what type of training one takes. It is quite possible that
a large part of the estimated net effect of training is due to some other variable
not included in the analysis. Whatever predisposes certain people to take job
training could also be responsible for much of their increased employment,
relative to non-trainees. [61]

Main did not estimate the costs of training, and consequently did not
calculate any benefit-cost ratios. However, Garth Mangum has estimated that the
average cost per enrollee in all institutional MDTA programs through 1966
was $1,570 and that the average cost per completer was $2,040 (Table 4-22).

Table 4–22
Estimated Costs of MDTA Training Through 1966

Average	Costs Per Trainee
Institutional only	
Average	$1,570
Completer	2,040
OJT only	420
Coupled Institutional	
and OJT	940

Source: Garth L. Mangum, *Contributions and Costs of Manpower Development and Training,* Policy Papers in Human Resources and Industrial Relations, no. 5, University of Michigan, Wayne State University and the National Manpower Policy Task Force (Washington, D.C.: The Institute of Labor and Industrial Relations, December 1967), table 16, p. 62.

Since Main conducted his interviews in 1966, the costs presented by Mangum can cautiously be applied to the benefits estimated by Main. Table 4–23 contains the benefit-cost ratios when this is done. All the ratios exceed one.[t] The lowest benefit-cost ratio is 1.5 when the discount rate is 10 percent and the time horizon ten years, and refers to those who completed training. In each case benefit-cost ratios for all trainees exceed comparably computed ratios for "completes." This means that lower benefit-cost ratios may be attributed to those who completed training than to those who dropped out. Without further research, it is dangerous to attribute too much significance to this finding (such as concluding that trainees should be encouraged to drop out, or programs shortened). The ratios are developed by combining data from several sources. Furthermore, a number of dropouts probably occurred because of job opportunities that were "too good to pass up." On the other hand, counselors should be careful about advising a trainee to stay in the training program in the face of such an opportunity.

A cost-benefit study by Planning Research Corporation, comparing the national experience of MDTA institutional training and OJT, found that the benefit-cost ratio from OJT was 3.3, and from institutional training 1.8, considering only first year earnings following completion of training.[62] The Planning Research Corporation used the "before and after" technique, however, measuring benefits as the total gain in trainees' earnings. Thus while it might be safe to conclude that these results suggest that OJT yields higher returns to society than institutional training (assuming trainees had similar characteristics), actual ratios may be substantially less than those reported.

[t]Several biases exist in the data. Assistance payments are included in cost figures, and this tends to overstate actual costs. Opportunity costs are left out. This introduces a downward bias in cost data. The net effect is unknown.

Table 4-23
Benefit-Cost Ratios for Institutional MDTA Training

	Discount Rate	10-Year Time Horizon	30-Year Time Horizon
All Trainees	5 percent	2.3	4.7
	10 percent	1.9	2.9
Completes	5 percent	1.9	3.8
	10 percent	1.5	2.3

Source: Calculated from tables 4-20 and 4-22.

Retraining in the Midwest

H. H. London has examined the experiences of 518 persons who participated in institutional MDTA training between October 1, 1964, and September
30, 1965, in St. Louis, Kansas City, and Joplin, Missouri. [63] His is not a cost-
benefit study, but many of the types of information he discusses would complement and confirm the results were such calculations made. Information for the
study was collected from MDTA records and interviews conducted six, twelve,
and eighteen months after completion of training. Participants in these programs
probably were not the really "hard core" unemployed. White males had
completed an average of 11 years of schooling, white females an average of
12.6 years. Similar figures for nonwhite males and females were 10.4 and 11.1
years. ". . . the bulk of . . . [the participants] had taken some form of pre-
employment vocational education, mostly for clerical occupations and the skilled
trades prior to MDTA training." [64] Nonwhites had an average I.Q. of 89.6,
and whites an average of 103.4. Nearly 21 percent of the trainees quit a job
to take MDTA training. Of the 21 percent who were on welfare when they
entered training, all but a few were women with dependent children.

Training was offered in a wide range of occupations including general office
skills, cooking, alterations tailoring, practical nursing, and several skilled
trades. Unemployment and earnings figures were not presented, but other
important aspects of the trainees' experiences were. The following discussion
comes from London's study. [65] The frequency of job change did not drop
dramatically immediately following training, but as time passed, job stability
increased. This trend, combined with a decrease in the frequency with which
ex-trainees were fired for poor work habits and attitudes, indicates that
they were becoming integrated into the mainstream of the labor force.

While trainees did not show any sudden increase in their standard of living,
their "life style" improved in several ways — they were saving more money,
owned more television sets, more of them purchased cars, and they spent more
on medical care. Additionally, eighteen months following graduation from

Table 4-24

MDTA Trainees' Success in Finding Jobs Similar to Those for Which They Had Trained in Three Cities

Occupation	Relative Success	Percent
Alterations Tailor	8 of 10	80
Auto Body Repair	7 of 28	25
Bookkeeper	5 of 16	37
Clerk (general office, steno, and typist)	99 of 142	69
Cook	11 of 12	92
Draftsman	11 of 14	79
Duplicating Machine Operator	5 of 14	36
Machine Operator	11 of 22	50
Practical Nurse	67[a] of 79	85
Presser, Machine	26 of 29	90
Combination Welder	29 of 40	72

Source: H. H. London, *How Fare MDTA Ex-Trainees? An Eighteen Months Follow-up Study of Five Hundred Such Persons* (Columbia, Mo.: Missouri University, December 1967), tables 64 to 77, pp. 158–73.

[a]Of these, 61 found jobs as nurses aides.

training 11 percent was taking some kind of further education, generally vocational training. In one area no improvement appeared. Welfare payments to trainees as a group did not decline following training. But since most of those receiving welfare were mothers, this is understandable (but contrary to findings of Hardin and Borus in Michigan).

Overall, about 48 percent of the trainees was employed in training-related occupations six months following training. However, as Table 4-24 shows, the percentages of participants finding work in occupations for which they had trained varied greatly among occupations. Most successful in this respect were those trained to be cooks (11 of 12). Those training as tailors (8 of 10), draftsmen (11 of 14), machine pressers (26 of 29) also were relatively successful. Somewhat less successful were these trained in office skills and skilled occupations. Auto body repair (7 of 28) was the most unrewarding area (with the possible exception of practical nursing) in which trainees sought jobs similar to their training.

London estimated that the average cost per trainee was $1,428.[u] While we can speak only in the most general terms since earnings are not known, some inferences can be made concerning relative costs and benefits of training offered in different occupations. First, training in office skills generally cost less than average training costs, yet these occupations offered above average

[u]This includes transportation and subsidy payments to the trainees, and costs reported by the schools in which they were trained (London, table LIV, p. 128).

probability to the trainees of finding training-related jobs. While training as a draftsman cost more than double the average ($3,568), this occupation offered a high probability of finding a job as a draftsman. On the other hand, training a person in auto body repair cost an average of $2,314, yet most of these trainees had to find work in other occupations. Training in practical nursing was the most expensive of all occupations ($3,784), and while most of those completing the training found "training-related" jobs, almost all were in the low-paid category of nurses aides. Were earnings and employment data for these occupational categories available, they could be compared with costs, and benefit-cost ratios could be computed. If earnings are positively related to placement in training-related jobs (and evidence exists that this is so), training in office skills and drafting may well give higher returns to society (and to the individual) than training in auto mechanics and practical nursing (as conducted in institutional programs). Additionally, to the extent that trainees desire to enter those occupations for which they have trained, placement in such jobs will add to their "psychic" incomes.

Several other study results are worth mentioning. Trainees were asked to identify most and least helpful aspects of the MDTA program in which they had participated. Results are shown in Table 4-25. Nearly 59 percent indicated that the practical skills they gained during training were most important. It would be surprising if this were not so. Two other most frequently mentioned features of MDTA training — technical information and pay — were listed considerably fewer times, 13.7 and 12.5 percent respectively. Aspects of the program considered least helpful by trainees — notice of job openings (41 percent), pretraining counseling (15 percent), and pretraining testing (13

Table 4-25

Most and Least Helpful Aspects of MDTA Programs in Three Cities as Identified by Ex-Trainees

	Percent Listing Aspect
Most Helpful	
Practical Skills	58.9
Technical Information Acquired	13.7
Pay During Training	12.5
Other	
Least Helpful	
Notice of Job Openings	41
Pre-Training Counseling	15
Pre-Training Testing	13
Other	31

Source: H. H. London, *How Fare MDTA Ex-Trainees? An Eighteen Months Follow-up Study of Five Hundred Such Persons* (Columbia, Mo.: Missouri University, December 1967), tables 60 and 61, pp. 142, 143.

percent) — probably can be credited with some of the lack of success in placing persons in training-related occupations. These latter aspects also may have caused some of the early post-training job turnover.

These responses, as well as placement and cost data, suggest some steps that might logically be taken to improve the value of MDTA training.

1. Training of mothers with dependent children should be examined closely, especially if no post-training child care is offered and other types of trainable applicants are being turned away for lack of funds.
2. More aid in development of good work habits should improve the post-training employment experience, especially immediately following training.
3. Better placement help should be provided.
4. Long-term vacancies should not be used blindly as a signal to train persons in those occupations unless there is a good likelihood that the training is adequate to satisfy employers' entry-level requirements.[v]

Benjamin Trooboff has conducted a non-cost-benefit case study of MDTA institutional training in Atlanta, Georgia.[66] He sampled 1,062 persons who had completed their training and 444 who had dropped out prior to completion. Trainees had participated in twenty-four different programs between 1963 and 1966. Those who completed the program were earning $.98 an hour just prior to entering it. They earned $1.76 an hour afterwards — an increase of $.78 an hour. Dropouts increased their earnings substantially less; from $1.07 to $1.51 an hour. Unfortunately, we cannot tell from these data how much training increased the participants' earnings. Earnings just prior to training almost certainly were depressed below their normal levels, and some earnings gain would have been made even in the absence of training. This is a normal problem with "before and after" data.

Two interesting details are available, however. First, although average earnings of the trainees increased, those of white males and females, and of black males, were not increased. The entire increase can be attributed to increases in the wage rates of black females. Second, no relationship appeared between the characteristics of trainees and the percent of time employed following training. The singular success of black females in increasing their earnings is difficult to explain. Possibly certain traditional barriers to employ-

---

[v]One type of information that seems essential in this regard, but is not available in enough detail, is why trainees failed to find a training-related job. That "no jobs were available," probably the most common reason, is not an adequate explanation. In fact it may suggest the wrong policy decision, depending on why "no jobs were available." Maybe there was an actual shortage of jobs. If so, then the occupational composition of training should be adjusted accordingly. On the other hand, if openings were available but trainees did not have the requisite skills or abilities, MDTA's training methods, length of training, and screening techniques for those occupations also should be reviewed. Auto body repair, duplicating machine operator, and practical nursing might come under scrutiny here.

ment were broken by the MDTA program, and their increased earnings were due to this rather than their increased skills.[67] But the lack of a regular relationship between personal characteristics and regularity of post-training employment implies that black females who experienced large increases in earnings may have done so through increased wage rates rather than through relatively better employment experience. Trooboff suggests that since personal characteristics are a poor predictor of post-training performance (excepting black females), they should not be used as a selection criterion.

Retraining in New Jersey

In 1965, Jack Chernick et al., sampled persons who participated in MDTA institutional retraining in Newark, New Jersey, between January 1964 and March 1965.[68] Four groups were sampled — those who entered and completed training, those who entered but dropped out, those who applied but were rejected, and those who were listed with the State Employment Service as looking for work sometime between January 1964 and March 1965.

As seen in Table 4-26, at the time of the interviews 67.9 percent of those completing the programs were employed, 26.4 percent were unemployed, and 1.9 percent were out of the labor force. These labor-market experiences, although not impressive, are better than those of any of the other groups sampled by Chernick. The employment record of the completers (and probably of dropouts) would undoubtedly have been better had more time passed between the time the program ended and the interviews. Only 56.8 percent of the dropouts, 42.5 percent of the rejects (rejected *by* MDTA), and 52.0 percent of those that did not come into contact with MDTA were employed. These employment experiences are comparable to those of the MDTA program in West Virginia shortly after the program ended (see Table 4-13, p. 83).

MDTA administrators were doing fairly well in screening out prospective trainees unlikely to stay in the labor force upon completion of training. Only 1.9 percent of those completing the program and none of those dropping out of the program withdrew from the labor force, while 10 percent of those rejected by MDTA training officials had withdrawn from the labor force by the time of the interviews. However, not all of this difference in withdrawal rates can be attributed to efficient screening operation. Chernick reports that many of those who were rejected were disappointed and discouraged. Some expressed bitterness toward the Employment Service.[69] This discouragement upon being rejected could account for part of the labor force withdrawal.[w]

---

[w]The only way to tell for sure would be to perform a controlled experiment by accepting at random some of those who normally would have been rejected, and compare the performance of the accepted "rejects" with those who actually were rejected.

Table 4-26
Labor Force Status of Sample Groups Employed at Time of Interview in Newark, New Jersey (percentage)

	Completers[a]	Dropouts[a]	Rejected by MDTA	Rejected MDTA	No Contact[a]
Employed (Full-Time)	67.9	56.8	42.5	59.2	52.0
Unemployed	26.4	40.5	47.5	35.5	36.7
Out of Labor Force	1.9	0.0	10.0	5.3	10.9

Source: Jack Chernick, Bernard P. Indik, and Roger Craig, *The Selection of Trainees Under MDTA*, report prepared for the Office of Manpower Policy, Evaluation and Research, U.S. Department of Labor (New Brunswick, N. J.: Institute of Management and Labor Relations, Rutgers State University, 1966), table 3.5, p. 103.

[a]Do not add to 100 due to undetermined status and part-time employment.

Comparing the relative employment success among groups following
training, Chernick found that both white and black "completes" did significantly
better than either the dropouts or the "no contacts." Females of both racial
groups, especially blacks, improved their labor-market performance more
than males.[70] [x] Women also had more success in increasing their wage rates
and in finding training-related jobs than the men. These results suggest that
job opportunities in occupations for which women were being trained were
better than those in occupations for which men were being trained (or that
barriers to employment were lower).

Conclusions

All cost-benefit studies of institutional retraining programs in Connecticut,
West Virginia, Massachusetts, and Michigan indicate that returns to society
exceed costs — that these programs pass the "economic" test.[y] Cost-benefit
calculations based on a national sample of institutional MDTA trainees reach the
same conclusion. Results from all these studies are summarized in Table 4-27.

Training programs administered under ARA and under state laws appear to
yield somewhat higher benefit-cost ratios than those conducted under MDTA.
Borus, Cain and Stromsdorfer, and Page suggest benefit-cost ratios for ARA and
state programs to be 5.9, 5.7, and 3.8, respectively, while Hardin and Borus,
and Main indicate MDTA institutional training programs yield benefit-cost
ratios of 1.5 and 1.9, respectively (using a 10 percent discount rate and a ten-
year time horizon). For several reasons, however, it would be dangerous to
conclude from these relative ratios that gains from retraining under MDTA are
less than those under state and ARA programs, or that if the decrease has
occurred, something is "amiss" with the later programs. First, earlier training
programs were directed more often toward *specific* job opportunities than
those conducted under MDTA. Training persons in occupations characterized
by labor shortages (common under MDTA) is not the same as training persons
for specific job openings (as was the case in the Cain and Stromsdorfer study of
programs in West Virginia).[71] Second, ARA training in Connecticut, as
reported by Borus, [72] was probably more a "preparation for job training"

---

[x]These results are consistent with Trooboff's, and they cloud the explanation proposed earlier for the better performances of black females (breakdown of racial discrimination) unless the same types of problems existed in Newark as in the southern cities studied
by both Trooboff and Walther.

[y]David O. Sewell ("Discussion," *Cost-Benefit Analysis of Manpower Policies. Proceedings of a North American Conference,* pp. 164–169), argues that since most income gains to
trainees came from decreased unemployment, programs were simply re-allocating unemployment (the displacement effect was operating) and net gains to society were near zero. Recall
that Taussig makes the same argument with respect to vocational education in New York,
as does Borus for the Connecticut programs he examines.

Table 4-27

Benefit-Cost Ratios of Institutional Retraining Programs Conducted Under State Legislation, ARA, and MDTA

Researcher and Discount Rate	10-Year Time Horizon	30-Year Time Horizon
Main – National		
5 percent		4.7
10 percent	1.9	
Hardin & Borus – Michigan		
5 percent		3.8
10 percent	1.5	
ARA Page – Massachusetts		
5 percent		9.4
10 percent	3.8	
ARA Cain & Stromsdorfer – West Virginia		
5 percent		16.8
10 percent	5.7	
ARA Borus – Connecticut		
5 percent		14.7
10 percent	5.9	

Source: Tables 4-8, 4-12, 4-17, 4-23, and p. 72.

than actual job training, so the real gains from those programs probably came from careful screening and placement, and from uncompensated OJT conducted by the firms. Last, the state- and ARA-offered courses examined in this chapter were relatively short. Hardin and Borus have reported that short MDTA courses in Michigan yielded a benefit-cost ratio of 17.3[z] — much greater than those of the early training programs. Lower overall ratios for MDTA thus could be the result of longer average courses. *It seems clear that training under MDTA is being conducted under different circumstances than the early training programs, and that generally lower benefit-cost ratios are not indicative of a decline in quality or efficiency.*[aa]

The ability of the early studies to predict general results of MDTA training programs was proven for aspects other than benefit-cost ratios.

1. They predicted that trainees of all ages, and trainees with widely divergent educational backgrounds would benefit from participation. Main, in his national study of MDTA training, found little relationship between the outcome of training and the participant's sex, educational level, age, race, previous unemployment experience, "main earner status" or marital

---

[z]While programs examined in Michigan by Hardin and Borus include some sponsored by ARA, the majority of program expenditures were under MDTA.

[aa]Differences in methodology also still exist in the calculations of the benefit-cost ratios contained in Table 4-27. Lower benefit-cost ratios of MDTA may partially reflect this.

status. These results were not due simply to the lack of differences in participants' characteristics. In 1966, for example, 49 percent of the MDTA trainees (including on-the-job trainees) were either under age twenty-two or over forty-four, and nearly 43 percent had less than twelve years of education.[73]

2. They suggested that a commitment to labor force attachment was an important variable in determining the economic value of training, and that women with dependent children were less likely to stay in the labor market following training. Results of the MDTA studies are ambiguous on this point. London's findings — that females who had been receiving welfare prior to participation (generally mothers with dependent children) were unlikely to leave the welfare roles following training — is the only evidence clearly consistent with the prediction. While Hardin and Borus also found that those receiving welfare support were likely to remain on it at least for a period following training, the benefit-cost ratio associated with this group was higher than that for those not receiving welfare income. Findings by Main (that sex and number of dependents did not materially affect the results), Trooboff (that black females were the only group to benefit from training), and Chernick (that females did better than males following training) indicated that sex was not a good predictor of subsequent labor force attachment or of employment success following training.

3. They predicted that black persons may make larger gains from training than white. Main suggested that race does not affect the size of training benefits. On the other hand, black females gained more than any other group in the programs studied by Trooboff and Chernick. Findings by Hardin and Borus are ambiguous on this point. Ability of the programs to break racial barriers to employment seemed an important consideration here.

4. They predicted that persons did not have to complete training programs in order to benefit, nor did the courses offered have to be long. These predictions were supported by Main and by Hardin and Borus.

5. They predicted that many gains from retraining would come from more regular employment. Main's national study of MDTA trainees could detect no "wage effect" from participation in MDTA — all observed income gains came from improvements in employment experience.

6. They predicted that gains from participation were not transitory. None of the studies examined covered a long enough time to test this prediction.

5 Other Manpower Programs

Introduction

Training programs discussed in the previous three chapters have emphasized classroom instruction as a means of making their participants employable. This chapter examines a wide range of programs, many of which include classroom education and skill training, but also utilize some type of sheltered employment experience to give participants the requisite job skills and work habits to compete in open labor markets. Studies are included of Neighborhood Youth Corps (NYC), Work Experience and Training Program (WEP), Job Corps, and On the Job Training (OJT) offered under MDTA and the Bureau of Indian Affairs (BIA). Also included are four other studies — one each of BIA institutional training (because of its close association with the study of BIA OJT), of a high school dropout-prevention program, of a high school counseling and job-placement program, and of a vocational rehabilitation program.

The highest benefit-cost ratios are associated with OJT and vocational rehabilitation programs. The study by Dale Rasmussen of MDTA OJT programs conducted in twenty-four metropolitan areas yields benefit-cost ratios that generally exceed one, and range as high as 10.7 under conservative interest-rate and time-horizon assumptions.[1] Loren Scott's study of OJT conducted by BIA in Oklahoma suggests a conservative ratio of 12.4.[2] Scott's companion study, done by Paul Blume, of institutional training sponsored by BIA in Oklahoma, yields a benefit-cost ratio of 2.4 — considerably lower than that of the OJT program.

Lower benefit-cost ratios are calculated for NYC and dropout-prevention programs. The only benefit-cost estimates available for NYC were made by Borus et al., in which they conclude that ratios for male participants were about 3; those for females a little less than 1. The only careful cost-benefit study of a dropout-prevention program was conducted by Burton Weisbrod.[3] He concludes that intensive counseling as a means of keeping students in school is not very efficient, and yields a benefit-cost ratio of less than one. No cost-benefit study of WEP has been made. However, the program appears to have had little impact on the labor-market performance of its participants.

Neighborhood Youth Corps

Michael Borus et al., studied the Neighborhood Youth Corps in urban Indiana as it was operated prior to the end of 1966.[4] NYC was authorized under the Economic Opportunity Act and had two stated goals: (1) to increase the employability of participants or enable them to continue (or resume) their education, and (2) to aid in conducting public and private programs for developing and conserving national resources and recreational areas. Three programs were being operated by NYC in this period — a part-time employment program for youths still in school, a summer employment program designed mainly for students, and an out-of-school program aimed primarily at dropouts.

The study by Borus et al. restricts its scope to the out-of-school program with a basic purpose ". . . to determine if the NYC program has effectively prepared the participants to be more productive or, as some have asserted, has only been an income maintenance or public works program for the period of participation."[5] Demographic data on participants and costs incurred in operating the program came from NYC records. The post-training experience of participants was compared to the experiences of a control group comprised of persons who were eligible for the program (as determined by the Employment Service), but who did not participate because, while they were qualified, they were never called to go to work, could not be reached when a job was available, or did not report for work when offered a job.[6] The study was conducted prior to the time when private employers began participating in the program, so all jobs provided during the training period were in the government sector.[7]

Borus et al. counted as benefits to society increases in aggregate output in the economy and increases in employability of the trainees attributable to the program. Both these criteria of success were measured primarily by participants' earnings experience following training. Wage data on both control group and participants came from Employment Security records of covered employers.[a]

In 1967, participants who had completed the program by the end of 1966 earned an average of $953. The control group earned $676, or a difference of $277. However, when earnings were controlled for age, sex and education of the two groups, the difference attributable to the program narrowed to $136, a difference not statistically significant. Borus et al. conclude that ". . . on the average the NYC out-of-school program did not have a demonstrably significant effect on the earnings of the program participants."[8] This conclusion — that the overall earnings increases were not statistically significant — does not preclude certain categories of participants from benefitting greatly, nor does it prohibit use of the earnings data to calculate benefit-cost ratios.

As seen in Table 5-1, high school dropouts of both sexes with nine or ten years of schooling benefitted more than participants with eight, eleven, *or twelve* years. However, males made substantially larger wage gains than females. Male trainees who had graduated from high school earned $.72 more an hour

---

[a]Borus et al. were aware that dependence upon Employment Security records eliminates from consideration persons who subsequently went to work in firms with three or less employees, for employers engaged in agriculture or nonprofit endeavors, for the government, as domestics, for immediate relatives, or who became self-employed.

Table 5–1ʼ
Hourly-Wage Rate Advantage of Indiana NYC Participants Over
Non-Participants by Years of School Completed and by Sex

Years School Completed	Male	Female
8	$ .97	$0.00
9	1.08	.16
10	1.08	.16
11	.96	.00
12	.72	.00

Source: Michael E. Borus, John P. Brennan, and Sidney Rosen, "A Benefit-Cost Analysis of the Neighborhood Youth Corps: The Out-of-School Program in Indiana," *Journal of Human Resources* 5, no. 2 (Spring 1970), pp. 148–49.

than male high school graduates who did not participate, a gain smaller than that made by those with only an eighth grade education. Male participants with nine or ten years of schooling did best, with a wage advantage following training of $1.08 an hour over their counterparts not participating in NYC. Female trainees benefitted little from participating in NYC. The only female subgroups to show any wage rate advantage at all ($.16 per hour) were those with nine and ten years of school. The gain was smaller than any gains made by males.

A number of benefit-cost ratios were computed based on highest grade completed and sex of the participant, depending on whether the wages received by participants during training were counted as benefits, and whether opportunity costs were included.[b] These ratios appear in Table 5–2. Understandably, benefit-cost ratios are highest when wages during training are counted as benefits and opportunity costs are assumed to be zero (columns 2 and 3). With these assumptions, the ratios for males range from 5.3 when they had graduated from high school, to 7.4 for those with nine or ten years of education. Similar ratios for females are 0.0 and 2.1. Even under the most severe set of assumptions (ignoring wages during training and counting opportunity costs), however, the benefit-cost ratios for males always exceed one (column 8). Under these assumptions the ratio for male high school graduates is 1.8, that for males with nine and ten years of school, 2.8. The benefit-cost ratios for female participants are substantially below those of males, and exceed one only under the more favorable assumptions (column 3). As a group, females who had completed high school did not benefit from participation. Their earnings failed to exceed those of females not in NYC.

[b]One might argue that since all of the participants were unemployed at the time they entered the program, opportunity costs (wages not earned from some other job) are zero. On the other hand, those in the control group were not unemployed all of the time, so the counter argument that participants would not have been unemployed all of the time could also be made.

Table 5-2
Benefit-Cost Ratios of the NYC Program in Indiana[a]

Years of School Completed	Wages During Program Counted as Benefits				Wages During Program Not Counted as Benefits			
	Opportunity Costs Excluded		Opportunity Costs Included		Opportunity Costs Excluded		Opportunity Costs Included	
Col. 1	Males Col. 2	Females Col. 3	Males Col. 4	Females Col. 5	Males Col. 6	Females Col. 7	Males Col. 8	Females Col. 9
8	6.7	1.5	3.0	.7	5.5	.3	2.5	.1
9	7.4	2.1	3.3	1.0	6.2	.9	2.8	.4
10	7.4	2.1	3.3	1.0	6.1	.9	2.8	.4
11	6.7	1.4	3.0	.6	5.4	.9	2.5	.1
12	5.3	0.0	2.4	0.0	4.1	0.0	1.8	0.0

Source: Michael E. Borus, John P. Brennan, and Sidney Rosen, "A Benefit-Cost Analysis of the Neighborhood Youth Corps: The Out-of-School Program in Indiana," *Journal of Human Resources* 5, no. 2 (Spring 1970), table 5, p. 156.

[a]First-year earnings gain assumed constant for ten years, then zero from then on, using a 10 percent discount rate and the assumption that displacement is zero.

Table 5-3
Recalculated Benefit-Cost Ratios of the NYC Program in Indiana[a]

Time Horizon	Discount Rate			
	10 Percent		5 Percent	
10-Year	Males	Females	Males	Females
10 years of school	3.3	1.0	4.1	1.3
12 years of school	2.4	0.0	3.0	0.0
30-Year				
10 years of school	5.0	1.5	8.2	2.5
12 years of school	3.7	0.0	6.0	0.0

[a]Including opportunity costs and wages during program participation, and assuming wage advantages constant over the relevant time horizon.

It is difficult to determine unequivocally which set of calculations is the "most reasonable." Opportunity costs should be included, since their exclusion probably understates the true costs of NYC programs. Whether to include wages during training as a benefit depends on one's assumption concerning the productivity of the trainees. If wage payments to trainees are regarded as transfer payments in lieu of subsistence allowances that would have been received in an institutional program, they are best excluded from the calculation. If, however, the trainees are working productively, output in the economy is being increased and their incomes should be regarded as wage payments and benefits of the program.[c] This appears to be the most reasonable assumption. Consequently, cols. 4 and 5 in Table 5-2 probably contain the most representative ratios. Utilizing data from this study, additional benefit-cost ratios are calculated using the time horizons and discount rates applied to studies in other parts of this book. The resulting ratios in Table 5-3 are relatively high for males (ranging from 2.4 to 8.2 depending on how much education they had completed and the computation assumptions), and low for females (with values from a low of 0.0 to a high of 2.5).

Given the nature of the training provided NYC enrollees, Borus et al. conclude that the benefits of NYC did not derive from its ability to give program participants significantly higher job skills; but that most improvements lay in changing other characteristics of trainees. They probably gained such attributes as "... getting to work on time, reporting regularly for work, neatness in appear-

---

[c]Two other possibilities present themselves. One could determine what portion of the wages represents payment for work performed and what portion represents subsidy and include as benefits only the wage portion. Or, even if trainees are employed productively, they may be displacing other persons who would have been hired in their places. The problem then is to estimate the extent to which this occurs. Any procedure will be partly arbitrary. However, the determination of the way wages during training are handled should be defended in each case study.

ance, ability to communicate with middle class persons, ability to accept supervision, and ability to accept responsibility."[9] If improved personal characteristics are the main sources of benefits, we might expect high school dropouts to benefit more than graduates because they probably need more of these characteristics to offset their disadvantage of not having completed school.

The NYC program in Indiana as studied by Borus et al. had selective success with its trainees. If efficiency is a goal, the large variability in the post-training job success among different groups of trainees makes monitoring of the program very important. If, for example, suitable participants exceed available openings in the program, the Indiana experience suggests that first enrollment opportunities (from an efficiency standpoint) should be given to those who have the highest probability of gaining the most — male high school dropouts. Male high school graduates should get second preference, with female dropouts and graduates following in that order.

In another (non-cost-benefit) examination of out-of-school NYC, Regis H. Walther and Margaret Magnusson have studied its operation in four urban areas in the South.[10] Their study included NYC participants who entered the program in the fall of 1965. They were interested in three separate aspects of the program — (1) employment experience of participants, (2) participants' views of the program, and (3) reductions in police "contacts" of participants. The control group utilized was composed of applicants for NYC who, for one reason or another, did not participate.

Participants clearly were more disadvantaged than the average twenty-year-old (mean age of those participating). Mean educational level was 9.8 years and average academic performance was 1.2 (on a 4 point scale with 4 high). Average I.Q. of male trainees was 79.4 and that of females 85.5. Police "contact" had been made by 50 percent of the males and 18 percent of the females at some time.[11] Of the trainees, 92 percent were black, and two-thirds of those were females (Table 5-4). Only 8 percent of the trainees were white (2 percent male and 6 percent female).

Table 5-5 shows that, at the time of the interview (early 1967), 56.7 percent of the male participants still in the civilian labor force were employed, compared to 51.2 percent of those in the control group.[12] On the other hand, hourly wages of the male control group in their most recent jobs exceeded those received by the trainees — $1.73 vs. $1.67.[13] The female experimental group did better in both the percent employed (50 percent vs. 32.5 percent) and hourly wage rates ($1.31 vs. $1.21). Clearly females were being aided more by the program than males. NYC participation tended to direct males into food service and cleaning and maintenance (janitorial) occupations following training (relative to the male control group). It tended to direct females into clerical and sales and professional aide occupations (relative to their control group). Apparently the occupational composition following training helped

Table 5-4
Race and Sex Composition of NYC Participants in Four Urban
Areas (percentage)

	Black	White	Total
Male	30	2	32
Female	62	6	68
Total	92	8	100

Source: Regis H. Walther and Margaret L. Magnusson, *A Retrospective Study of
the Effectiveness of Out of School Neighborhood Youth Corps Programs in Four
Urban Sites* (Washington, D. C.: George Washington University, Social Research
Group, November 1967), table 2, p. 20.

Table 5-5
1966 Employment Experiences of NYC Trainees in Four Urban Areas

	Experimental			Control		
	Male	Female	Average	Male	Female	Average
Hourly Wages	$1.67	$1.31	$1.47	$1.73	$1.21	$1.46
Percent Employed	56.7	50	52.5	51.2	32.5	40

Source: Calculated from Regis H. Walther and Margaret L. Magnusson, *A Retro-
spective Study of the Effectiveness of Out of School Neighborhood Youth Corps
Programs in Four Urban Sites* (Washington, D. C.: George Washington University,
Social Research Group, November 1967), p. 61.

increase females' wages more than males' (relative to their appropriate control
groups).[d] However, the program was not successful in taking women off welfare
rolls.[14]

Females' apparent post-training advantage may be explained by reference
to the following factors: First, numbers of white and black participants were
unequal. Black males and females together made up 92 percent of the total
sample. The proportion of white participants (18 percent) is probably too low
to have much impact on the results. What Walther and Magnusson's study
probably measures, then, is the ability of NYC to aid black males and females.
Second, geographic location of the study may have influenced the results. Since
programs examined were all conducted in southern cities, it is possible that the
barriers faced by black females to occupations in which they trained were lower

[d]It is interesting to note that NYC participation did not help males get jobs in the
machine trades (though 23 percent of both the control and experimental groups found
such work), nor into the construction industry, in which only 4 percent of the male participants and 2 percent of their control group were employed at the time of the interview.

than for black males.[e] Third, differences in personal characteristics of trainees have not been controlled for. While both males and females tended to be below the average worker in terms of "desirability" to employers, the latter group's disadvantage was smaller. Women's average I.Q. was higher (85.5 vs. 79.4), their average education better (10.2 years vs. 9.6 years), their academic performance better, they spent more time in the program (8.4 months vs. 6.9 months),[f] and had had fewer police contacts (18 percent vs. 50 percent).[15] Walther and Magnusson state that in addition to the above characteristics,

It seems probable that part of the explanation for the favorable finding with respect to Negro females is that they are easier to work with than are males; they have more interest in improving themselves, and they have a more difficult time obtaining job training or job placement without assistance.[16]

Last, females appeared to get "better service" from NYC than did males. Work assignments they received while in NYC were for more "preferable" occupations in terms of pay and status in the community, and their occupational goals and training were more closely matched than was the case for males. As seen in Table 5-6 over half (58 percent) of the males were placed in training jobs within NYC that prepared them for cleaning and maintenance (janitorial positions), yet only 1 percent of the participating males had indicated this occupational area as a career choice. Another 42 percent of the males indicated their career goals included occupations as mechanics, craftsmen, or machine operators, and only 5 percent were assigned those jobs in NYC.

The poor matching job of assignments within NYC and the career choices of trainees is not necessarily a bad reflection on NYC administration. The career goals may have been completely unrealistic, and the training given by NYC more in line with the participants' capabilities. None of the preferred types of training jobs may have been available, so that in order to participate, trainees had to take what training was within the scope of NYC. Last, there may not have been a shortage of desired skills in the private sector, so that giving trainees experience in jobs requiring those skills would not have helped them get jobs after leaving NYC.

The picture for females is somewhat different. Of the females, 49 percent

---

[e]Borus, who participated in the Indiana NYC study, also notes that the racial composition of persons participating in NYC programs examined by Walther and Magnusson—given the geographic location of the programs—probably introduced biases into the results [Michael E. Borus, John P. Brennan, and Sidney Rosen, "A Benefit-Cost Analysis of the Neighborhood Youth Corps: The Out-of-School Program in Indiana," *Journal of Human Resources* Vol. 5, 2 (Spring 1970): 158.], so that his (Borus') conclusion that males benefitted most is not necessarily contradicted by Walther's opposite conclusion.

[f]Recall that Borus ("A Benefit-Cost Analysis of the Neighborhood Youth Corps") found a positive relationship between length of time spent in the program and participants' benefits.

Table 5-6
NYC Work Assignments in Four Urban Areas (percentage)

Occupational Category	Male	Female
Professional Aide	19	56
Clerical	4	28
Food Preparation and Service	2	8
Mechanic, Craftsman and Machine Operator	5	0
Cleaning and Maintenance	58	7
Unskilled Labor	5	1
Other	7	0

Source: Regis H. Walther and Margaret L. Magnusson, *A Retrospective Study of the Effectiveness of Out of School Neighborhood Youth Corps Programs in Four Urban Sites* (Washington, D. C.: George Washington University, Social Research Group, November 1967), table 8, p. 29a.

had indicated career choices as professionals or professional aides, and 56 percent were assigned work as professional aides. Another 28 percent were assigned clerical work, matching exactly the percentage indicating this career are as a goal. (Of course, we do not know whether this was the same 28 percent.) Only 7 percent of the females were assigned cleaning and maintenance jobs.[17] Additionally, women enjoyed their NYC jobs more than men, felt their work was more important, had slightly more helpful supervisors, met with counselors more often, and received more placement help.[18][g]

The post-participation evaluation of the ways NYC helped male and female trainees is consistent with the different treatment they received while in NYC. When asked to list ways in which NYC helped them, 52 percent of the females and 36 percent of the males listed "learning job skills" (Table 5-7). The item most frequently listed by males was "learning work habits." Only 29 percent of the males felt that placement was helpful to them (relative to 40 percent of the females).

When other aspects of the post-training experiences of participants are examined, a mixed picture emerges. NYC participation appears to increase ex-trainees' interest in further career advancement. At the time of the interview, 39 percent of the male participants and 49 percent of the female participants were attending some type of evening classes (mostly vocational) compared to 12 percent and 28 percent respectively in the control group (Table 5-8). Overall, 44 percent and 21 percent in the control and experimental groups respectively

[g] John Glass, in an unpublished dissertation ("Organization Dilemmas in the War on Poverty: Contrasts in the Neighborhood Youth Corps," Ph.D. dissertation, University of California, 1968.), concludes that NYC was better suited to women than men because a larger proportion of training-type jobs are available for women than for men. Thus his conclusion is consistent with the experiences in these four NYC sites.

Table 5-7
NYC Characteristics Judged "Helpful" by Participants

	Male (Percentage Identifying)	Female (Percentage Identifying)
Learning Work Habits	40	45
Learning Job Skills	36	52
Classroom Work	8	17
Counseling	12	20
Placement	29	40
Money	37	46

Source: Regis H. Walther and Margaret L. Magnusson, *A Retrospective Study of the Effectiveness of Out of School Neighborhood Youth Corps Programs in Four Urban Sites* (Washington, D. C.: George Washington University, Social Research Group, November 1967), table 18, p. 40.

Table 5-8
Post-NYC Education of the Experimental and Control Groups (percentages)

	Experimental			Control		
Type of School	Male	Female	Total	Male	Female	Total
Night or vocational	39	49	44	12	28	21
Full-Time School	1	3	2	3	7	5

Source: Regis H. Walther and Margaret L. Magnusson, *A Retrospective Study of the Effectiveness of Out of School Neighborhood Youth Corps Programs in Four Urban Sites* (Washington, D. C.: George Washington University, Social Research Group, November 1967), table 27, p. 53.

were attending night school. Since one of NYC's goals is to enable participants to continue with their education, this is a significant finding. The control group attended full-time school more than the experimental group (5 percent vs. 2 percent), possibly because of the less firm labor-force attachment of the females in the control group. But the NYC program was not successful in reducing frequency of police contacts among male participants, and only managed a small reduction in such contacts among females.[19]

Several other aspects of this study should be mentioned. Walther and Magnusson are critical of the way manpower programs in these urban areas are administered relative to each other. They state that all NYC, MDTA, and Job Corps programs are designed to aid the same general group of persons, yet there is little interaction and no cooperation among them. "The MDTA establishments in the several sites were impressive — and frustrating to NYC and MDTA personnel. MDTA wanted more trainees, and NYC wanted to place enrollees as trainees; but procedural problems stood in the way."[20] (Unfortunately, Walther does not identify these problems.) Lack of coordination between NYC and MDTA seems to be the result of administrative rules imposed from a higher administrative level on cities' operations of MDTA. This apparently is not the case with the Job Corps. On the other hand, there has been no systematic evaluation of the needs of trainees during screening procedures to determine whether they are directed to NYC or Job Corps programs; decisions appear to be random.[21]

John Glass, [22] who examines NYC out-of-school programs in a "Western City," reaches conclusions that parallel those of Walther and Magnusson. Glass finds that females are aided more than males, and that this results from differences in characteristics of the participants, from the types of training opportunities open in public employment, and from the way the private job market operates. Females participating in NYC in the "Western City" were better educated than their male counterparts; 32 percent of the females and 16 percent of the males had graduated from high school. This educational advantage held by females is accentuated by the types of training jobs they received in NYC. A large percentage of training jobs open to females were clerical, and offered better career possibilities than jobs (mainly maintenance work) offered males. Glass feels that males also faced greater problems in the form of institutional barriers upon leaving NYC than females; that unions, apprenticeship requirements, and strict hiring qualifications of both private firms and government agencies prevented males from being hired for jobs they might be able to perform.[23]

While Walther and Magnusson are critical of the apparent lack of coordination among the various manpower programs, Glass criticizes the operation of NYC — its failure to alter the characteristics of the training program to help offset the relatively greater problems of male participants — and of the subsequent employers' (both public and private) unwillingness to relax hiring standards.[h] He states that since NYC is more successful with black females than with black males (due to attitudes of the community as well as to the manner in which NYC is operated), ". . . NYC perpetuates, even exaggerates, the existing gap between the success of Negro males and females in the labor market."[24]

Again, as was the case for conclusions of the previous study, those by Glass must be looked at carefully. NYC in the "Western City" trained mostly blacks and Mexican-Americans, with these groups comprising around 90 percent of total enrollment.[25] Consequently Glass also is comparing NYC's ability to aid nonwhite females relative to nonwhite males. Additionally, Glass failed to control for personal characteristics of the trainees. The greater success of females

---

[h]The *1970 Manpower Report of the President* indicates that increased coordination among programs now allows participants to receive aid from the combination of services most beneficial for them.

may be due to their more "favorable" characteristics. Consequently, although both Walther and Magnusson, and Glass reach similar conclusions (that NYC aids nonwhite females more than males) they do not necessarily conflict with a different conclusion reached by Borus et al. — that males, relative to their control groups, experience greater postparticipation earnings increases than do females relative to their control groups.

Work Experience and Training Program

Worth Bateman has discussed operation of the Work Experience and Training Program (WEP) in 1966. WEP, like NYC, was authorized under the Economic Opportunity Act of 1964 and provided jobs in public and nonprofit agencies. Rather than being youth-oriented, however, it was developed to serve family heads receiving public assistance (primarily Aid for Dependent Children), or nonrecipients with similar characteristics. In its operation, WEP clearly served the type of person for which it was designed. In 1966, there were 101,000 participants equally divided between males and females. Of these, 60 percent were married, 90 percent were heads of households with four or more dependents, 80 percent were between twenty-one and forty-nine years old, 30 percent were high school dropouts, and 50 percent had completed only one to eight years of schooling.[26] In calculating the costs of WEP, Bateman includes as costs the opportunity costs of the participants, additional administrative costs, work-related expenses (travel, clothing, etc.), and public assistance payment.[27][1] Using this framework, the costs ranged from $639 to $1,489 per participant.[28]

Three months after training was completed the average income of participants *who were employed* was $250 a month. Unfortunately, only 42 percent of those who went through the program were employed at this time. Under the assumption that their employment experience without WEP would have been about like that of MDTA trainees prior to training, Bateman does not feel the level of unemployment was reduced much by participation.[29]

No benefit-cost ratios are calculated in this study. However, Bateman did indicate the percentage increase in earnings that males who participated in Kentucky would have had to experience in order for the benefit-cost ratio to equal one. These percentages ranged from a low of 1.1 percent for males aged twenty-five with twelve years of education, to a high of 2.9 percent for

---

[1]The public assistance payments—" . . . AFDC, allowances provided under Title V of the Economic Opportunity Act, or General Assistance are the most important [of these] . . . " (Worth Bateman, "An Application of Cost-Benefit Analysis to the Work-Experience Program," *American Economic Review* 57, no. 2 (May 1967), pp. 80–81)—were included as costs because he felt they were an investment in the future productivity of the participants and not simply transfer payments (*Ibid.*, pp. 85–86). Including these payments as social costs runs counter to normal practice.

males aged fifty-five with zero to seven years of education.[30] Consequently, while WEP only modestly affected trainees' post-participation experiences, only modest impact is required for benefits to exceed costs.

Assume for a moment that actual WEP benefits exceeded costs by enough to yield relatively high benefit-cost ratios. Could we then conclude that WEP (now phased into the Work Incentive and Training Program — WIN), is preferred over some other program with higher costs. higher gross benefits, but a lower benefit-cost ratio? Not necessarily. If the reduction of poverty and redistribution of income are important goals, a program yielding greater benefits to participants, but lower net benefits to society, might be preferred to one yielding lower gross benefits to participants, but greater net benefits to society.

MDTA-Sponsored OJT

Since early state-supported training and retraining programs, and those programs supported by the Area Redevelopment Act and the Manpower Development and Training Act were initially concerned with institutional-type training, it is reasonable that most of the studies examining these programs should be concerned with institutional training. Only one thorough cost-benefit study of MDTA OJT has been found by this writer. This study, a dissertation written in 1969 by Dale Rasmussen, utilizes a sample of MDTA OJT trainees from twenty-four Standard Metropolitan Statistical Areas (SMSA's), and finds relatively high benefit-cost ratios attributable to such training in most locations. Rasmussen selected his experimental sample from persons who had completed MDTA OJT (including "coupled" training, where OJT was preceded by an institutional training course) between 1964 and 1966 in each of twenty-four SMSA's. He was interested not only in determining if such training offered attractive returns to society, but also in his ability to identify broad characteristics of the SMSA's that affected the rate of return to training.

The size of his study and the difficulties of selecting a control group of OJT participants forced Rasmussen to utilize a unique methodology. He first classified all trainees' pre- and post-training occupations into six broad classifications — professional-managerial, clerical-sales, service, skilled, semi-skilled, and unskilled. Utilizing the 1–1,000 1960 Census sample, he then calculated earnings of the six broad occupational classifications by SMSA, and adjusted these earnings for known wage differentials in each SMSA, by the known unemployment experiences of the trainees and by their race, sex, and education characteristics. These earnings estimates based on pre-training occupations were taken as what trainees would have earned had they not participated in OJT. OJT usually resulted in the trainees changing their broad occupational classification from lower- to higher-paid classifications, making the post-training occupational profile differ from the pre-training profile. New earnings estimates then were made based on the new occupational classifications. The differences between the earnings estimates based on the post-training profile less those based on the pre-training profile were taken as an approximation of the direct benefits of OJT. Rasmussen thus was utilizing a "before and after" analysis, but attempting to avoid its inherent problems. Specifically, since pre-training earnings usually are abnormally depressed for program participants, and since OJT practically guarantees jobs following training, use of the actual earnings data would likely overstate benefits due to skill change. Additionally, follow-up earnings data were not collected regularly.[31]

Direct OJT costs were computed using Bureau of Apprenticeship Training records for 1965. Subsistence and travel payments to trainees were included. From these figures were subtracted the estimated portion of support that would have been received as transfer payments (welfare and unemployment) had training not been undertaken. Costs borne by the State Employment Services were not included [32] (Rasmussen indicates that no additional manpower was required by the various State Employment Service offices due to the OJT program). Costs by broad occupational category of OJT are presented in Table 5-9. It is interesting that OJT for the skilled trades lasted fewer weeks (18.0 vs. 21.8) and cost less ($466 vs. $611) than for semi-skilled trades. Least expensive occupational classes in which to offer OJT were unskilled and service occupations. The classification in which most trainees were being trained was semi-skilled, with 42.2 percent of the total trainees. Next was skilled with 24.8 percent and service at 18.6 percent. Unskilled (4.5 percent) and clerical-sales (2.6 percent) were the least frequently offered. The general combination of occupations for which participants were given OJT appears rational on the surface, because the occupational categories least offered — unskilled and clerical-sales — probably offer the least opportunity for increased earnings.

Rasmussen computed the rates of return for OJT in each of the twenty-four SMSA's for which complete data were available. Utilizing his time horizon (the number of years between the average age of the trainees in each SMSA until age sixty-five), Rasmussen's data can be converted into benefit-cost ratios. These ratios appear in Table 5-10. With a relatively low discount rate and long time horizon, OJT in nearly every city can be attributed with a benefit-cost ratio greater than one. Five cities — Miami (27.7), New Orleans (18.0), Los Angeles (15.6), Charlotte (14.1) and Chicago (12.2) have benefit-cost ratios exceeding 10. Providence and Seattle are the only urban areas where the calculated ratios are less than one. (It is possible that the same classification problems were operating in these cities that were apparent in Portland, but this is unknown.)

Benefit-cost ratios are recalculated for six of the urban areas (Table 5-11) using the discount rates (5 and 10 percent) and time horizons (ten and thirty years) utilized throughout the book to facilitate comparisons. The ratios in the second column — 10 percent discount rate with a time horizon of ten years —

Table 5-9

Costs Per Trainee of MDTA OJT in Twenty-Four Urban Sites[a]

Occupational Classification	Weeks of OJT Training (average)	Average per-Trainee Cost[b]	Percent of Total Trainees
Professional, Managerial	33.3	$429	5.4
Clerical-Sales	10.6	477	2.6
Service	6.6	253	18.6
Skilled	18.0	466	24.8
Semi-Skilled	21.8	611	42.2
Unskilled	7.6	150	4.5

Source: Dale Bruce Rasmussen, "Determinants of Rates of Return to Investment in On-the-Job-Training," Ph.D. dissertation, Southern Methodist University, 1969, table 4, p. 74.

[a]OJT training only; excludes institutional portion when training is coupled.
[b]Including dropouts.

Table 5-10

Benefit-Cost Ratios of MDTA On-The-Job Training in Twenty-Four SMSA's, 1964-1966

Urban Area	Benefit-Cost Ratio[a]	Average Age of Trainees	Urban Area	Benefit-Cost Ratio[a]	Average Age of Trainees
Akron	1.7	20	Minneapolis-St. Paul	1.5	25
Atlanta	5.6	26	Newark	8.3	24
Baltimore	7.0	35	New Haven	3.4	26
Birmingham	5.8	33	New Orleans	18.0	28
Boston	6.7	27	Norfolk-Portsmouth	5.5	23
Charlotte	14.1	25	Phoenix	6.4	35
Chicago	12.2	21	Pittsburgh	3.7	29
Dallas	7.6	28	Portland	b	38
Denver	5.0	28	Providence-Pawtucket	.9	29
Detroit	.6	21	Seattle	2.7	27
Los Angeles	15.6	23	Utica-Rome	9.0	24
Miami	27.7	29	Wichita	4.6	24

Source: Dale Bruce Rasmussen, "Determinants of Rates of Return to Investment in On-the-Job Training," Ph.D. dissertation, Southern Methodist University, 1969, table 5, pp. 84-86.

[a]Five percent discount rate.

[b]Portland evidently classified skills in a different manner than other training sites, so that the post-training occupational profile was identical to that of the pre-training profile. Hence, the methodology employed by Rasmussen resulted in zero benefits being attributed to the training.

Table 5-11
Recalculated Benefit-Cost Ratios of MDTA OJT in Six Urban
Areas, 1964–1966

	10-Year Time Horizon		30-Year Time Horizon	
Urban Area	5% Discount Rate	10% Discount Rate	5% Discount Rate	10% Discount Rate
Boston	3.1	2.5	6.1	3.7
Dallas	3.5	2.8	6.9	4.2
Detroit	.3	.2	.6	.3
Miami	12.9	10.3	25.7	15.7
New Haven	1.5	1.2	3.0	1.8
Phoenix	3.2	2.6	6.4	3.9

Source: Calculated from Dale Bruce Rasmussen, "Determinants of Rates of Return to Investment in On-the-Job Training," Ph.D. dissertation, Southern Methodist University, 1969, table 5, pp. 84–86.

may be regarded as extremely conservative estimates. The lowest benefit-cost ratio is .3 in Detroit. Miami's is the highest at 10.3. MDTA in Phoenix has a ratio of 2.6. Extending the time horizon to thirty years and lowering the discount rate to 5 percent increases these ratios to .6 in Detroit, 25.7 in Miami, and 6.4 in Phoenix.

The greatest portion of the variability in the ratios among the various areas may be attributed to differences in trainee and SMSA characteristics. First, some differential may have resulted from differences in the ways the pre- and post-training occupations were classified into the six broad skill areas by program administrators at each of the training sites. Second, Rasmussen found that higher returns were associated with greater proportions of nonwhites taking the training. Greater skill jumps for nonwhites than whites between pre- and post-training occupations, and reductions in discrimination against nonwhite persons participating in training could account for this. Third, higher rates of population growth in urban areas were associated with higher returns. Fourth, structural unemployment (as measured by the rate wages in skilled occupations increase relative to the rate they change in unskilled occupations) and the returns to OJT were positively related. This is consistent with our expectations. Structural unemployment implies co-existence of unemployment and job vacancies. The greater the extent of surplus labor and unfilled jobs, the greater the opportunities for training people in desirable occupations. Fifth, contrary to what might be expected, high percentages of employment in manufacturing were associated with lower rates of return. Rasmussen suggests that this might be explained by slower-than-average increases in demand for labor in the manufacturing sector than in others. Since most OJT was conducted in manufacturing, slower growth implies less wage pressure.[33]

An alternative, but untested explanation is proposed. If urban areas characterized by rapid growth had been experiencing most of that growth in the nonmanufacturing sectors, then urban areas with a high percentage of employment in manufacturing would tend to be the slower-growing ones. Those with low percentages of employment in manufacturing then would be the faster growing ones. Thus, the percentage of employment in manufacturing could be just a proxy for the inverse of the growth rate of the urban areas.

Rasmussen's study is valuable because it gives some empirical support to the supposition that the returns to society from MDTA-sponsored OJT are relatively large,[j] it allows us to compare the experiences of OJT in various urban centers around the country, and it indicates several characteristics of urban areas associated with "successful" OJT programs – high structural unemployment and rapid growth.

Job Corps

The Office of Economic Opportunity (OEO) has made several estimates of benefit-cost ratios of some of the programs it oversees. One such study, written in May 1967, computes a series of ratios for the Job Corps based on differing assumptions concerning levels of costs and benefits. These ratios ranged from .58 to 1.88, with ratios from 1 05 to 1.69 resulting from what OEO felt to be a set of realistic, conservative assumptions.[34] Other estimates of benefit-cost ratios were made by OEO for the Job Corps and the out-of-school NYC using "before and after" data.[k] The pay-back period for both was esimated to be about five years. Assuming the earnings differentials apparently calculated by the OEO remain constant, a five-year pay-back period implies benefit-cost ratios for Job Corps falling somewhere between 2 and 4; a range of ratios somewhat higher than the 1.05 to 1.69 noted above.

The short calculated pay-back period of five years probably overstates the real gains attributable to training. While Job Corps trainees who completed training were earning $.34 an hour more ($680 a year) six months after leaving training than they had earned prior to training, dropouts from the program were earning $.21 an hour ($420 a year) more than before, and qualified persons who did not participate were earning $.14 an hour ($240 a year) more. Weighting

---

[j] Jacob Mincer used Census data to compare the rate of return associated with OJT in industry with that of attending college and found they were about the same ["On-the-Job Training: Costs, Returns and Some Implications," *Journal of Political Economy,* Supplement, 70 (October 1962): 50–79].

[k] OEO recognizes that this is not a wholly satisfactory technique. Its methodology for calculating Job Corps costs is acceptable. It includes operating costs of the Centers and of the program in general, and foregone earnings of the participants while they are at the Centers. From these costs it subtracts the value of output produced (or projects completed) by enrollees and the value of transfer payments received by enrollees.

the wage gains of "completes" and dropouts by the number of persons in each category yields an improvement of only $.12 an hour ($240 a year) over the qualified nonparticipants. With an expected unemployment rate of 18.75 percent, estimated income gains are only $203 a year.[35] However, favorable employment-unemployment experiences of Job Corps participants relative to nonparticipants would increase this income gain. In fact, if it is assumed that participants will maintain the 4 percentage points employment advantage held by them six months after leaving the Job Corps, an additional $114 income advantage accrues to participants. Thus $317 a year is probably a realistic figure for computing gains attributable to Job Corps.

Per-trainee costs of operating the Job Corps depend largely on the average length of stay in the program. Table 5-12 contains per trainee costs of two alternative lengths of stay in the program — five months and nine months. Per trainee costs over five months are $3,169; those over nine months, $5,130. A number of benefit-cost ratios can be computed with alternative earnings gains and cost estimates. These appear in Table 5-13. The first set of ratios is calculated from reported earnings gains. The second set is based on census data by estimating expected income gains from the measured change in educational levels of Job Corps participants. Most of the benefit-cost ratios are less than one; only the most liberal earnings gain measurement and calculation assumptions yield a ratio greater than this amount. Note that the ratios associated with a nine-month stay in the program exceed those of a five-month stay. In this case, predicted income gains resulting from educational gains increase more rapidly than costs as participants stay in the program (at least over the range of five to nine months).

From an economic standpoint, Job Corps as a training program is less attractive than other programs, although given that Job Corps trainees are very young, a thirty-year time horizon may not be unreasonable. Additionally, its advantages as a welfare and income redistribution program have not been evaluated here; nor has it yet been demonstrated that more efficient programs are available, capable of serving the same groups of persons as Job Corps.

BIA-Sponsored Retraining

Loren Scott has calculated benefit-cost ratios for a Bureau of Indian Affairs (BIA) on-the-job training (OJT) program in Oklahoma. The BIA initiated OJT programs in the U.S. in 1958. Scott's study analyzes the effectiveness of the program in Oklahoma as conducted between 1960 and 1966.[36] The OJT program is administered locally by BIA, which screens Indians who wish to receive training and matches them with employers willing to participate. BIA subsidizes employers up to one-half the federal minimum wage, although actual subsidization rate and training period are negotiated with each employer. In

Table 5-12
Job Corps Costs Per Trainee of a Five-Month and a Nine-Month
Training Period

Cost Category	Length of Training Period	
	5 Months	9 Months
Direct Operating Costs	$3,300	$5,414
Administrative Overhead	293	460
Opportunity Costs	644	1,179
Less:		
Transfer Payments Received by Trainees	-804	-1,448
Value of Output Produced During Training	-264	- 475
Total Costs	$3,169	$5,130

Source: Graeme M. Taylor, "Office of Economic Opportunity: Evaluation of Training Programs," Program Budgeting and Benefit-Cost Analysis, ed. Harley H. Hinrichs and Graeme M. Taylor (Pacific Palisades, Calif.: Goodyear Publishing Co., Inc., 1969), exhibit 6, p. 326.

Table 5-13
Benefit-Cost Ratios of the Job Corps

Source of Wage Data	Period of Participation	10-Year Time Horizon		30-Year Time Horizon	
		Discount Rate			
		5 Percent	10 Percent	5 Percent	10 Percent
Questionnaire[a]	5 Months	.8	.6	1.5	.9
Census[b]	5 Months	.4	.3	.8	.5
	9 Months	.5	.4	.9	.6

Source: Calculated from table 5-12; and Graeme M. Taylor, "Office of Economic Opportunity: Evaluation of Training Programs," Program Budgeting and Benefit-Cost Analysis, ed. Harley H. Hinrichs and Graeme M. Taylor (Pacific Palisades, Calif.: Goodyear Publishing Co., 1969), exhibit 7, p. 327.

[a]Assuming average income gain is constant at $317 over the time horizon.

[b]Assuming the educational-level changes were between grades 8-10. Lower grades result in slightly lower benefit-cost ratios.

each case, Indians are hired for entry-level jobs, and training given is specific to performance of that job.[37]

Costs of operating the program between 1960 and 1966 were estimated at $82,000 for administration at all levels and $146,159 for subsidies to participating firms. Because of the absence of what Scott regards as adequate control groups, benefits were estimated by the "before and after" method

(controlled for age, marital status, number of dependents, and changes in level
of economic activity.[38] Scott found that the average trainee increased his
earnings from $186 a month to $317 a month, and was employed 10.7 months
a year following training, as compared to 7.3 months before training (Table
5–14). Net effect on income was to increase it from $1,358 a year to $3,392 a
year (measured two years after the completion of training).[39] Benefit-cost
ratios in Table 5–15 resulting from these data suggest that economic returns from
the BIA projects are quite high. Over a ten-year period the benefit-cost ratios
range from about 12 to 15 depending on the discount rate used. If the time
horizon is stretched to thirty years, the ratios increase to 19 and 31 for 5 percent
and 10 percent discount rates, respectively.

When employers were asked to compare BIA trainees with their regular
employees, the trainees were rated about normal with respect to turnover.
Their absenteeism rates were higher, and they were not as punctual as other
employees.[1] However, trainees were rated as having better work habits and
higher productivity than other workers.[40] It seems clear that the trainees did
not have a problem with respect to attitude or incentive.

Discussions by Scott in his study lead one to suspect that many of the
earnings gains by the Indians were due to placement (through the inducement
of subsidies to firms) rather than any OJT they might have received. Negotiated
training periods ranged from 6 to 78 weeks. The training periods over which
firms were reimbursed and the length of time trainees indicated it took to learn
their jobs are compared in Table 5–16. In only one case did the average trainee
require the full training period or longer to learn his assigned job. Over half
the trainees responding indicated they learned their job in two weeks or less, and
less than 20 percent of the trainees required more than a month. The short
training time required, combined with Scott's statement that "Only two of the
firms visited indicated they had any sort of established training program."[41]
and his suggestion that the trainees' productivity was probably increased by only
a small amount [42] are consistent with the possibility that placement was
more important than training in increasing the Indians' earnings.[43]

In the companion study to Scott's, Paul Blume performed a cost-benefit
study of insitutional retraining programs supported by BIA in Oklahoma
between 1958 and 1966.[44] Training was offered in a wide range of occupations with the courses lasting from one to twenty-four months, all conducted in
established vocational training institutions. The 672 persons participating in
the program received subsistence payments as well as free training.

Program costs were calculated by adding direct instructional expenditures,
subsidies, and administrative costs of selecting, testing and placing participants.
Blume estimated that average training and subsidy, and average administrative
costs were $3,925 and $1,547 respectively, [45] although there was a wide

---

[1]These traits are often noted in disadvantaged employees generally, though the
Indians' characteristics in these respects are more widely publicized.

Table 5–14
Pre- and Post-Training Earnings of Indians in the BIA OJT Program in Oklahoma

Period	Earnings Per Month[a]	Months Employed Per Year	Annual Income
Pre-Training	$186	7.3	$1,358
Post-Training	317	10.7	3,392

Source: Loren C. Scott, "The Economic Effectiveness of On-the-Job Training: The Experience of the Bureau of Indian Affairs in Oklahoma," *Industrial and Labor Relations Review* 23, no. 2 (January 1970), pp. 223–34.

[a]Adjusted for exogenous factors.

Table 5–15
Benefit-Cost Ratios of the BIA OJT Program in Oklahoma

Discount Rate	10-Year Time Horizon	30-Year Time Horizon
5 percent	15.6	31.0
10 percent	12.4	18.9

Source: Loren C. Scott, "The Economic Effectiveness of On-the-Job Training: The Experience of the Bureau of Indian Affairs in Oklahoma," *Industrial and Labor Relations Review* 23, no. 2 (January 1970), table 7, p. 235.

Table 5–16
Negotiated Training Periods Compared With Trainees' Statement of the Period It Took to Learn Their Job

Training Period Negotiated (weeks)	Average Time Period Trainees Indicated They Needed (weeks)
6	14[a]
8	3
11	1
12	3 1/3
13	2 1/4
14	3 1/2
26	1 2/3
32	8
39	2
46	5
52	6
78	4 2/3

Source: Loren C. Scott, "The Economic Effectiveness of On-the-Job Training: The Experience of the Bureau of Indian Affairs in Oklahoma," *Industrial and Labor Relations Review* 23, no. 2 (January 1970), table 1, p. 223.

[a]One of two trainees required 24 weeks.

variance in the average length of training and subsidy size depending on the skills in which training was offered. Table 5-17 contains selected occupations for which Indians were trained and the nonadministrative costs associated with them. The most expensive skill to offer was T.V. electronics and the cheapest was meat cutting, costing $6,231 and $656, respectively. Office skill and personal services occupations were substantially less expensive to offer than were skilled trades.

Benefits of the program, as measured by the difference between pre- and post-training earnings,[m] averaged $1,929 a year when adjusted for age and changes in general economic activity.[46] Post-training earnings periods extended up to 100 months, depending on what year training was completed. Using a 5 percent discount rate and a ten-year time horizon, the resulting benefit-cost ratio for the overall institutional program is 2.4. This ratio must be interpreted carefully when evaluating the program and making recommendations for future action. Blume's conclusion that the ratio is high enough to justify expanding the BIA's institutional retraining program is open to question.[47]

Blume encountered both conceptual and methodological difficulties when he calculated costs and benefits. First, he included transfer payments in the form of subsidies as a cost, while ignoring the opportunity costs to society of temporarily withdrawing trainees from the labor force. Unless transfer payments were equal to opportunity costs, some unknown bias is introduced into his cost figures. Second, he failed to accrue interest costs for training and administrative costs when courses lasted more than a year. This introduces a small downward bias into costs. Third, Blume estimated administrative costs at $1,547 per trainee, an amount including much of the operating expenses of numerous employment assistance offices that aid many persons not participating in the retraining program. He notes that this probably overstates these costs, but makes no adjustment.

Fourth, Blume has depended on a "before and after" comparison of earnings to determine benefits. While he does make an adjustment for effects of age and changes in general economic conditions, it is not clear that these adjustments adequately answer objections to this methodology. When the observation period is short, pre-training earnings are likely to be abnormally depressed. When the observation period is long, high school attendance and military service could be a factor in reducing pre-training earnings of younger persons, and inflation becomes a more important factor. These problems introduce an upward bias to the estimates.

Last, although Blume attempted to follow-up all 672 persons no longer in

---

[m]Blume gathered data so that the length of the two periods were the same for each trainee. If postparticipation earnings data were available over twenty-four months, the average earnings immediately preceding program participation were measured. If the postparticipation observation was forty-eight months, forty-eight months was selected for the preparticipation period.

Table 5-17
Training and Subsistence Costs of the BIA Institutional Retraining
Program by Occupation, 1958-1966[a]

Occupation	Costs	Occupation	Costs
Accounting	$4,279	Dry Cleaning	$3,659
Auto Body Repair	4,917	Electronic Engineering	4,409
Auto Mechanics	5,402	Furniture Upholstery	2,473
Banking	3,644	Industrial Electrical	
		Maintenance	5,132
Barber	1,080	Industrial Electronics	5,096
Building Construction	5,864	Letterpress Printing	3,834
Business Machine		Lithographic Printing	3,997
Operator	1,971		
Commercial Art	6,428	Meat Cutting	656
Cosmetician	1,220	Refrigeration and Air	
		Conditioning	4,689
Culinary Arts	4,006	Secretarial	2,502
Diesel Mechanic	5,168	Stenography	2,105
Drafting	3,659	T.V. Electronics	6,231

Source: Paul Rountree Blume, "An Evaluation of Institutional Vocational Training Received by American Indians Through the Muskogee, Oklahoma Area Office of the Bureau of Indian Affairs," PH.D. dissertation, Oklahoma State University, 1968, appendix L, pp. 235-36.
[a]Direct training expenses and subsistence payments are not presented separately.

the training program, only 210 questionnaires were returned. Of course, only 138 utimately were used to estimate training benefits. Blume notes that those completing training were more likely to return questionnaires than dropouts, but makes no adjustments to compensate for the likely bias this introduces. Consequently, the "average" income gain measured in the study ($1,929), is probably overstated. The net effect of all the possible biases noted above is not known, but this writer suspects the benefit-cost ratios are overstated.

Characteristics of the trainees relative to the rest of the Indian population in Oklahoma also may have acted to overstate probable benefits of the program were it expanded. Blume notes that "The average trainee was far better educated than the average Oklahoma Indian, surpassing him by almost three full years of school."[48] As seen in Table 5-18, over 60 percent of the trainees had completed twelve or more years of school, and another 12 percent eleven years. These are the persons most easily trained. Through 1966, then, the BIA institutional retraining program may be characterized as having trained the "cream of the crop" among Indians. Expansion of the program to include larger proportions of Indians with greater education handicaps is likely to make training more difficult and lower the benefits per dollar spent.

The above considerations (a possible upward bias in the calculated benefit-cost ratio and a probable decline in the calculated ratio were the program

Table 5-18

Highest Grade Completed by Participants in BIA Institutional Retraining Programs in Oklahoma, 1958-1966

Highest Grade Completed	Percent of Trainees
13+	2.8
12	59.1
11	11.9
10	9.8
9	7.1
8	6.5

Source: Paul Rountree Blume, "An Evaluation of Institutional Vocational Training Received by American Indians Through the Muskogee, Oklahoma Area Office of the Bureau of Indian Affairs," Ph.D. dissertation, Oklahoma State University, 1968, table 5-2, p. 104.

expanded), plus the recognition that OJT conducted by BIA during the same period resulted in a benefit-cost ratio about six times larger than institutional retraining conducted by that Agency (15.6 vs. 2.4), suggest that greater efforts should be made toward expanding BIA OJT rather than institutional training. Blume cannot be blamed for reaching the conclusion he does — that BIA institutional training should be expanded — because Scott's study evidently had not yet been completed. Blume's reaching what seem to be a premature conclusion, however, points out the danger of making judgments on the basis of one case study (a danger recognized by those who have analyzed vocational education in high schools). *Although one approach to training a certain group of persons may yield a benefit-cost ratio exceeding one, alternate approaches may yield even larger ratios.*

When examining the training program in greater detail, Blume notes that it suffered from a 35 percent dropout rate,[n] and he indicates that overall performance of the program could be improved if this were reduced.[49] A brief rundown of the reasons trainees failed to complete the program is instructive. Table 5-19 summarizes reasons participants failed to complete their training. About 50 percent of those not completing their training did so for "miscellaneous" reasons — illness, misconduct, marriage, alcohol, family problems, unknown reasons, and "other" reasons. Solving these types of problems probably would entail expanding the program beyond its envisioned scope or coordinating it with other social services available through other agencies.

The remaining 50 percent either found work or did not make satisfactory progress. Those who dropped out because of an especially good job opportunity cannot be regarded as program failures. In fact, trainees might rightly be

---

[n]The national noncompletion rate was 42 percent.

Table 5-19

Reasons for Trainees Not Completing the BIA Institutional
Retraining Program

Reason	Percent of Total
Lack of Progress	37.7
Found Work	14.6
Unknown	12.9
Family Problems	11.6
Alcohol	9.9
Marriage	4.3
Misconduct	4.3
Illness	1.7
Other	3.0

Source: Paul Rountree Blume, "An Evaluation of Institutional Vocational Training Received by American Indians Through the Muskogee, Oklahoma Area Office
of the Bureau of Indian Affairs," Ph.D. dissertation, Oklahoma State University,
1968, table 5-7, p. 119.

counseled to take a promising job. Those who went to work because they needed
extra money could have been kept in the program by increasing the level of
subsidies. Of the 37.7 percent who left the program because they failed to make
satisfactory progress, Blume reports that "many" were dropped by administrators.[50] Some who failed to progress well because they were not interested
might have been retained with better initial counseling. The "many" who were
administratively dropped, and the others who became discouraged and dropped
on their own initiative, may have been victims of the conditions under which
training was offered — in regular classes of already-established vocational
schools. If the pace of training suitable for regular students was too fast for
BIA-sponsored students, individual courses designed for the latter might have
reduced their dropout rate.

Increased subsidies, better counseling that allows the trainee to follow
his interests more closely,[o] and courses that move at a slower pace suggest
themselves as means to increase the completion rate within the framework of
the existing program. Beyond these suggestions, enlarging the program's
functions or coordinating it with other social and welfare programs are additional
possible avenues for reducing the noncompletion rate. Increased costs of these
alternatives would have to be compared with their expected benefits to see
which of them (or other unlisted alternatives) should be pursued.

Blume examines wage rates earned by the trainees after leaving the

[o]Blume reports that GATB scores were unable to predict the likelihood of a person
completing training (Paul Rountree Blume, "An Evaluation of Institutional Vocational
Training Received by American Indians Through the Muskogee, Oklahoma Area Office of
the Bureau of Indian Affairs," Ph.D. dissertation, Oklahoma State University, 1968).

program, and finds that many were employed at jobs paying less than $250 a month.[51] Reasoning that such incomes were too low to support a family, he recommends avoiding offering training in the low-paying occupations — furniture upholstering, meat cutting, cosmetology, stenography, secretarial sciences, and building maintenance.[52] Since over 90 percent of the females in the program were trained in these low-paying occupations, he suggests the higher-paying occupations of accounting-bookkeeping, business machines operations, culinary arts, licensed practical nursing and registered nursing as alternatives.

Surely the problem is not quite so simple. An income of $250 a month in 1964 may not have been enough to support a family, but it would have supported a single person, and been a welcome addition to total family income, were a husband present and working. Even if it were the sole source of family support, $250 in 1964 (the "average" year over which earnings were measured) is the equivalent of about $335 a month now (assuming a 4 percent rate of inflation). It therefore is not clear that $250 a month was too low an income in 1964. Another consideration is whether the women would accept training in the alternate occupations suggested by Blume. Accounting-bookkeeping and business machines operations may be substitutes for stenography or secretarial sciences, but nursing requires a different set of skills and preferences.

If training in the "low wage" occupations identified by Blume is not necessarily preparing Indians for employment at poverty-level incomes, cost-benefit considerations become more important in evaluating the desirability of offering training in those occupations. Blume does not attempt to calculate benefit-cost ratios for individual occupations, but his unadjusted data can be used to estimate these ratios. The results appear in Table 5-20. Unexpectedly, barbering and meat cutting head the list, with ratios of 5.0 and 4.6 respectively. The rest of the occupations with ratios over 3 (with the exception of cosmetology) are in the skilled trades. None of the occupational offerings is associated with a benefit-cost ratio less than one, including those occupations Blume recommends avoiding because of the "low" incomes they produce. In fact, these latter occupations yield ratios of 4.6 (meat cutting), 3.1 (cosmetology), 2.2 (stenography), and 1.7 (secretarial sciences).[p] High benefit-cost ratios and low incomes are not contradictory. A benefit-cost ratio measures size of the income gain relative to cost necessary to achieve that gain. A high ratio is consistent with a small income gain if costs are smaller yet, and consistent with a low final income if initial income was low. The high benefit-cost ratios in those low income occupations singled out by Blume result from both low initial incomes and training costs. Similarly, high final incomes do not guarantee high benefit-cost ratios, as high initial incomes (implying small income gains) and high

[p]Sufficient data were not available to estimate benefit-cost ratios for furniture upholstery and building maintenance.

Table 5-20

Benefit-Cost Ratios of Various Occupations Offered in BIA
Institutional Retraining Program, 1958–1966

Occupation	Benefit-Cost Ratio
Barbering	5.0
Meat Cutting	4.6
Electronic Engineering	3.8
Drafting	3.6
Refrigeration and Air Conditioning	3.6
Lithographic Printing	3.6
Industrial Electronics	3.1
Letterpress Printing	3.1
Cosmetology	3.1
T.V. and Electronics	2.6
Diesel Mechanics	2.6
Auto Body Repair	2.2
Culinary Arts	2.2
Stenography	2.2
Building Construction	1.9
Dry Cleaning	1.9
Industrial Electrical Maintenance	1.7
Secretarial Skills	1.7
Auto Mechanics	1.4
Business Machine Operator	1.0

Source: Calculated from Burton A. Weisbrod, "Preventing High School Drop-outs," Measuring Benefits of Government Investments, ed. Robert Dorfman (Washington, D.C.: The Brookings Institution, 1965), table 6-2, pp. 173–74; table 6-3, p. 176; appendix L, pp. 235–36; and pp. 128–29.

training costs can be factors off-setting the apparent advantage of high final incomes. The occupations Blume suggest as alternatives (for which benefit-cost ratios could be calculated) yield ratios of 2.2 (auto body repair) and 1.0 (business machine operations), somewhat lower ratios than the "low income" occupations listed above.

These findings (that the occupations Blume recommends avoiding apparently had higher benefit-cost ratios than those he suggests as alternatives) do not indicate that Blume's recommendations are incorrect. A wage rate of $250 a month associated with even moderate unemployment experiences may yield an unacceptably low income. Even if an income of $250 were not too low, it may be derived from occupations other than those for which the persons were trained. If this were the case, training should be offered directly in those occupations. An expected conclusion again is reached — the decision concerning which occupations to offer in a training program should rest on a number of considerations, all of which should be investigated. Dependence upon a sole criterion — e.g., monthly wage rate or benefit-cost ratio — may lead to incorrect choices.

Dropout-Prevention

B.A. Weisbrod has developed a framework to test the economic efficiency of a special program for preventing dropouts conducted in St. Louis in 1961–1962.[53] A group of students who had been identified as "potential dropouts" were selected on the basis of personal characteristics and performance in school. They were randomly divided into a control and an experimental group of 385 and 429 students respectively. The experimental group received special counseling during the last two years of high school and job placement help following graduation. The control group received normal school counseling and placement services.

After two years, 189 (44 percent) of the original 429 students in the experimental group and 200 (52 percent) of the original 385 students in the control group had dropped from school.[54] Thus the program might be regarded as "successful." However, when the expected economic benefits to society of the program were compared to the costs of conducting it, the dropout-prevention program was not an efficient use of resources.

The cost per dropout prevented (34 in all) was $8,200 — $7,300 for personnel and $900 in additional education costs.[55] Benefits, calculated from the 1950 census as the difference between the discounted lifetime earnings of persons with twelve years of education and the dropouts, were estimated to be $2,700 (in 1950 prices) per dropout "saved."[56] Weisbrod used a 5 percent discount rate and a time horizon stretching to age sixty-five. The result is a benefit-cost ratio of .4. Thomas Ribich discusses Weisbrod's study in detail, and recalculates the benefit-cost ratios using 1960 census data. Using assumptions like Weisbrod's, the benefit-cost ratios derived by Ribich range from .64 to .69 depending on whether median income of central cities or mean income of North and West U.S. is used (Weisbrod used the latter).[57]

Weisbrod does not conclude that the ratio he calculated (.4) accurately represents the returns to society from the dropout-prevention program. One of the important considerations in manpower and poverty programs is the way they affect the distribution of income in society.[q] In fact, some income maintenance programs are conducted in which not any explicit monetary benefits are expected, let alone a one-for-one (or greater) pay-back. To the

---

[q]It should be clear that "manpower" and "poverty" programs are not mutually exclusive. Rather, they go hand in hand and are sometimes indistinguishable from each other.

extent that potential dropouts were kept in school and thus experienced increased incomes, the distributional goal has been achieved at least partly. There are additional benefits to society noted by Weisbrod. (1) Crime and delinquency are probably reduced. (2) The students may become better citizens by participating more in community affairs than they would have otherwise. (3) There may be some "intergeneration" effects, in which graduates impart better attitudes and opportunities to their children. (4) Keeping a student in school who otherwise might have dropped out may keep others in also. (5) The increased earnings of graduates who were prevented from dropping out will reduce the transfer payments they would have received otherwise. While this last item in itself is not an economic benefit to society, the reduction in the administrative costs of those transfer payments programs *is* a benefit to society.[58] All the above factors act to increase the benefits to society of such a program, but have not been included in the calculations.

Even the existence of extremely large nonmeasured benefits of the sort identified above by Weisbrod does not mean that the dropout program should be continued. Instead, it implies that a more efficient dropout program (in terms of dollar costs per dropout prevented) should be sought for. A less expensive dropout-prevention program presumably would have all the unmeasured benefits of the more expensive program, but would have the advantage of using resources more efficiently. Weisbrod suggests that the "dropout problem" may be indicative of problems with the school curriculum and the way it is offered — that the problem might be better ". . . solved by a re-orientation of school programs rather than by direct action toward the student."[59]

Weisbrod's conclusion that the counseling program appears to be an inefficient way to keep students in school is consistent with some research findings cited by Ribich, who notes that economic problems are not the prime reason for students leaving school. "The most important reason seems to be the students' open dislike for school. Counselors also cite unfavorable parental attitudes toward education."[60] Thus an intensive counseling program designed to aid the students with personal problems, and to give them greater economic incentives to stay in school is likely to "fail." Ribich notes that two types of changes have occurred in the treatment of the dropout problem. The first is the recognition that nonacademic training is needed for those who do not respond well to traditional education, and is illustrated by programs like NYC and Job Corps (for those already out of school), and work-study and cooperative education (for those still in school). The second is the recognition that dropout-prevention is going to have to begin prior to high school.[61]

Arthur Corazzini, in his study of vocational education at the high school level, attacked the problem of estimating the ability of a vocational program to reduce the number of high school dropouts.[62] The main difficulty he encountered was in determining the number of students who would have dropped out of school but for the availability of vocational education, and when they would have dropped out.[r] Based on his estimates of the number of dropouts prevented, and the known costs of vocational education, Corazzini suggests that the benefit-cost ratios of vocational education when its effects on reducing dropouts are included are only slightly higher than without the consideration of dropouts.

High School Job Placement Services

Larry Singell examined the job-search and subsequent labor-market behavior of 1963 Detroit high school graduates.[63] His sample was drawn from three high school districts; one each in neighborhoods characterized as having residents with low, median and high social and economic characteristics, as measured by median family income, median years of education, and the percent of the labor force employed in professional and managerial occupations. He found that the graduates from the "best" neighborhoods had consistently better labor market experiences than those from the "worst" neighborhoods. As Table 5-21 shows, 65 percent of the graduates from District #1 found jobs immediately upon high school graduation, while only 40 percent and 15 percent of those from Districts #2 and #3, respectively, were as successful. All of the graduates from District #1 found jobs within six months following graduation. Fifteen percent of those from District #3 still had not found jobs by that time. One year following graduation, the graduates of Districts #1, #2 and #3 were experiencing unemployment rates of 5, 10, and 30 percent, respectively. Graduates from Districts #2 and #3 who were employed at that time were earning less than those from the remaining district ($1.66 and $1.73 an hour vs. $1.90 an hour, respectively), and were more likely to be employed as unskilled laborers in factories (17 and 40 percent vs. 11 percent).

An examination of the job-search behavior of graduates of all three districts revealed that they were utilizing inefficient methods of looking for jobs. About 60 percent of them sought and found jobs through connections of relatives and friends. The next most frequently used approach was direct application (almost always to an employer close to home), and was used by nearly 20 percent of the graduates. Graduates used the State Employment Service to find jobs a little less than 10 percent of the time, and generally attempted to avoid it. Newspapers and private and high school placement offices provided the remaining 11 percent of productive job leads.[64] Additionally, most persons

---

[r]Knowing when a student would have dropped out is important because a student's staying in school when he might have dropped out adds two kinds of costs to the program—the additional schooling costs attributable to the student, and opportunity costs of wages given up to stay in school. Thus, the more effective the dropout program the more it costs to operate.

Table 5-21

Labor-Market Performance of Graduates from Three High School
Districts in Detroit, 1963-1964

Labor-Market Performance Characteristic	School District		
	#1[a]	#2[a]	#3[a]
Found an Immediate Job	65%	40%	15%
Found a Job Within 6 Months Following Grad.	100%	95%	85%
Unemployed at Time of Interview (one year following graduation)	5%	10%	30%
Employed in Factories as Unskilled Labor	11%	17%	40%
Hourly Wage Rate One Year Following Graduation	$1.90	$1.66	$1.73

Source: Larry Duane Singell, "Economic Opportunity and Juvenile Delinquency: A Case Study of the Detroit Juvenile Labor Market," Ph.D. dissertation, Wayne State University, 1965, table 3, p. 87, and pp. 88-89.
[a]District #1 ranked highest in Detroit by the criteria used by Singell; #2 was the median District, and #3 was the lowest District.

accepted the first job offered rather than "shopping around" for the best
job they could find.[s]

Use of relatives and friends, or direct application, certainly are not the most
efficient methods of exposing oneself quickly to a large number of job openings.
Newspapers and public and private placement services can do this better. Besides
being inefficient, the job sources actually utilized by graduates acted to provide
graduates from poor neighborhoods with less desirable jobs, and do it slower,
than the same job sources for graduates from more wealthy neighborhoods.
Poorer neighborhoods were characterized by relatively low percentages of
employment in managerial and professional occupations, and hence offered
fewer "connections" to aid the graduates in their search for work. Students from
poor neighborhoods also were characterized by relatively low educational
achievement, so that graduates in those neighborhoods were competing more
often with unemployed older workers for entry-level jobs. Those two factors
explain much of the difficulty experienced by graduates from Districts #2 and
#3 in finding jobs. Since they were slower finding their initial jobs (and, as noted
earlier, were not slower because they were comparing alternative opportunities),

[s]Singell shows that since the costs of job-search must be balanced against the
probable higher earnings of a better job, and since job-search costs for unemployed high
school graduates are high, graduates are rational to accept the first "reasonable" job offer
(Larry Duane Singell, "Economic Opportunity and Juvenile Delinquency: A Case Study
of the Detroit Juvenile Labor Market," Ph.D. dissertation, Wayne State University, 1965,
p. 141).

Table 5-22

Calculation of the Benefit-Cost Ratio of Establishing State Employment
Offices in Detroit Schools

Cost Calculation		Benefit Calculation	
Number of placements required to reduce youth unemployment by 1%	281	Expected reduction in the number of delinquents resulting from a reduction in unemployment of 281	15
Total costs of placement (281 x $250)	$70,250	Reduction in crime costs from reducing delinquency by 15 (15 x $776)	$11,640[a]
		+ Additional earned income of the 281 persons placed (281 x $4,000)	$1,124,000[a]
		Total benefits	$1,135,640

$$\text{Benefit-Cost Ratio} = \frac{\$1,135,640}{\$70,250} = 16.2$$

Source: Larry Duane Singell, "Economic Opportunity and Juvenile Delinquency:
A Case Study of the Detroit Juvenile Labor Market," Ph.D. dissertation, Wayne
State University, 1965.

[a]Assumed to occur the first year following high school graduation.

they could be expected to be earning lower wages a year following graduation.

Singell concludes that offering better job information to students while
they are in school (especially in poverty neighborhoods) may be an efficient way
of reducing unemployment among recent graduates. He suggests early counseling
on long-run employment opportunities in occupations being considered by
students (something schools currently are unable to offer) as well as better
placement help. The latter could be accomplished by establishing school and
neighborhood placement offices.[65]

Singell's "impressionistic" cost-benefit calculation of intensified counseling
and placement activities in high schools results in a benefit-cost ratio of about
16. Costs are comprised of placement costs incurred by the public employment
service in placing graduates, and are estimated to be $250 per placement.
Benefits include the increased earnings resulting from reduced unemployment
and the expected savings of less crime.[t] Results of these calculations are contained in Table 5-22.

---

[t]Singell is careful to establish a case for tying reduced unemployment to reduced
crime. He estimates the statistical relationship between unemployment and the incidence
of crime among youth and suggests that a 1 percent reduction of unemployment among
them will reduce the number committing crimes by about 6 percent.

While there are many omissions in these calculations likely to affect the results,[u] Singell did not intend to perform a complete analysis. The interesting part of his study is the estimate of savings attributable to reduced crime associated with less unemployment. His is the only study this writer found while surveying research for this book which made such a calculation. Taking his figures at face value, placement of high school graduates reduces crime costs by an average of $41 per placement ($11,640 ÷ 281).[v] This study is important because it indicates that while significant net benefits (at least in the short run) may be achieved from placement efforts in high schools, high school placement services are cited frequently as inadequate.

Vocational Rehabilitation

Frank Grella has performed a cost-benefit study of vocational rehabilitation in Connecticut as conducted between July 1, 1966 and June 30, 1967.[66] Besides showing that vocational rehabilitation has a large probable economic payoff, he illustrates a broad methodology for applying the cost-benefit technique in the internal management of the program. Grella's study included all 1,545 persons who were in the program and completed it during that year. While he computed benefit-cost ratios for a number of different groups, only the private and social ratios are discussed here.[w] The methodology Grella adopted to estimate benefits conforms quite closely to that of a cost-benefit study conducted by the Vocational Rehabilitation Administration in 1967. Both studies utilize the "before and after" technique to estimate the economic benefits of rehabilitation.

---

[u]For example, Singell estimates that 281 placements could reduce the unemployment rate of Detroit youth by 1 percent. If the placement services are performed in the high schools, many of those being placed by the Employment Service could have found jobs on their own; thus more than 281 placements would be required to achieve a net reduction in unemployment of one percent. Youths also might have to be placed more than once in order to keep them employed. Both these factors increase costs. But the benefits may also be understated. Income benefits attributable to placement probably last more than a year, and many of the youths who do not commit crimes because they are employed, would have committed more than one. These factors increase benefits. The omissions noted above are not a complete list, but with errors in both directions, net bias is not known.

[v]This is not strictly correct, because the calculated relationship between reduced unemployment and crime was not linear—reducing unemployment from initially high levels has a greater effect on crime than reducing it from lower levels (Frank Carmen Grella, "An Application of Cost-Benefit Theory and Systems Theory to Vocational Rehabilitation in Connecticut," Ph.D. dissertation, University of Massachusetts, 1969).

[w]Grella closely followed generally accepted methodology when examining the program from the "private" viewpoint. However, he departed significantly from this methodology when viewing it from the "public" standpoint. Although there are still important areas for argument, Grella's data on social costs and benefits have been modified to approximate more closely more common methodology.

Unlike other manpower programs, the major portion of private costs of vocational rehabilitation is comprised of lost benefits ($14,073,059) rather than foregone earnings ($807,888). Table 5-23 shows that the greatest part of these lost benefits to participants is in the form of decreased institutional care. Private benefits came from two sources — increased earnings *net* of taxes, and the imputed value of the increased labor services in the homes of those who remain out of the labor force following participation. The labor force participation rate following rehabilitation is amazingly high — nearly 96 percent — and accounts in part for the high estimated earnings that more than offset the lost forms of public assistance. The private benefit-cost ratio resulting from the data in Table 5-23 is 4.2.

Social costs involved in the vocational rehabilitation program are direct rehabilitation costs (including all phases of vocational rehabilitation) and opportunity costs. The total social costs of $3.4 million imply an expenditure of about $2,200 per person.[x] Social benefits are equal to the sum of the increase in expected earnings of the participants, the imputed value of those who voluntarily stay in the home and the savings in resources achieved through reduced demands for institutional care.[y] Using $3.4 million as the total estimated social costs and $87.6 million as the estimated present value of social benefits yields a social benefit-cost ratio of 25.8.

The Connecticut program dramatically changed the labor-market performance of its participants. Prior to participation, 85 percent of the rehabilitants reported zero income (Table 5-24). Only 9 percent were earning $60 or more a week. Following rehabilitation, only 6 percent reported no earnings and 64 percent reported earning $60 or more a week. The increased earnings did not result from employment within the vocational rehabilitation program. Of the 1,475 persons who were employed after leaving the program, only 78 were employed in sheltered workshops and 1 by the state government. Another 13 were self-employed. The remaining 1,390 were working in the competitive labor market.[67]

Sar Levitan and Garth Mangum argue that the earnings estimates based on short-term "before and after" data substantially overstate the income gains experienced by rehabilitants.[68] They suggest that earnings are likely to be unusually depressed just prior to entry into the program and unusually high immediately following it.[z] Adjusting for these tendencies reduced a benefit-cost ratio calculated in the Vocational Rehabilitation Administration study men-

---

[x]Since it is a continuing program with persons entering and leaving throughout the year, a study covering several years would be necessary to get an accurate per-person cost.

[y]There is disagreement over whether society captures these last two sources of benefits.

[z]Their remarks were actually directed at the Vocational Rehabilitation Administration's study, but since Grella utilized the same methodology, the comments also apply in general to Grella's study.

Table 5-23
Costs and Benefits of Vocational Rehabilitation in Connecticut, 1966–1967

Costs[a]		Benefits[a]	
Private			
Loss of Public Assistance	$ 1,896,584	Increase in Expected Lifetime Earnings[b]	$74,499,395
Loss of Institutional Care	11,560,527	Increase in Value of Homemakers and Unpaid Family Workers	1,500,000
Loss of Social Security Disability Payments	615,948	(Less Increased Taxes Attributable to Increased Incomes)	–12,868,800
Foregone Earnings[c]	807,888		
	$14,880,947		$63,130,595
Social			
Direct Rehabilitation Costs	$ 2,588,978	Increase in Expected Lifetime Earnings[b]	$74,499,395
Opportunity Costs[c]	807,888	Increase in Value of Homemakers and Unpaid Family Workers	1,500,000
	$ 3,397,466	Reduced Costs of Institutional Care	11,560,527
			$87,559,922

Source: Frank Carmen Grella, "An Application of Cost-Benefit Theory and Systems Theory to Vocational Rehabilitation in Connecticut," Ph.D. dissertation, University of Massachusetts, 1969, table 23, p. 154; table 24, p. 170; and table 25, p. 182.

[a]Discounted at 4 percent.

[b]Adjusted for the probability of withdrawal from the labor force, death, and increased earnings at 3 percent a year.

[c]Based on earnings at time of entry into the program.

144 COST-BENEFIT ANALYSIS

Table 5-24
Weekly Earnings of Participants in the Connecticut Vocational
Rehabilitation Program Before and After Participation (percentage)

Weekly Earnings Range	Before	After
$ 0	85	6
1–19	1	3
20–39	1	6
40–59	4	21
60–79	4	34
80–99	3	17
100+	2	13

Source: Frank Carmen Grella, "An Application of Cost-Benefit Theory and Systems Theory to Vocational Rehabilitation in Connecticut," Ph.D. dissertation, University of Massachusetts, 1969, table 20, p. 128.

tioned earlier from 35 to 12. If the ratio calculated by Grella were reduced by a similar magnitude through these adjustments, it would be reduced from 25.8 to 8.8 — still a relatively high ratio compared to those of other manpower programs. Levitan and Mangum conclude

. . . that the same could be true with the most seriously socially and environmentally handicapped. It also demonstrates that even a proven payoff and an apparent federal willingness to supply larger amounts of matching funds cannot attract support for services to more than a fraction of those eligible.[69]

Conclusions

The programs examined in this chapter generally achieved benefit-cost ratios greater than one. Least successful from this standpoint were the dropout-prevention programs conducted in St. Louis and the Job Corps as it was operated nationally. A benefit-cost ratio greater than one did not result in the former program even with the most favorable assumptions. Further analyses by Weisbrod, Ribich and Corazzini suggest that counseling and traditional vocational education are not efficient ways to prevent dropouts.[aa] On the other hand, counseling and job placement of graduating high school students may yield substantial net benefits.

Training given by Job Corps nationally, and by BIA in vocational schools in Oklahoma, yielded lower benefit-cost ratios than their counterparts — NYC and BIA OJT, respectively. These and other ratios are summarized in Table 5-25.

[aa]This does not imply that dropout-prevention cannot be thought of as a "side" benefit of these activities.

Table 5-25
Benefit-Cost Ràtios of Various Manpower Programs

Program and Researcher	10-Year Time Horizon 10 Percent Discount Rate	30-Year Time Horizon 5 Percent Discount Rate
NYC-Indiana, Bateman		
Males		
High School Graduates	2.4	6.0
9–10 years of school	3.3	8.2
Females		
High School Graduates	0.0	0.0
9–10 years of school	1.0	2.5
MDTA OJT-SMSA's, Rasmussen		
New Haven	1.2	3.0
Phoenix	2.6	6.4
Miami	10.3	25.7
Job Corps-National, O.E.O.		
Questionnaire data	.6	1.5
Census data	.4	.9
BIA OJT-Oklahoma, Scott	12.4	31.0
BIA Institutional-Oklahoma, Blume	1.9	4.8
Dropout-Prevention-St. Louis, Weisbrod[a]	.2	.6
Counseling and Placement-Detroit, Singell[b]	16.2	
Vocational Rehabilitation- Connecticut, Grella[c]	8.8-25.8	

Source: Tables 5-3, 5-11, 5-13, 5-15 and 5-22; and pages 181–82, 190–91, and p. 202.

[a]Ratios are based on earnings data developed by Ribich from 1960 Census.

[b]Includes only one year earnings data.

[c]Ratios include lifetime expected earnings of persons of various ages.

The benefit-cost ratio associated with OJT supported by BIA was about six times as great as that associated with that agency's institutional training. Ratios for NYC averaged about three times those achieved by the Job Corps.

MDTA OJT can be compared with MDTA institutional training discussed in the last chapter (Table 4-27). While Rasmussen's study of MDTA OJT was limited to SMSA's, and benefit-cost ratios calculated for only 23 of those, an unweighted average of those 23 ratios is about 1.5 times as great as the overall benefit-cost ratio of MDTA institutional training nationally (2.7 vs. 1.9 using a 10 percent discount rate and a ten-year time horizon). Thus evidence from three sets of studies (Job Corps vs. NYC; BIA institutional vs. BIA OJT; and MDTA institutional vs. MDTA OJT) consistently suggests that OJT yields greater economic benefits relative to costs than institutional training. Uncertainty concerning the effects of different research methodologies and trainee charac-teristics within each set of studies prevents a conclusion that OJT can be substituted for institutional training and still be successful. Research aimed at reducing these uncertainties should receive high priority.

Vocational rehabilitation may well be the most efficient large scale manpower program. "Adjusted" benefit-cost ratios of 9 and 12 for the Connecticut and national programs, respectively, are higher than all except isolated ratios associated with several case studies of other manpower programs. Whether the processes used in vocational rehabilitation are transferable to programs serving groups with other disadvantages is not clear. This writer suspects that an important part of the vocational rehabilitation program's relative success has been employers' greater willingness to accept persons with physical rather than social handicaps. If so, further education of employers may improve the measured efficiency in other programs.

6 Review and Conclusions

Conclusions from Cost-Benefit Analysis

Within the manpower area, cost-benefit analysis has been applied formally to secondary and post-secondary vocational education, and retraining programs conducted under state legislation, ARA, MDTA (both institutional and OJT components), Economic Opportunity Act, Social Security Act (vocational rehabilitation), and Public Law 959 (training conducted by the Bureau of Indian Affairs). Data from the majority of cost-benefit studies examined in chaps. 2 through 5 suggest that social benefits of programs examined exceeded social costs. Thus, manpower programs designed to enhance the employability and income of their participants, as they were conducted in the 1960s, may have returned net economic benefits to society. That is, they have returned net benefits to society as measured by the methodology commonly employed in cost-benefit analysis. Discussions concerning whether retraining actually increases national income or only redistributes job opportunities are voluminous, and are likely to continue for some time.

Vocational Education

Morris Ullman, et al., have suggested that

... if funds were allocated on the basis of economic efficiency alone, all vocational education dollars available might be invested in post-secondary programs which, by certain criteria, yield the greatest marginal return per extra dollar invested.[1]

They do not cite evidence that led them to this conclusion. Studies examined in chaps. 2 and 3 suggest the opposite — that investment in vocational education at the high school level yields greater net benefits (relative to costs) than such education in post-secondary institutions.

Four cost-benefit studies of vocational education at the secondary level, and two of vocational education at the post-secondary level, were examined and their methodologies adjusted to make their results as comparable as possible. Utilizing a time horizon of thirty years and a 5 percent discount rate,[a] social

---

[a]The long time horizon is used here and elsewhere in this chapter with the justification that studies which followed graduates' post-participation earnings experiences for several years measured no significant decrease in participants' earnings advantage over nonparticipants. [Michael E. Borus "Time Trends in the Benefits From Retraining in Connecticut," *Proceedings of the Twentieth Annual Winter Meeting of the Industrial Relations Research*

148 COST-BENEFIT ANALYSIS

benefit-cost ratios ranged from 1.5 to 27.1 (Table 6-1). Each of the studies of vocational education at the secondary level compared vocational education in a vocational-technical school as an alternative to general education. The two studies of vocational education at the post-secondary level compared such education to entering the labor force following high school graduation.

Benefit-cost ratios of vocational education in high schools exceed those for vocational education in post-high school institutions. The lowest ratio at the high school level − 3.3 − is more than 30 percent greater than the unweighted average of ratios (2.4) at the higher level. And the unweighted average of those at the lower level are more than four times greater than that of post-secondary training (10.1 vs. 2.4). We may conclude that *available evidence from cost-benefit analysis consistently suggests that vocational education in vocational-technical secondary schools yields higher returns than such education in post-secondary institutions*. Examination of data developed in these studies indicates that the largest single factor contributing to the lower returns at the post-secondary level is the high opportunity cost associated with withdrawing participants from the labor force to attend post secondary schools.

Out-of-School Programs

A variety of institutional and OJT retraining programs for persons out of school has been examined. Results of institutional training programs are summarized in Table 6-2. The three studies of ARA-sponsored training yielded benefit-cost ratios ranging from 9.4 to 16.8, substantially higher than the 3.8 to 4.8 ratios from the three studies of MDTA- and BIA-sponsored training. *Evidence from cost-benefit studies suggests that institutional training conducted under ARA yielded higher returns than institutional training under either MDTA or BIA*. Explanations for the differential probably lie with (1) the extremely short-term nature of classes conducted under ARA and (2) the greater amount of job-placement guarantee associated with ARA training, rather than with differences in efficiency with which programs were operated.

Association, Madison, Wisc., 1967; A. B. Carroll and L. A. Ihnen, "Costs and Returns for Two Years of Post-Secondary Technical Schooling," Journal of Political Economy 75, no. 6 (December, 1967): 862–873; Jacob J. Kaufman et al., "A Cost-Effectiveness Study of Vocational Education," *A Comparison of Vocational and Non-vocational Education in Secondary Schools,* (University Park, Penn.: Institute for Research on Human Resources, Pennsylvania State University, March, 1969); and Kaufman and Morgan V. Lewis, *The Potential of Vocational Education: Observations and Conclusions* (University Park, Penn.: Institute for Research on Human Resources, Pennsylvania State University, 1968]. Gerald G. Somers' and Graeme H. McKechnie's conclusion that advantages of retraining may disappear after several years of economic expansion refers to *employment,* not *earnings,* advantage. ["Vocational Retraining Programs for the Unemployed," *Proceedings of the Industrial Relations Research Association* (December, 1967).] No special justification exists for using a 5 percent discount rate in this final chapter. Ratios for a 10 percent discount rate may be approximated by multiplying ratios in this chapter by 0.6.

Table 6-1

Benefit-Cost Ratios for Vocational Education Conducted in Secondary and Post-Secondary Schools

Study	Benefit-Cost Ratio
Secondary Level	
Corazzini	3.3
Kaufman et al.	10.5 and 27.1
Kaufman	5.4
Taussig	4.3
Unweighted Average	10.1
Post-Secondary Level	
Corazzini	1.5
Carroll and Ihnen	1.5–4.2
Unweighted Average	2.4

Source: Tables 2-3, 2-9, 2-11, 2-15, 3-5, and 3-6.

Table 6-2

Summary of Benefit-Cost Ratios Relating to Institutional Retraining Programs

Program and Scope	Benefit-Cost Ratio[a]
MDTA – National	4.7
MDTA – Michigan	3.8
BIA – Oklahoma	4.8
ARA – Massachusetts	9.4
ARA – West Virginia	16.8
ARA – Connecticut	14.7

Source: Tables 4-8, 4-12, 4-17, 4-23, 5-25, and p. 72.
[a]Using a 5 percent discount rate and a 30-year time horizon.

Results of the three studies of programs in which OJT played a major role appear in Table 6-3. BIA-conducted OJT appears to yield the highest benefit-cost ratio – 31.0 – and NYC the lowest – 3.7. Of the three programs, only NYC offered work training in public agencies. *Evidence from cost-benefit analysis suggests that OJT conducted by BIA yields greater returns than MDTA and NYC-sponsored OJT, and that work training offered in the private sector yields greater returns than such training offered in public employment.* Measured advantages of some OJT programs over others may be explained by (1) unreconcilable methodological differences among the studies, and (2) greater job guarantees associated with work training in the private sector where the employment relationship continues unbroken following training.

Table 6–3
Summary of Benefit-Cost Ratios Relating to OJT Programs

Program and Scope	Benefit-Cost Ratio[a]
MDTA – SMSA's	6.7[b]
NYC – Indiana	3.7
BIA – Oklahoma	31.0

[a]Using a 5 percent discount rate and a 30-year time horizon.
[b]Estimated taking an unweighted average of the ratios for each SMSA.

Comparisons of benefit-cost ratios for institutional retraining with ratios
for OJT are difficult to make. Because of methodological differences, only
the Borus et al. study of NYC [2] lends itself to comparison with any of the
studies of institutional retraining; and only Hardin's and Borus' study of MDTA
in Michigan [3] contains sufficient detail to allow the comparison to be
based on similar groups. Results of this comparison appear in Table 6–4. A
benefit-cost ratio of 5.3 is associated with persons having ten years of school
in the NYC program, compared to a ratio of 15.7 for similar persons in MDTA.
Ratios for those with twelve years of school in the NYC and MDTA programs
respectively are 3.0 and 11.5. While the two programs are not identical with
respect to the groups they are designed to serve (NYC containing more young,
nonwhite persons), and education classifications of the two studies are not
identical, MDTA institutional training seems to yield greater returns than does
NYC.

Job Corps training appears to yield the lowest benefit-cost ratio of all
out-of-school retraining programs aimed at the economically and educationally
disadvantaged. Even so, a ratio of 1.5 was achieved when a 5 percent discount
rate and thirty-year time horizon were used. If economic efficiency were
the only goal, one might argue that Job Corps activities should be reduced
relative to other types of training programs. *Evidence from cost-benefit analysis
suggests that NYC yields greater economic returns than Job Corps, and that
institutional MDTA training aimed at those with nine through twelve years of
school yields even greater returns than NYC.* Differences in these ratios may
result from unmeasured differences in characteristics of participants.

Vocational rehabilitation, while of a somewhat different nature than other
manpower programs, appears to yield impressive benefit-cost ratios. Vocational
rehabilitation in Connecticut achieved a ratio somewhere between 9 and 25
in 1966–1967. While methodological differences prevent direct comparison of
these results with those of other programs, it seems clear that reducing physical
handicaps and offering training when needed enables persons to be absorbed
into the labor force at costs substantially below their future contribution
to output. Thus, *cost-benefit analysis suggests that vocational rehabilitation
yields high returns to society.*

Table 6-4
Benefit-Cost Ratios of NYC in Indiana and MDTA in Michigan by
Educational Level of Participants

Training Program	Educational Level	Benefit-Cost Ratio[a]
NYC	9 and 10 years	5.3
	12 years	3.0
MDTA	9-11 years	15.7
	12 years and more	11.5

[a]Five percent discount rate and 30-year time horizon.

High School Dropout and Placement Programs

High school dropout-prevention programs were seen to be inefficient means of increasing incomes of persons who, without them, would have dropped out of school. A major difficulty in operating "efficient" dropout-prevention programs lies in identifying future dropouts "before the fact." Inability to do this requires that "treatment" be given to many who would not have dropped out anyway. In the face of a 0.6 benefit-cost ratio for dropout-prevention as studied by Weisbrod, [4] and of the higher ratios achieved by MDTA, NYC, and Job Corps programs providing training and education to persons who *did* drop out of high school, a more *efficient* course to pursue than to keep students in school through counseling would be to aid these persons *after* they have dropped out. On the other hand, Singell's impressionistic cost-benefit study of school placement activities indicates that they may yield a benefit-cost ratio around 16.[5] Consequently, we might conclude that *fragmentary evidence suggests that schools increase their students' future incomes more efficiently through training and placement of those willing and able to stay in school than through counseling students who have been identified as potential dropouts*. As stressed in chap. 5, this conclusion does not imply that counseling is an unimportant activity nor that counseling to keep students in school should be discontinued.

Cost-Benefit Analysis' Contribution to Program Evaluation

Manpower activities examined earlier can be ranked according to their benefit-cost ratios. Based on results surveyed in earlier chapters, such a ranking (in descending order of ratios) lists:[b]

[b]Ratios which were comprised of only one type of program—vocational rehabilitation, secondary and post-secondary vocational education, Job Corps, and dropout-prevention— were determined by entering the calculated ratio if there was only one study, and by taking an unweighted average of ratios if there were more than one study. Ratios comprised of

1.   Vocational rehabilitation (9–25)
2.   Vocational education in vocational-technical high schools (10.1)
3.   Programs utilizing OJT (5.0)
4.   Out-of-school institutional retraining (4.7)
5.   Post–high school vocational education (1.5–4.2)
6.   Job Corps (1.5)
7.   Dropout-prevention programs (0.6).

If program priorities were determined solely on the basis of the above rankings, programs would be funded in that order, and dropout-prevention programs of the sort examined by Weisbrod would be abandoned. Expanded funding for various OJT programs in the last several years — cooperative education and work-study for in-school youth; and JOBS, WIN and Public Service Careers (a kind of JOBS program in the public sector), for out-of-school persons — is consistent with this ranking; as are expanded efforts in vocational education at the secondary level. This writer does not know if cost-benefit studies were influential in redirecting manpower activities toward programs aimed at giving OJT experience, or if legislators were influenced primarily by other factors.

Cost-benefit studies (and data developed from them) have done more than simply indicate relative efficiency of broad programs. In many cases, studies have provided information that could aid program administrators in setting internal operating priorities. A sampling of the conclusions of this nature reached in studies examined in earlier chapters are:

1.   NYC in Indiana was most efficient in aiding male high school dropouts, and least efficient in aiding female high school graduates
2.   MDTA-sponsored OJT in urban areas was more efficient in aiding black, than white, persons
3.   Job Corps was more efficient in aiding persons who remained in the program nine months than those remaining only five months
4.   MDTA institutional retraining in Winona, Michigan, was most efficient in training persons for general office skills, and least efficient in training them in automobile repair skills
5.   MDTA institutional training in Michigan was highly efficient when courses were no longer than 200 hours in length, and highly inefficient when courses exceeded 200 hours in length

---

more than one type of program—out-of-school OJT and institutional training—were determined by weighting individual programs by the estimated total federal expenditures on
those programs between 1963 and 1969. Because of the problems inherent in cost-benefit
analysis and the procedures followed in arriving at the above ranking, the order in which
programs are listed must be interpreted carefully.

6. MDTA institutional training in Michigan was most efficient when aiding
    nonwhites of both sexes and white females, and least efficient when aiding
    white males
7. Comprehensive high school vocational programs may be most efficient
    in offering "low-cost" programs such as business education, and least
    efficient in offering "high-cost" programs such as electronic repair
8. Vocational education in post–high school institutions is more efficient when
    programs are offered in skills not available in high school programs

    This list could be extended at great length, but the point should be made by
now. Carefully designed cost-benefit analysis can suggest important avenues
for increasing the economic efficiency with which programs are operated.

    Assessing the relative efficiency of different programs has proven to be a
formidable task. Since studies were conducted by many different researchers, a
wide variety of methodologies was encountered. Scott [6] and Blume, [7]
for example, used the "before and after" technique in their studies of retraining
sponsored by BIA. Rasmussen, who examined MDTA OJT utilized the "before
and after" method, but rather than measuring *observed* earnings changes, he
measured *predicted* earnings changes resulting from the altered occupational
profile of those participating in training. His results may not be comparable to
those of the above studies nor to those of Main's "snowball" method of
measuring the impact of MDTA institutional programs.[8] Other differences
among the studies included the manner of collecting and extrapolating benefit
data, calculating administrative and opportunity costs, and handling vacuum
and displacement effects. In three studies (Corazzini, [9] Taussig [10] and
Kaufman et al. [11]), it was not clear that the researchers were using the
concepts they claimed to be using. When sufficient data were presented, this
writer made rough adjustments to make the studies' methodologies more
comparable. When they were not presented, the nature of the biases introduced
by methodologies used were explored. Some of these adjustments were made
easily; such as changes in discount rates and time horizons. Capital costs
(when presented separately) were simply subtracted from calculated total costs,
as in the case of Taussig's and Corazzini's respective studies of vocational
high schools in New York and Worcester. Others were made with more difficulty.
Adjusting Taussig's methodology in his study of post-secondary vocational
education in Worcester so that his results could be compared with other studies
necessitated using two other sources to alter both his cost and benefit calculations. These adjustments do not reduce the uncertainties inherent in interpret-
ing any given benefit-cost ratio, but they do provide a better ground for making
comparisons between ratios.

    Complaints concerning the inability of cost-benefit analysis to measure
accurately benefits of an activity are more significant than similar complaints

concerning costs. Complaints revolving around cost errors tend more to be methodological (such as poor accounting data), whereas those relating to benefits are more conceptual. In fact, most complaints center, in one way or another, on the use of earnings as the measure of benefits. Frequently listed benefits claimed unmeasured by earnings are:

1. reduction in crime
2. increased productivity through better health
3. increased earnings of children of trainees (intergeneration effect)
4. nonwage job benefits
5. increased productivity of other resources
6. consumption value of training activities
7. benefits to society of improved citizenship
8. personal satisfaction of succeeding in selected occupation
9. value of options opened up by better education and training
10. value of income redistribution.

The importance of these sources of benefits relative to earnings is a serious consideration in assessing the value of cost-benefit analysis as it has been applied to manpower programs. The larger the unmeasured benefits, the less confidence we can have in calculated benefit-cost ratios. Several studies (most included in preceding chapters) help throw some light on the importance of items neglected by traditional analysis. Results suggest that their significance lies more in how their magnitudes vary among programs than in their absolute magnitudes. The following discussion is not meant to be a complete analysis of this issue; but is meant only to indicate how serious some of the objections are and how cost-benefit analysis can meet them.

The value of crime reduction was broached by Singell, who estimated the effects of reducing unemployment on the incidence of juvenile delinquency. His calculations suggest that savings to society in reduced property damage and theft were around $24 for each graduating high school student placed in a job.[c] Applying this figure to other manpower programs suggests that society saves relatively little from reduced crime for each participant who becomes successfully employed as a result of program participation. Relative to the wage gains already measured, neglect of this small total sum does not result in substantial understatement of benefits. Society also benefits from crime reduction because persons who otherwise would have committed crimes and been sent

---

[c]This figure is low despite the fact that for each person induced to "stay out of crime" the savings are large. The low savings per participant result from the same problem operating to make dropout-prevention programs inefficient—inability to identify those who will act in an undesirable fashion (in this case, commit crime) before those acts have been committed. Reduced crime as a source of benefits undoubtedly would be significantly larger for programs aimed at persons with previous "records" than for those without.

to prison can be employed productively. But this source of benefits has already been measured by participants' earnings. No estimate has been made for income lost by others resulting from bodily injury, or losses from property damage; both sources of benefits when crime is reduced. Savings in crime control costs as crime is reduced also have not been measured.

Economic benefits resulting from better health have largely already been measured. If better health results in decreased absenteeism from work, this is reflected in earnings. Savings in the form of reduced medical care costs are redistributions of income from society's viewpoint. When income redistribution is an important goal, however (or when private benefit-cost ratios are calculated), this source of savings is relevant.

The intergeneration effect has been estimated by Swift and Weisbrod.[12] Their data, summarized in Table 6-5, suggest that a parent who receives some high school education increases the present value of his child's lifetime increased earnings by about $550 at a 5 percent discount rate and about $90 at an 8 percent discount rate. Completing high school increases these figures to $1,000 and $160, respectively. Increasing the discount rate to 10 percent would wipe out most gains from intergeneration effects. Consequently, depending on what is considered to be the appropriate discount rate, intergeneration effects may be an important source of benefits.

Carroll and Ihnen have estimated the value of some nonwage benefits accruing to junior college graduates.[13] Annual value to these persons of lower required overtime, longer paid vacations and more paid holidays was put at $440. This gain is sizable and would substantially alter any benefit-cost ratios in which it was included.[d] While values of other nonwage gains were not estimated by Carroll and Ihnen, gains from such things as employer-paid benefits could be estimated. Failure of cost-benefit studies to include these benefits probably results from the methodology commonly used to collect wage data — questionnaires.[e]

Increased productivity of other resources has been neglected, and the importance of this benefit is unknown. Part of this benefit, however, is reflected back into wage increases for trainees; increases that are measured in normal analysis.[f]

Consumption value of training and education likewise has been left unmeasured. The importance of this factor is unknown.

Benefits to society of improved citizenship probably defy measurement.

---

[d]For example, the present value of a $440 annual stream of income using a 10 percent discount rate and a ten-year time horizon is $2,780. Combined with the already calculated earnings benefits, this amount would increase benefit-cost ratios for vocational education in Worcester post-secondary institutions by over 50 percent, and those in Gastonia by over 30 percent.

[e]Respondents usually are unable to supply dependable information of this sort. Cost considerations probably restrict researchers from getting this information from employers.

[f]Most intermediate-level economic theory texts explain why this is so.

Table 6-5

Present Value of Male Child's Increased Earnings Resulting From Further Education of Parent[a]

Increment to Parent's Education	Present Value of Child's Increased Earnings	
	5 Percent Discount Rate	8 Percent Discount Rate
Some High School	$ 550	$ 90
Completing High School	1,000	160
Some College	591	95

Source: Calculated from W. J. Swift and B. A. Weisbrod, "On the Monetary Value of Education's Intergeneration Benefits," *Journal of Political Economy*, vol. 83 (December 1965), pp. 643–49.

[a]Calculated using a time horizon lasting until child's retirement, and assuming education costs of child are $704 a year.

However, Kaufman et al. found that voting behavior (a kind of index for community spirit) was not affected by vocational education in high school. Whether this is the case in other manpower activities has yet to be seen, but such data could be collected in routine follow-ups of ex-trainees.

Personal satisfaction of succeeding in a selected occupation is another nebulous benefit. A good portion of it is already reflected in increased earnings that come with being successful. Furthermore, vocational education in high school may not give persons large benefits from this source. Kaufman found that an unexpectedly low percentage of vocational high school graduates was able to find employment in selected occupations, and that vocational graduates were no more satisfied with their first jobs than were nonvocational graduates.[14]

Value of options created by participating in manpower programs may be large, but to the extent these options are exercised, most of this value is already measured by earnings. The satisfaction one gets merely from having options available is not measured.

Value of income redistribution is a social decision. There is no way for cost-benefit analysis to determine such a value independently. Myrick Freeman has developed a framework for integrating the value of income redistribution into the benefit calculation.[15] It involves attaching arithmetic weights to income gains which vary with the absolute incomes achieved by manpower program participants. As noted above, officials first must indicate what value they wish placed on income redistribution.

Of the claimed "unmeasured" benefits accruing from manpower programs, we have seen that many of the benefits of decreased crime, improved health, wider options, personal satisfaction of succeeding, and increased productivity of other resources are already included in earnings. Three other sources of benefits – decreased property loss from crime, intergeneration effects and benefits of improved citizenship — may not be very large. Nonwage benefits may be large, but most are readily susceptible to measurement. Value of income redistribution has not been measured, but a methodology exists for integrating it into the calculation as soon as its relative importance is specified. The remaining item — consumption value of the training — is not measured; and it is not clear how it should be measured.

Thus, cost-benefit analysis may not ignore as many benefits as often claimed. Some ignored benefits are not significant relative to those measured. Other are readily measurable, and are not ignored because of a basic inadequacy cost-benefit analysis, but simply because available data have not been collected. If the relative size of unmeasured benefits do not vary widely among different broad programs, the ranking of these programs by benefit-cost ratios which exclude them will not differ much from a ranking which includes them. Decisions based on either set of ratios will be "correct."[g]

Even if unmeasured benefits do vary widely among programs (and thus reduce our confidence in a ranking of ratios when they are excluded), their variance among participants *within* a given program normally will be substantially less because of the greater homogeneity of participants. Thus even the presence of large and varying unmeasured benefits among programs does not prevent use of benefit-cost ratios for internal management of programs.

Conclusion

Cost-benefit studies have been made of manpower programs operating under a number of different settings serving many different groups. Most numerous are studies of institutional training conducted under ARA and MDTA. Without exception, these training programs were seen to yield benefit-cost ratios greater than one. Likewise, cost-benefit studies of vocational rehabilitation, vocational education in vocational high schools and in post–high school institutions; of institutional and OJT programs sponsored by BIA; and of NYC and Job Corps all resulted in benefit-cost ratios exceeding one. Only dropout-prevention programs in high school achieved a ratio less than one.

Vocational rehabilitation appears to yield the highest benefit-cost ratios (9–25), followed by programs involving vocational education in vocational high schools (10.1), OJT (5.0), out-of-school institutional retraining programs (4.7), post-secondary vocational education (1.5–4.2), Job Corps (1.5), and dropout-prevention programs (0.6). Dangers of making such a ranking are recognized, but differences in the ratios between the first four types of programs

---

[g]This would not be true if ignoring those extra benefits results in a ratio less than one, and including them increases the ratio to greater than one. Of all the manpower programs examined in this paper, only dropout-prevention programs might be affected by this consideration.

ranked above and the next three are sizable. Some confidence may be attached to the conclusion that vocational rehabilitation, on-the-job training, high school vocational education and out-of-school retraining programs are more "efficient" means of increasing persons' incomes than post-secondary vocational education, Job Corps and dropout-prevention programs. But neither most of those conducting cost-benefit studies nor this writer are willing to recommend that manpower training approaches be redirected toward programs with higher benefit-cost ratios unless it can be shown that such redirection is consistent with national priorities. For example, it is possible that Job Corps serves a unique group of persons which other current programs are unable to aid. Discussions by Glass, and by Walther and Magnusson indicate that NYC is not a good substitute for Job Corps. Eliminating Job Corps might leave a group of disadvantaged with no program suited to their needs. Another example: even though vocational education in high school appeared more efficient than vocational education in post-secondary schools, the elimination of vocational education following high school would place great constraints on options available to high school graduates and could result in even greater inefficiencies. Additionally, the implied expansion of high school vocational education could well reduce its relatively high benefit-cost ratio. Clearly enlightened decisions to alter the composition of manpower programs can be made only after a great number of factors have been considered in light of a well-defined set of social and economic priorities.

Comparisons of manpower programs are hindered by economists' failure to agree on a common methodology for conducting cost-benefit research, the existence of unmeasured benefits and costs, the absence of good cost data, and an insufficient economic commitment to conduct cost-benefit analysis as reflected in the relatively small number of studies that have been made.[h] Whatever their sources, however, deficiencies in cost-benefit analysis appear to be minimized when the analysis is directed at the internal operation of programs. It is in this direction that cost-benefit analysis particularly needs to be developed.

---

[h]Although few cost-benefit studies have been performed, analysis of one kind or another accompanies most manpower programs; and a large number of Research and Demonstration, and Experimental and Demonstration projects have been conducted under Manpower Acts. Evaluation is an integral part of these projects.

Notes

Notes to Chapter 1

1. U.S. Department of Labor, *Manpower Report of the President* (Washington, D.C.: G.P.O., 1970), p. 70.
2. *Manpower Report*, 1970.
3. William R. Dymond, "The Role of Benefit/Cost Analysis in Formulating Manpower Policy," *Cost-Benefit Analysis of Manpower Policies: Proceedings of a North American Conference*, ed. G. G. Somers and W. D. Wood (Ontario: Industrial Relations Centre, Queen's University at Kingston, 1969), p. 50.
4. Glen G. Cain and Robinson G. Hollister, "Evaluating Manpower Programs for the Disadvantaged," *Ibid.*, pp. 149–150.
5. Peter H. Rossi, "Boobytraps and Pitfalls in the Evaluation of Social Action Programs," *Proceedings of the Social Statistics Section* (Washington, D.C.: American Statistics Assn., 1966), p. 129.
6. Cain and Hollister, "Evaluating Manpower Programs."
7. Bruce F. Davie, "Benefit/Cost Analysis of Vocational Education: A Survey," *Occupational Education: Planning and Programming*, ed. Arnold Kotz, Vol. II (Menlo Park, Calif.: Stanford Research Institute, September, 1967).
8. Robert A. Parnes, "Discussion," *Cost-Benefit Analysis of Manpower Policies*, p. 222; and Davie, "Using Benefit-Cost Analysis in Planning and Evaluating Vocational Education," prepared for David S. Bushnell, Director, Division of Adult and Vocational Research, Bureau of Research, U.S. Office of Education (Washington, D.C.: G.P.O., November 1965), mimeo, p. 10.
9. Jacob J. Kaufman, Teh-wei Hu, Maw Lin Lee, and Ernst W. Stromsdorfer, "A Cost-Effectiveness Study of Vocational Education," *A Comparison of Vocational and Non-vocational Education in Secondary Schools* (University Park, Penn.: Institute for Research on Human Resources, Pennsylvania State University, March 1969) (hereafter cited as "Kaufman").
10. Clyde E. Sullivan and Wallace Mendess, *Restoration of Youth Through Training*, Staten Island Mental Health Society, U. S. Department of Labor, Manpower Administration (Washington, D.C.: G.P.O., 1968).
11. David O. Sewell, "A Critique of Cost-Benefit Analysis of Training," *Monthly Labor Review* 90, no. 9 (September 1967), p. 51.
12. Robert Spiegelman, "Benefit/Cost Analysis of Education," *Occupational Education: Planning and Programming*, p. 352.
13. Sewell, "A Critique of Cost-Benefit Analysis," p. 51.
14. Glen G. Cain and Ernst W. Stromsdorfer, "An Economic Evaluation of Government Retraining Programs in West Virginia," *Retraining the Unemployed*, ed. Gerald G. Somers (Madison, Wis.: University of Wisconsin Press, 1968).
15. Arthur J. Corazzini, "The Decision to Invest in Vocational Education: An

Analysis of Costs and Benefits," *Journal of Human Resources*, vol. 3 (Supp. 1968), pp. 88–120.

16. Michael K. Taussig, "An Economic Analysis of Vocational Education in the New York City High Schools," *Ibid.*, pp. 59–87.

17. See Einar Hardin, "Summary Guide for Effectiveness/Cost and Benefit-Cost Analyses of Vocational and Technical Education," *Cost-Benefit Analysis of Manpower Policies*, pp. 100–103 for a more complete discussion of this problem.

18. Sar A. Levitan, "What's Happening, Baby? — Essential Research for the War on Poverty," *Proceedings of the Social Statistics Section* (Washington, D.C.: American Statistical Assn., 1966), p. 355.

19. Cain and Hollister, "Evaluating Manpower Programs," pp. 125–126.

20. Rossi, "Bobbytraps and Pitfalls."

21. Einar Hardin, "Summary Guide for Effectiveness/Cost and Benefit-Cost Analyses of Vocational and Technical Education," *Occupational Education: Planning and Programming*, p. 106.

22. *Ibid.*

23. *Ibid.*, p. 107.

24. Richard J. Solie, "Employment Effects of Retraining the Unemployed," *Industrial and Labor Relations Review* 21, no. 2 (January 1968), pp. 210–225.

25. Cain and Hollister, "Evaluating Manpower Programs," pp. 126–127.

26. David A. Page, "Retraining Under the Manpower Development Act: A Cost-Benefit Analysis," *Public Policy*, ed. John D. Montgomery and Arthur Smithies, vol. 13 (Cambridge: Harvard University Press, 1964).

27. Earl D. Main, "Nationwide Evaluation of M.D.T.A. Institutional Job Training," *Journal of Human Resources*, 3, no. 2 (Spring 1968), pp. 159-170.

28. Paul Rountree Blume, "An Evaluation of Institutional Vocational Training Received by American Indians Through the Muskogee, Oklahoma Area Office of the Bureau of Indian Affairs," Ph. D. dissertation (Oklahoma State University, 1968).

29. Michael E. Borus, "A Benefit-Cost Analysis of the Economic Effectiveness of Retraining the Unemployed," *Yale Economic Essays* 4, no. 2 (Fall 1964), pp. 371–429.

30. See, for example, Jacob J. Kaufman and Morgan V. Lewis, *The Potential of Vocational Education: Observations and Conclusions* (University Park, Penn.: Institute for Research on Human Resources, Pennsylvania State University, February 1967); and A. B. Carroll and L. A. Ihnen, "Costs and Returns for Two Years of Post-Secondary Technical Schooling," *Journal of Political Economy* 75, no. 6 (December 1967), pp. 862–873.

31. Burton A. Weisbrod, "Preventing High School Dropouts," *Measuring Benefits of Government Investments*, ed. Robert Dorfman (Washington, D.C.: The Brookings Institution, 1965).

32. *Ibid.*

33. Ernst W. Stromsdorfer, "Economic Benefits and Criteria for Investment in Vocational and Technical Education," *Occupational Education: Planning and Programming*, p. 344.

34. Robert S. Goldfarb, "The Evaluation of Government Programs: The Case of New Haven's Manpower Training Activities," *Yale Economic Essays* 9, no. 2 (Fall 1969), pp. 59–104.
35. Davie, "Using Benefit-Cost Analysis," p. 10.

Notes to Chapter 2

1. Arthur J. Corazzini, "The Decision to Invest in Vocational Education: An Analysis of Costs and Benefits," *Journal of Human Resources*, Vol. 3 (Supp. 1968), pp. 88–120.
2. *Ibid.*, table 3, p. 99.
3. *Ibid.*, p. 120.
4. *Ibid.*, pp. 108–109.
5. Max U. Eninger, *The Process and Product of T. & I. High School Level Vocational Education in the United States: The Product* (Pittsburgh: American Institutes for Research, 1965).
6. Jacob J. Kaufman, Teh-wei Hu, Maw Lin Lee, and Ernst W. Stromsdorfer, "A Cost-Effectiveness Study of Vocational Education," *A Comparison of Vocational and Non-vocational Education in Secondary Schools* (University Park, Penn.: Institute for Research on Human Resources, Pennsylvania State University, March 1969), (hereafter cited as "Kaufman et al.").
7. *Ibid.*, pp. 147–196.
8. *Ibid.*, pp. 237–238.
9. Jacob J. Kaufman and Morgan V. Lewis, *The Potential of Vocational Education: Observations and Conclusions* (University Park, Penn: Institute for Research on Human Resources, Pennsylvania State University, 1968), (hereafter cited as "Kaufman").
10. *Ibid.*, pp. 105–106.
11. *Ibid.*, pp. 108–109.
12. *Ibid.*, table 46, p. 90.
13. *Ibid.*, p. 129.
14. *Ibid.*, tables 51 and 52, pp. 96–97.
15. *Ibid.*, table 55, p. 99.
16. *Ibid.*, pp. 116–117.
17. Michael K. Taussig, "An Economic Analysis of Vocational Education in the New York City High Schools," *Journal of Human Resources* 3 (Supp. 1968), pp. 59–87.
18. Corazzini, "The Decision to Invest"; Kaufman et al.; and Kaufman.
19. Taussig, p. 64.
20. *Ibid.*, p. 79.
21. *Ibid.*, pp. 79–80.
22. *Ibid.*, p. 71.
23. *Ibid.*, p. 75.
24. *Ibid.*, p. 77.
25. *Ibid.*, p. 76.

26. *Ibid.*, pp. 86–87.
27. *Ibid.*, p. 82.
28. *Ibid.*, pp. 84–85.
29. Corazzini, "The Decision to Invest."
30. Max U. Eninger, *The Process and Product of T. & I. High School Level Vocational Education in the United States: The Product* (Pittsburgh: American Institutes for Research, 1965).
31. *Ibid.*, table 77, p. 5–38.
32. Chester J. Swanson, *Leadership Role, Functions, Procedures and Administration of Vocational-Technical Education Agencies at the State Level* vol. 3, *Program-Cost Analyses of Vocational-Technical Education in a Junior College and in a Unified School District* (Berkeley, Calif.: School of Education, University of California, March 1969).

Notes to Chapter 3

1. Arthur J. Corazzini, "When Should Vocational Education Begin?" *Journal of Human Resources* 2, no. 1 (Winter 1967), pp. 41–50.
 2. Adger B. Carroll and Loren A. Ihnen, "Costs and Returns for Two Years of Post-Secondary Technical Schooling," *Journal of Political Economy* 75, no. 6 (December 1967), pp. 862–873.
 3. Corazzini, "When Should Vocational Education Begin?", p. 45.
 4. *Ibid.*, pp. 45–46.
 5. *Ibid.*, p 46.
 6. *Ibid.*, p. 48.
 7. Max U. Eninger, *The Process and Product of T. & I. High School Level Vocational Education in the United States: The Product* (Pittsburgh, American Institutes for Research, 1965).
 8. Corazzini, "When Should Vocational Education Begin?", p. 49.
 9. *Ibid.*
10. Carroll and Ihnen, pp. 14–15.
11. *Ibid.*, pp. 16–19.
12. *Ibid.*, table 7, p. 41.
13. *Ibid.*, pp. 28–32.
14. *Ibid.*, p. 31.
15. *Ibid.*, p. 25.
16. *Ibid.*, pp. 25–28.
17. Corazzini, "When Should Vocational Education Begin?"; and Corazzini, "The Decision to Invest in Vocational Education: An Analysis of Costs and Benefits," *Journal of Human Resources* 3 (Supp. 1968), pp. 88–120.

Notes to Chapter 4

1. Garth L. Mangum, *Contributions and Costs of Manpower Development and Training*, Policy Papers in Human Resources and Industrial Relations, no. 5, University of Michigan, Wayne State University and the National

Manpower Policy Task Force (Washington, D.C.: The Institute of Labor and Industrial Relations, December 1967).

2. Dale Bruce Rasmussen, "Determinants of Rates of Return to Investment in On-the-Job Training," Ph. D. dissertation (Southern Methodist University, 1969).

3. Benjamin Michael Trooboff, "Employment Experience After MDTA Training: A Study of the Relationships Between Selected Training Characteristics and Post-Training Employment Experience," Ph. D. dissertation (Georgia State College, 1968).

4. Michael E. Borus, "A Benefit-Cost Analysis of the Economic Effectiveness of Retraining the Unemployed," *Yale Economic Essays* 4, no. 2 (Fall 1964), pp. 371–429.

5. Glen G. Cain and Ernst W. Stromsdorfer, "An Economic Evaluation of the Government Retraining Programs in West Virginia," *Retraining the Unemployed*, ed. Gerald G. Somers (Madison Wis.: University of Wisconsin Press, 1968).

6. Einar Hardin and Michael E. Borus, *Economic Benefits and Costs of Retraining* (Lexington, Mass.: D. C. Heath and Company, 1971).

7. David A. Page, "Retraining Under the Manpower Development Act: A Cost-Benefit Analysis," *Public Policy*, ed. John D. Montgomery and Arthur Smithies, vol. 3 (Cambridge: Harvard University Press, 1964).

8. Borus, "Benefit-Cost Analysis."

9. *Ibid.*, pp. 395–396.

10. *Ibid.*, p. 405.

11. *Ibid.*, p. 399.

12. *Ibid.*, p. 375.

13. *Ibid.*, p. 399.

14. *Ibid.*, pp. 399–400.

15. Einar Hardin, "Benefit-Cost Analysis of Occupational Training Programs: A Comparison of Recent Studies," *Cost-Benefit Analysis of Manpower Policies, Proceedings of a North American Conference*, ed. G. G. Somers and W. D. Wood (Ontario: Industrial Relations Centre, Queen's University at Kingston, 1969), table 1, p. 113.

16. Michael E. Borus, "Time Trends in the Benefits From Retraining in Connecticut," *Proceedings of the Twentieth Annual Winter Meeting of the Industrial Relations Research Association* (Madison, Wisconsin, 1967).

17. *Ibid.*, p. 41.

18. *Ibid.*, p. 45.

19. *Ibid.*, p. 46.

20. *Ibid.*, pp. 421–422.

21. Other studies do not reach this conclusion. For example, Cain and Stromsdorfer "An Economic Evaluation"; and Benjamin Michael Trooboff, "Employment Experience After MDTA Training: A Study of the Relationships Between Selected Training Characteristics and Post-Training Employment Experience," Ph.D. dissertation, (Georgia State College, 1968).

22. Borus, "Time Trends," p. 46.

23. Michael K. Taussig, "An Economic Analysis of Vocational Education in the New York City High Schools," *Journal of Human Resources* 3 (Supp. 1968), pp. 59–87.
24. Cain and Stromsdorfer, "An Economic Evaluation," pp. 302–303.
25. *Ibid.*, p. 327.
26. Harold A. Gibbard and Gerald G. Somers, "Government Retraining of the Unemployed in West Virginia," *Retraining the Unemployed*, p. 29.
27. Cain and Stromsdorfer, "An Economic Evaluation," table IX.2, p. 313.
28. *Ibid.*, p. 320.
29. *Ibid.*, p. 319.
30. *Ibid.*, p. 318.
31. Gerald G. Somers and Graeme H. McKechnie, "Vocational Retraining Programs for the Unemployed," *Proceedings of the Industrial Relations Research Association* (December 1967), table 3, p. 33.
32. *Ibid.*, p. 34.
33. Adger B. Carroll and Loren A. Ihnen, "Costs and Returns for Two Years of Post-Secondary Technical Schooling," *Journal of Political Economy* 75, no. 6 (December 1967), pp. 862–873; and Ernst W. Stromsdorfer, "Determinants of Economic Success in Retraining the Unemployed," *Journal of Human Resources*, 3 (Spring 1968), pp. 139–158.
34. Gerald G. Somers and Ernst W. Stromsdorfer, "A Benefit-Cost Analysis of Manpower Retraining," *Proceedings of the Industrial Relations Research Association*, (Winter meeting 1964), p. 178.
35. Cain and Stromsdorfer, "An Economic Evaluation," p. 310.
36. Page, "Retraining Under the MDA," p. 266.
37. *Ibid.*, exhibit 1, p. 261.
38. *Ibid.*, pp. 261–262.
39. *Ibid.*, p. 263.
40. Borus, "Time Trends."
41. Page, "Retraining Under the MDA," p. 267.
42. Richard J. Solie, "Employment Effects of Retraining the Unemployed," *Industrial and Labor Relations Review* 21, no. 2 (January 1968), pp. 210–225.
43. *Ibid.*, pp. 221–222.
44. *Ibid.*, pp. 222–223.
45. *Ibid.*, table 4, p. 218.
46. *Ibid.*, p. 213.
47. *Ibid.*, p. 214.
48. Borus, "Benefit-Cost Analysis" and "Time Trends."
49. Svetozar Pejovich and William Sullivan, "The Role of Technical Schools in Improving the Skills and Earnings of Rural Manpower, a Case Study," Final Report to the Office of Manpower Policy, Evaluation and Research, U. S. Dept. of Labor (Washington, D.C.: G.P.O., September 1966).
50. U. S. Department of Labor, *Cost Effectiveness Analysis of On-the-Job and Institutional Training Courses*, Office of Manpower Policy, Evaluation and Research (Washington, D.C.: Planning Research Corporation, 1967).
51. Earl D. Main, "Nationwide Evaluation of M.D.T.A. Institutional Job

Training," *Journal of Human Resources* 3, no. 2 (Spring 1968): pp. 159–170.

52. Hardin and Borus, *Economic Benefits*, p. 1.

53. *Ibid.*, table 5:2, p. 94.

54. *Ibid.*, pp. 122–123.

55. *Ibid.*, calculated from table 7:2, p. 152 and table 4:2, p. 82.

56. *Ibid.*, pp. 330–334.

57. Pejovich and Sullivan, "Role of Technical Schools," p. 5.

58. *Ibid.*, p. 3.

59. *Ibid.*, p. 19.

60. Main, "Nationwide Evaluation of M.D.T.A.," p. 165.

61. *Ibid.*, p. 168.

62. U. S. Department of Labor, *Cost Effectiveness Analysis of On-the-Job and Institutional Training Courses.*

63. H. H. London, *How Fare MDTA Ex-Trainees? An Eighteen Months Follow-up Study of Five Hundred Such Persons* (Columbia, Mo.: Missouri University, December 1967).

64. *Ibid.*, p. 4.

65. London, *How Fare MDTA Ex-Trainees?* pp. 7–17.

66. Trooboff, "Employment Experience After MDTA Training."

67. Regis H. Walther and Margaret L. Magnusson, *A Retrospective Study of the Effectiveness of Out of School Neighborhood Youth Corps Programs in Four Urban Sites* (Washington, D.C.: George Washington University, Social Research Group, November, 1967), in their study of NYC in several southern cities indicated that black females did better than other groups. This supports the above supposition. An identical conclusion is reached by John Franklin Glass, "Organization Dilemmas in the War on Poverty: Contrasts in the Neighborhood Youth Corps," Ph.D. dissertation, (University of California, 1968), in his study of the Neighborhood Youth Corps.

68. Jack Chernick, Bernard P. Indik, and Roger Craig, *The Selection of Trainees Under MDTA*, Report prepared for the Office of Manpower Policy, Evaluation and Research, U. S. Department of Labor (New Brunswick, N. J.: Institute of Management and Labor Relations, Rutgers State University, 1966).

69. *Ibid.*, p. 98.

70. *Ibid.*, p. 106.

71. Cain and Stromsdorfer, "An Economic Evaluation of Government Retraining Programs in West Virginia."

72. Borus, "A Benefit-Cost Analysis."

73. U. S. Department of Labor, *Manpower Report of the President* (Washington, D.C.: GPO, 1969), table F-5, p. 241.

Notes to Chapter 5

1. Dale Bruce Rasmussen, "Determinants of Rates of Return to Investment in On-the-Job Training," Ph.D. dissertation (Southern Methodist University, 1969).

2. Loren C. Scott, "The Economic Effectiveness of On-the-Job Training: The Experience of the Bureau of Indian Affairs in Oklahoma," *Industrial and Labor Relations Review* 23, no. 2 (January 1970), pp. 220–236.
3. Burton A. Weisbrod, "Preventing High School Dropouts," *Measuring Benefits of Government Investments*, ed. Robert Dorfman (Washington, D.C.: The Brookings Institution, 1965).
4. Michael E. Borus, John P. Brennan, and Sidney Rosen, "A Benefit-Cost Analysis of the Neighborhood Youth Corps: The Out of School Program in Indiana," *Journal of Human Resources*, 5, no. 2 (Spring 1970), pp. 139–159.
5. *Ibid.*, p. 141.
6. *Ibid.*, pp. 142–143.
7. *Ibid.*, p. 142.
8. *Ibid.*, p. 147.
9. *Ibid.*, pp. 158–159
10. Regis H. Walther and Margaret L. Magnusson, *A Retrospective Study of the Effectiveness of Out of School Neighborhood Youth Corps Programs in Four Urban Sites* (Washington, D.C.: George Washington University, Social Research Group, November 1967).
11. *Ibid.*, tables 4 and 5, p. 247.
12. *Ibid.*, p. 61.
13. *Ibid.*, table 25, p. 50.
14. *Ibid.*, table 26, p. 51.
15. *Ibid.*, table 4, p. 24; and table 5, p. 30.
16. *Ibid.*, p. 6.
17. *Ibid.*, table 8, p. 29a; and table 28, p. 55.
18. *Ibid.*, pp. 32–52.
19. *Ibid.*, p. 52.
20. *Ibid.*, pp. 64–65.
21. *Ibid.*, pp. 63–64.
22. John Franklin Glass, "Organization Dilemmas in the War on Poverty: Contrasts in the Neighborhood Youth Corps," Ph.D. dissertation (University of California, 1968).
23. *Ibid.*, p. 143.
24. *Ibid.*
25. Glass, "Organization Dilemmas," table 1, p. 136.
26. Worth Bateman, "An Application of Cost-Benefit Analysis to the Work-Experience Program," *American Economic Review*, 57, no. 2 (May 1967), p. 81.
27. *Ibid.*, pp. 85–86.
28. *Ibid.*, pp. 89–90.
29. *Ibid.*
30. *Ibid.*, table 1, p. 89.
31. Rasmussen, "Determinants of Rates of Return to Investment," p. 29.
32. *Ibid.*, pp. 75–76.
33. *Ibid.*, pp. 96–102.

34. Graeme M. Taylor, "Office of Economic Opportunity: Evaluation of Training Programs," *Program Budgeting and Benefit-Cost Analysis,* ed. Harley H. Hinrichs and Graeme M. Taylor (Pacific Palisades, Calif.: Goodyear Publishing Company, 1969), p. 318.
35. *Ibid.,* exhibit 8, p. 328.
36. Scott, "Economic Effectiveness," p. 220.
37. *Ibid.,* pp. 222–223.
38. *Ibid.,* pp. 225–227.
39. *Ibid.,* pp. 233–234.
40. *Ibid.,* table 2, p. 224.
41. *Ibid.,* p. 222.
42. *Ibid.,* p. 233.
43. For further discussions of this study, see Steven L. Barsby, "The Economic Effectiveness of On-the-Job Training: The Experience of the Bureau of Indian Affairs in Oklahoma: Comment," *Industrial and Labor Relations Review* 24, no. 2 (January 1971), pp. 265–268; and Loren C. Scott, "Reply," *Ibid.,* pp. 268–269.
44. Paul Rountree Blume, "An Evaluation of Institutional Vocational Training Received by American Indians Through the Muskogee, Oklahoma Area Office of the Bureau of Indian Affairs," Ph. D. dissertation (Oklahoma State University, 1968).
45. *Ibid.,* p. 166.
46. *Ibid.,* p. 183.
47. *Ibid.,* p. 191.
48. *Ibid.,* p. 147.
49. *Ibid.,* pp. 128–129.
50. *Ibid.,* p. 120.
51. *Ibid.,* table 6-3, p. 176.
52. *Ibid.,* p. 192.
53. Weisbrod, "Preventing High School Dropouts."
54. *Ibid.,* p. 140.
55. *Ibid.,* p. 144.
56. *Ibid.,* p. 142.
57. Thomas I. Ribich, *Education and Poverty* (Washington, D.C.: The Brookings Institution, 1968), pp. 53–59.
58. Weisbrod, "Preventing High School Dropouts," pp. 135–136.
59. *Ibid.,* p. 133.
60. Ribich, p. 52, f.n.
61. Weisbrod, "Preventing High School Dropouts," p. 60.
62. Arthur J. Corazzini, "The Decision to Invest in Vocational Education: An Analysis of Costs and Benefits," *Journal of Human Resources,* vol. 3 (Supp. 1968), pp. 88–120.
63. Larry Duane Singell, "Economic Opportunity and Juvenile Delinquency: A Case Study of the Detroit Juvenile Labor Market," Ph. D. dissertation (Wayne State University, 1965).
64. *Ibid.,* table 5, p. 92; and pp. 93–97.

65. *Ibid.*, pp. 141–151.
66. Frank Carmen Grella, "An Application of Cost-Benefit Theory and Systems Theory to Vocational Rehabilitation in Connecticut," Ph.D. dissertation (University of Massachusetts, 1969).
67. *Ibid.*, p. 156.
68. Sar A. Levitan and Garth L. Mangum, *Federal Training and Work Programs in the Sixties* (Ann Arbor, Michigan: Institute of Labor and Industrial Relations, University of Michigan, 1969), pp. 322–323.
69. *Ibid.*, p. 323.

Notes to Chapter 6

1. Morris Ullman, Bernard Michael, and Marc Matland, "The Needs for Vocational Education Data," *Proceedings of the Social Statistics Section* (Washington, D.C.: American Statistics Association, 1968), p. 140.
2. Michael E. Borus, John P. Brennan, and Sidney Rosen, "A Benefit-Cost Analysis of the Neighborhood Youth Corps: The Out-of-School Program in Indiana," *Journal of Human Resources* vol. 5, no. 2 (Spring 1970), pp. 139–159.
3. Einar Hardin and Michael E. Borus, *The Economic Benefits and Costs of Retraining* (Lexington, Mass.: D. C. Heath and Company, 1971).
4. Burton A. Weisbrod, "Preventing High School Dropouts," *Measuring Benefits of Government Investments*, ed. Robert Dorfman (Washington, D.C.: The Brookings Institution, 1965).
5. Larry Duane Singell, "Economic Opportunity and Juvenile Delinquency: A Case Study of the Detroit Juvenile Labor Market," Ph.D. dissertation (Wayne State University, 1965).
6. Loren C. Scott, "The Economic Effectiveness of On-the-Job Training: The Experience of the Bureau of Indian Affairs in Oklahoma," *Industrial and Labor Relations Review* 23, no. 2 (January, 1970), pp. 220–236.
7. Paul Rountree Blume, "An Evaluation of Institutional Vocational Training Received by American Indians Through the Muskogee, Oklahoma Area Office of the Bureau of Indian Affairs," Ph. D. dissertation (Oklahoma State University, 1968).
8. Earl D. Main, "Nationwide Evaluation of M.D.T.A. Institutional Job Training," *Journal of Human Resources* 3, no. 2 (Spring 1968), pp. 159–170.
9. Arthur J. Corazzini, "When Should Vocational Education Begin?" *Journal of Human Resources* 2, no. 1 (Winter, 1967), pp. 41–50.
10. Michael K. Taussig, "An Economic Analysis of Vocational Education in the New York City High Schools," *Journal of Human Resources*, vol. 3 (Supp. 1968), pp. 59–87.
11. Jacob J. Kaufman, Teh-wei Hu, Maw Lin Lee, and Ernst W. Stromsdorfer, "A Cost-Effectiveness Study of Vocational Education," *A Comparison of Vocational and Non-vocational Education in Secondary Schools*

(University Park, Penn.: Institute for Research on Human Resources, Pennsylvania State University, March 1969).

12. W. J. Swift and Burton A. Weisbrod, "On the Monetary Value of Education's Integeneration Benefits," *Journal of Political Economy*, vol. 83 (December 1965), pp. 643–649.

13. Adger B. Carroll and Loren A. Ihnen, "Costs and Returns for Two Years of Post-Secondary Technical Schooling," *Journal of Political Economy* 75, no. 6 (December 1967), pp. 862–873.

14. Jacob J. Kaufman and Morgan V. Lewis, *The Potential of Vocational Education: Observations and Conclusions* (University Park, Penn.: Institute for Research on Human Resources, Pennsylvania State University, 1968).

15. Myrick A. Freeman, III, "Project Design and Evaluation With Multiple Objectives," *The Analysis and Evaluation of Public Expenditures: The PPB System*, vol. 1, Joint Economic Committee (Washington, D.C., 1969).

Bibliography

Arrow, Kenneth J. "The Social Discount Rate." *Cost-Benefit Analysis of Manpower Policies. Proceedings of a North American Conference.* G. G. Somers and W. D. Wood, eds. Ontario: Industrial Relations Centre, Queen's University at Kingston, 1969.

Barsby, Steven L. *An Analysis of Data Requirements for Cost-Effectiveness and Cost-Benefit Analysis.* Report to the Arizona Research Coordinating Unit, Arizona. Jan. 1970. Mimeo.

——. "The Economic Effectiveness of On-the-Job Training: The Experience of the Bureau of Indian Affairs in Oklahoma: Comment." *Industrial and Labor Relations Review* 24, No. 2 (January, 1971), pp. 265–268.

Bateman, Worth. "An Application of Cost-Benefit Analysis to the Work Experience Program." *American Economics Association Proceedings.* Menasha, Wisconsin, 1966; Also *American Economic Review* 62, No. 2 (May 1967), pp. 80–90.

Baumol, William J. "On the Discount Rate for Public Expenditures." *The Analysis and Evaluation of Public Expenditures: The PPB System.* Vol.1. Joint Economic Committee. Washington, D.C.: G.P.O., 1969.

Besen, Stanley M.; Fechter, Alan E.; and Fisher, Anthony C. "Cost-Effectiveness Analysis for the 'War on Poverty.' " *Cost-Effectiveness Analysis, New Approaches in Decision-Making.* Thomas A. Goldman, ed. New York: Frederick A. Praeger, 1967.

Blume, Paul Rountree. "An Evaluation of Institutional Vocational Training Received by American Indians Through the Muskogee, Oklahoma Area Office of the Bureau of Indian Affairs." Ph.D. dissertation. Oklahoma State University, 1968.

Borus, Michael E. "A Benefit-Cost Analysis of the Economic Effectiveness of Retraining the Unemployed." *Yale Economic Essays* 4, no. 2 (Fall 1964), pp. 371–429.

——. "Time Trends in the Benefits From Retraining in Connecticut." *Proceedings of the Twentieth Annual Winter Meeting of the Industrial Relations Research Association.* Madison, Wisconsin, 1967.

——, Brennan, John P.; and Rosen, Sidney. "A Benefit-Cost Analysis of the Neighborhood Youth Corps: The Out-of-School Program in Indiana." *The Journal of Human Resources* 5, No. 2 (Spring 1970), pp. 139–159.

Cain, Glen G., and Hollister, Robinson G. "Evaluating Manpower Programs for the Disadvantaged." *Cost-Benefit Analysis of Manpower Policies. Proceedings of a North American Conference.* G. G. Somers and W. D. Wood, eds. Ontario: Industrial Relations Centre, Queen's University at Kingston, 1969.

—— and Stromsdorfer, Ernst W. "An Economic Evaluation of Government Retraining Programs in West Virginia." *Retraining the Unemployed.* Gerald G. Somers, ed. Madison, Wis.: University of Wisconsin Press, 1968.

Carroll, Adger B., and Ihnen, Loren A. "Costs and Returns for Two Years of Post-Secondary Technical Schooling." *Journal of Political Economy* 75,

No. 6 (December 1967), pp. 862–873. Also in *Costs and Returns of Technical Education: A Pilot Study*. Department of Economics, North Carolina State University at Raleigh. Prepared for Office of Manpower Policy, Evaluation and Research. U. S. Department of Labor. Washington, D.C., 1966.

Chamberlain, Neil W. "Some Further Thoughts on the Concept of Human Capital." *Cost-Benefit Analysis of Manpower Policies. Proceedings of a North American Conference*. G. G. Somers and W. D. Wood, eds. Ontario: Industrial Relations Centre, Queen's University at Kingston, 1969.

Chase, Samuel B., ed. *Problems in Public Expenditure Analysis*. Washington, D.C.: The Brookings Institution, 1968.

Chernick, Jack; Indik, Bernard P.; and Craig, Roger. *The Selection of Trainees Under MDTA*. Report prepared for the Office of Manpower Policy, Evaluation and Research. U. S. Department of Labor. New Brunswick, New Jersey: Institute of Management and Labor Relations, Rutgers State University, 1966.

Chesler, Herbert A. "The Retraining Decision in Massachusetts: Theory and Practice." *Retraining the Unemployed*. G. G. Somers, ed. Madison, Wis.: University of Wisconsin Press, 1968.

Corazzini, Arthur J. "The Decision to Invest in Vocational Education: An Analysis of Costs and Benefits." *Journal of Human Resources* 3, (Supplement 1968), pp. 88–120.

——. "When Should Vocational Education Begin?" *Journal of Human Resources* 2, No. 1 (Winter 1967), pp. 41–50.

Davie, Bruce F. "Benefit/Cost Analysis of Vocational Education: A Survey." *Occupational Education: Planning and Programming*. Arnold Kotz, ed. vol. 2. Menlo Park, Calif.: Stanford Research Institute. September, 1967.

——. "Using Benefit-Cost Analysis in Planning and Evaluating Vocational Education." Prepared for David S. Bushnell, Director. Division of Adult and Vocational Research. Bureau of Research. U. S. Office of Education. Washington, D.C., November, 1965. Mimeo.

Dymond, William R. "The Role of Benefit/Cost Analysis in Formulating Manpower Policy." *Cost-Benefit Analysis of Manpower Policies. Proceedings of a North American Conference*. G. G. Somers and W. D. Wood, eds. Ontario: Industrial Relations Centre, Queen's University at Kingston, 1969.

Enninger, Max. U. *The Process and Product of T. & I. High School Level Vocational Education in the United States: The Product*. Pittsburgh: American Institutes for Research, 1965.

Freeman, Myrick A., III. "Project Design and Evaluation With Multiple Objectives." *The Analysis and Evaluation of Public Expenditures: The PPB System*. Vol. 1, Joint Economic Committee. Washington, D.C.: G.P.O., 1969.

Gibbard, Harold A., and Somers, Gerald G. "Government Retraining of the Unemployed in West Virginia." *Retraining the Unemployed*. Gerald G. Somers, ed. Madison, Wis.: University of Wisconsin Press, 1968.

Glass, John Franklin. "Organization Dilemmas in the War on Poverty: Contrasts in the Neighborhood Youth Corps." Ph.D. dissertation, University of California, 1968.

Goldfarb, Robert S. "The Evaluation of Government Programs: The Case of New Haven's Manpower Training Activities." *Yale Economic Essays* 9, No. 2 (Fall 1969), pp. 59–104.

Goldman, T., ed. *Cost-Effectiveness Analysis*. Washington Operations Research Council. New York: Frederick A. Praeger, 1967.

Grella, Frank Carmen. "An Application of Cost-Benefit Theory and Systems Theory to Vocational Rehabilitation in Connecticut." Ph.D. dissertation, University of Massachusetts, 1969.

Grosse, Robert. "The Program Budget: Its Value to Education at Federal, State, and Local Levels." *Occupational Education: Planning and Programming*. Arnold Kotz, ed. vol. 2. Menlo Park, Calif.: Stanford Research Institute (September, 1967), 229–248.

Harberger, Arnold C., and Reuber, Grant L. "Discussion: Professor Arrow on the Social Discount Rate." *Cost-Benefit Analysis of Manpower Policies. Proceedings of a North American Conference*. G. G. Somers and W. D. Wood, eds. Ontario: Industrial Relations Centre, Queen's University at Kingston, 1969.

Hardin, Einar. "Benefit-Cost Analysis of Occupational Training Programs: A Comparison of Recent Studies." *Cost-Benefit Analysis of Manpower Policies. Proceedings of a North American Conference*. G. G. Somers and W. D. Wood, eds. Ontario: Industrial Relations Centre, Queen's University at Kingston, 1969.

——. "Summary Guide for Effectiveness/Cost and Benefit-Cost Analyses of Vocational and Technical Education." *Occupational Education: Planning and Programming*. Arnold Kotz, ed. vol. 2. Menlo Park, Calif.: Stanford Research Institute (September, 1967), 379–386.

Hardin, Einar, and Borus, Michael E. *The Economic Benefits and Costs of Retraining*. Lexington, Mass.: D. C. Heath and Company, 1971.

——. "An Economic Evaluation of the Retraining Program in Michigan: Methodological Problems of Research." *Proceedings of the Social Statistics Section*. Washington, D.C.: American Statistics Association, 1966.

Hinrichs, Harley H., and Taylor, Graeme M., eds. *Program Budgeting and Benefit-Cost Analysis*. Pacific Palisades, Calif.: Goodyear Publishing Co., 1969.

Hoos, Ida R. *Retraining the Work Force*. Berkeley: University of California Press, 1967.

Horowitz, Morris A., and Herrnstadt, Irwin L. "Manpower and its Education and Training." *Proceedings of the Industrial Relations Research Association*. Dec. 1967.

Jenness, Robert A. "Manpower Mobility Programs." *Cost-Benefit Analysis of Manpower Policies. Proceedings of a North American Conference*. G. G. Somers and W. D. Wood, eds. Ontario: Industrial Relations Centre, Queen's University at Kingston, 1969.

Joint Economic Committee. *The Analysis and Evaluation of Public Expenditures: The PPB System*. A Compendium of Papers. Washington, D.C.: G.P.O., 1969.

Judy, Richard W. "Costs: Theoretical and Methodological Issues." *Cost-Benefit Analysis of Manpower Policies. Proceedings of a North American Conference*. G. G. Somers and W. D. Wood, eds. Ontario: Industrial Relations Centre, Queen's University at Kingston, 1969.

Kaufman, Jacob J., et al. *The Preparation of Youth for Effective Occupa-*

tional Utilization, the Role of the Secondary Schools in the Preparation of Youth for Employment. University Park, Penn.: Institute for Research on Human Resources, Pennsylvania State University, February, 1967.

——; Hu, Teh-wei; Lee, Maw Lin; and Stromsdorfer, Ernst W. "A Cost-Effectiveness Study of Vocational Education." *A Comparison of Vocational and Non-vocational Education in Secondary Schools*. University Park, Penn.: Institute for Research on Human Resources, Pennsylvania State University, March, 1969.

——, and Lewis, Morgan V. *The Potential of Vocational Education: Observations and Conclusions*. University Park, Penn.: Institute for Research on Human Resources, Pennsylvania State University, 1968.

Kotz, Arnold, ed. *Occupational Education: Planning and Programming*. 2 Vols. Menlo Park, Calif.: Stanford Research Institute (September, 1967).

Kraft, Richard H. P. *Cost/Effectiveness Analysis of Vocational-Technical Education Programs*. Tallahassee, Fla.: Department of Educational Administration, Educational Systems and Planning Center, The Florida State University, 1969.

Levine, Abraham S. "Cost-Benefit Analysis of the Work Experience Program." *Welfare in Review* 4, August-September, 1966, pp. 1–9.

Levine, Robert A. "Manpower Programs in the War on Poverty." *Cost-Benefit Analysis of Manpower Policies. Proceedings of a North American Conference*. G. G. Somers and W. D. Wood, eds. Ontario: Industrial Relations Centre, Queen's University at Kingston, 1969.

Levitan, Sar A. "What's Happening, Baby? – Essential Research for the War on Poverty." *Proceedings of the Social Statistics Section*. Washington, D.C.: American Statistical Association, 1966.

——, and Mangum, Garth L. *Federal Training and Work Programs in the Sixties*. Ann Arbor, Mich.: Institute of Labor and Industrial Relations, University of Michigan, 1969.

London, H. H. *How Fare MDTA Ex-Trainees? An Eighteen Months Follow-up Study of Five Hundred Such Persons*. Columbia, Missouri: Missouri University, December, 1967.

Maass, Arthur. "Benefit-Cost Analysis: Its Relevancy to Public Investment Decisions." *Quarterly Journal of Economics* Vol. 79 (May, 1966): 208–226.

Main, Earl D. "Nationwide Evaluation of M.D.T.A. Institutional Job Training." *Journal of Human Resources* Vol. 3, No. 2 (Spring, 1968): 159–170.

Mangum, Garth L. *Contributions and Costs of Manpower Development and Training*. Policy Papers in Human Resources and Industrial Relations, No. 5. University of Michigan, Wayne State University, and the National Manpower Policy Task Force. Washington, D.C.: The Institute of Labor and Industrial Relations, December, 1967.

——. "Determining the Results of Manpower and Antipoverty Programs." *The Analysis and Evaluation of Public Expenditures: The PPB System*. vol 3. Joint Economic Committee. Washington, D.C., 1969.

——. "Evaluating Vocational Education: Problems and Priorities." *Occupational Education: Planning and Programming*. Arnold Kotz, ed. vol. 1. Menlo Park, Calif.: Stanford Research Institute, September, 1967.

———. *MDTA Foundation of Federal Manpower Policy*. Baltimore, Md.:
The Johns Hopkins Press, 1968.

———. "Manpower Programs in the Anti-Poverty Effort."
Examination of the War on Poverty. Staff and Consultant Reports. Prepared
for the Subcommittee on Employment, Manpower and Poverty. United States
Senate. 90th Congress, 1st Sess., August, 1967.

March, Michael S. "Comments on Burton A. Weisbrod, 'Preventing High
School Dropouts'." *Measuring Benefits of Government Investments*. Robert
Dorfman, ed. Washington, D.C.: The Brookings Institution, 1965.

McKechnie, Graeme H. "Discussion." *Cost-Benefit Analysis of Manpower
Policies. Proceedings of a North American Conference*. G. G. Somers and W. D.
Wood, eds. Ontario: Industrial Relations Centre, Queen's University at
Kingston, 1969.

Miller, Herman P. "Comments on Burton A. Weisbrod 'Preventing High
School Dropouts'." *Measuring Benefits of Government Investments*. Robert
Dorfman, ed. Washington, D.C.: The Brookings Institution, 1965.

Mills, Guy H. "Preliminary Phase: Effects of Vocational Training and
Other Factors on Employment Experience." Minneapolis, Minn.: North Star
Research and Development Institute, April, 1966.

Mincer, Jacob. "On-the-Job Training: Costs, Returns and Some Implications." *Journal of Political Economy* Supp. 70 (October, 1962), 50–79.

Page, David A. "Retraining Under the Manpower Development Act:
A Cost-Benefit Analysis." *Public Policy*. John D. Montgomery and Arthur
Smithies, eds. vol. 13. Cambridge: Harvard University Press, 1964.

Parnes, Robert A. "Discussion." *Cost-Benefit Analysis of Manpower
Policies. Proceedings of a North American Conference*. G. G. Somers and W. D.
Wood, eds. Ontario: Industrial Relations Centre, Queen's University at Kingston,
1969.

Pejovich, Svetozar and Sullivan, William. "The Role of Technical Schools
in Improving the Skills and Earnings of Rural Manpower, a Case Study." Final
Report to the Office of Manpower Policy, Evaluation and Research. U.S.
Department of Labor. Washington, D.C.: G.P.O., September, 1966.

Rasmussen, Dale Bruce, "Determinants of Rates of Return to Investment
in On-the-Job Training." Ph.D. dissertation, Southern Methodist University,
1969.

Raynauld, Andre. "Discussion." *Cost-Benefit Analysis of Manpower
Policies. Proceedings of a North American Conference*. G. G. Somers and W. D.
Wood, eds. Ontario: Industrial Relations Centre, Queen's University at Kingston,
1969.

Ribich, Thomas I. *Education and Poverty*. Washington, D.C.: The Brookings
Institution, 1968.

Rossi, Peter H. "Boobytraps and Pitfalls in the Evaluation of Social Action
Programs." *Proceedings of the Social Statistics Section*. Washington, D.C.:
American Statistics Association, 1966.

Schultz, T. W. "Education and Economic Growth." *Social Forces Influenc-
ing American Education*. Chicago: National Society for the Study of Education,
1961.

Scott, Loren C. "The Economic Effectiveness of On-the-Job Training: The Experience of the Bureau of Indian Affairs in Oklahoma." *Industrial and Labor Relations Review* Vol. 23, No. 2 (January, 1970): 220–236.

——. "Reply." *Industrial and Labor Relations Review* Vol. 24, No. 2 (January, 1971): 268–269.

Sewell, David O. "A Critique of Cost-Benefit Analysis of Training." *Monthly Labor Review* Vol. 90, No. 9 (September, 1967): 45–51.

——. "Discussion." *Cost-Benefit Analysis of Manpower Policies. Proceedings of a North American Conference.* G. G. Somers and W. D. Wood, eds. Ontario: Industrial Relations Centre, Queen's University at Kingston, 1969.

Singell, Larry Duane. "Economic Opportunity and Juvenile Delinquency: A Case Study of the Detroit Juvenile Labor Market." Ph.D. dissertation, Wayne State University, 1965.

Solie, Richard J. "Employment Effects of Retraining the Unemployed." *Industrial and Labor Relations Review* Vol. 21, No. 2 (January, 1968): 210–225.

Somers, Gerald G., ed. *Retraining the Unemployed.* Madison, Wis.: The University of Wisconsin Press, 1968.

——. "Training the Unemployed." *In Aid of the Unemployed.* Joseph M. Becker, ed. Baltimore, Md.: Johns Hopkins University Press, 1965.

—— and McKechnie, Graeme H. "Vocational Retraining Programs for the Unemployed." *Proceedings of the Industrial Relations Research Association.* December, 1967.

—— and Stromsdorfer, Ernst W. "A Benefit-Cost Analysis of Manpower Retraining." *Proceedings of the Industrial Relations Research Association.* Winter Meeting, 1964.

—— and Wood, W. D., eds. *Cost-Benefit Analysis of Manpower Policies. Proceedings of a North American Conference.* Ontario: Industrial Relations Centre, Queen's University at Kingston, 1969.

Spiegelman, Robert. "Benefit/Cost Analysis of Education." *Occupational Education: Planning and Programming.* Arnold Kotz, ed. Vol. 2. Menlo Park, Calif.: Stanford Research Institute, September, 1967.

Stromsdorfer, Ernst W. "Determinants of Economic Success in Retraining the Unemployed." *Journal of Human Resources* Vol. 3 (Spring, 1968): 139–158.

——. "Discussion." *Cost-Benefit Analysis of Manpower Policies. Proceedings of a North American Conference.* G. G. Somers and W. D. Wood, eds. Ontario: Industrial Relations Centre, Queen's University at Kingston, 1969.

——. "Economic Benefits and Criteria for Investment in Vocational and Technical Education." *Occupational Education: Planning and Programming.* Arnold Kotz, ed. Vol. 2. Menlo Park, Calif.: Stanford Research Institute, September, 1967.

——; Hu, Teh-wei; and Lee, Maw Lin. "Theoretical and Empirical Problems in the Analysis of the Economic Costs of Vocational Education." *Proceedings of the Social Statistics Section.* Washington, D.C.: American Statistics Association, 1968.

Sullivan, Clyde E. and Mendess, Wallace. *Restoration of Youth Through Training*. Staten Island Mental Health Society. U.S. Department of Labor. Manpower Administration, Washington, D.C., 1968.

Swanson, Chester J. *Leadership Role, Functions, Procedures and Administration of Vocational-Technical Education Agencies at the State Level*. Vol. 3. *Program-Cost Analyses of Vocational-Technical Education in a Junior College and in a Unified School District*. Berkeley, Calif.: School of Education, University of California, March, 1969.

Swift, W. J. and Burton A. Weisbrod. "On the Monetary Value of Education's Intergeneration Benefits." *Journal of Political Economy*, Vol. 83 (December, 1965): 643–649.

Taussig, Michael K. "An Economic Analysis of Vocational Education in the New York City High Schools." *Journal of Human Resources* Vol. 3, Supp. (1968), 59–87.

Taylor, David P. "Discussion of 'Time Trends in the Benefits From Retraining in Connecticut,'" by Michael E. Borus. *Proceedings of the Twentieth Annual Winter Meeting of the Industrial Relations Research Association*. Madison, Wis., 1967.

Taylor, Graeme M. "Office of Economic Opportunity: Evaluation of Training Programs." *Program Budgeting and Benefit-Cost Analysis*. Harley H. Hinrichs and Graeme M. Taylor, eds. Pacific Palisades, Calif.: Goodyear Publishing Company, 1969.

Trooboff, Benjamin Michael. "Employment Experience After MDTA Training: A Study of the Relationships Between Selected Training Characteristics and Post-Training Employment Experience." Ph.D. dissertation, Georgia State College, 1968.

Ullman, Morris; Michael, Bernard; and Matland, Marc. "The Needs for Vocational Education Data." *Proceedings of the Social Statistics Section*. Washington, D.C.: American Statistics Association, 1968.

U. S. Department of Health, Education and Welfare. *An Exploratory Cost-Benefit Analysis of Vocational Rehabilitation*. Vocational Rehabilitation Administration. Washington, D.C.: G.P.O., 1967.

——. *HEW Annuals*. Washington, D.C.: G.P.O., Various Issues.

——. *Vocational and Technical Annual Report-Fiscal Year 1968*. Office of Education. Washington, D.C.: G.P.O., Various Issues.

U.S. Department of Labor. *Cost Effectiveness Analysis of On-the-Job and Institutional Training Courses*. Office of Manpower Policy, Evaluation and Research. Washington, D.C.: Planning Research Corporation, 1967.

——. *Manpower Report of the President*. Washington, D.C.: G.P.O., 1969.

——. *Manpower Report of the President*. Washington, D.C.: G.P.O., 1970.

——. *Statistics on Manpower*. Washington, D.C.: G.P.O., March, 1969.

——. "The Neighborhood Youth Corps: A Review of Research." *Manpower Research Monograph No. 13*. Washington, D.C.: G.P.O., 1970.

U.S. Treasury Department. *Annual Report of the Secretary of the Treasury*. Washington, D.C.: G.P.O., Various Issues.

Walther, Regis H., and Magnusson, Margaret L. *A Retrospective Study of the*

Effectiveness of Out of School Neighborhood Youth Corps Programs in Four Urban Sites. Social Research Group. Washington, D.C.: George Washington University, November, 1967.

Weisbrod, Burton A. "Benefits of Manpower Programs: Theoretical and Methodological Issues." *Cost-Benefit Analysis of Manpower Policies. Proceedings of a North American Conference*. G. G. Somers and W. D. Wood, eds. Ontario: Industrial Relations Centre, Queen's University at Kingston, 1969.

——. "Concepts of Costs and Benefits." *Problems in Public Expenditure Analysis*. S. B. Chase, Jr., ed. Washington, D. C.: The Brookings Institution, 1968.

——. "Investing in Human Capital." *Journal of Human Resources* Vol. 1, No. 1 (Summer, 1966), 1–21.

——. "Preventing High School Dropouts." *Measuring Benefits of Government Investments*. Robert Dorfman, ed. Washington, D.C.: The Brookings Institution, 1965.

Wiseman, Jack. "Cost-Benefit Analysis in Education." *Southern Economic Journal* Vol. 32, No. 1, Part 2, Supp. (July, 1965): 1–12.

Index

179